W9-BEF-210

MIKE MEYERS' CERTIFICATION
Passport ⋆

CCNA™

EXAM 640-507

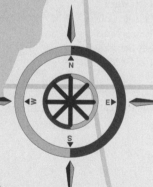

LOUIS ROSSI AND
RON ANTHONY

 OSBORNE

New York • Chicago • San Francisco
Lisbon • London • Madrid • Mexico City
Milan • New Delhi • San Juan
Seoul • Singapore • Sydney • Toronto

McGraw-Hill/Osborne
2600 Tenth Street
Berkeley, California 94710
U.S.A.

To arrange bulk purchase discounts for sales promotions, premiums, or fund-raisers, please contact McGraw-Hill/Osborne at the above address. For information on translations or book distributors outside the U.S.A., please see the International Contact Information page immediately following the index of this book.

Mike Meyers' CCNA™ Certification Passport (Exam 640-507)

1 2 3 4 5 6 7 8 9 0 DOC DOC 0 1 9 8 7 6 5 4 3 2 1

Book p/n 0-07-219599-1 and CD p/n 0-07-219598-3
parts of
ISBN 0-07-219365-4

Publisher	**Acquisitions Coordinator**	**Design and**
Brandon A. Nordin	Jessica Wilson	**Production**
		epic
Vice President &	**Technical Editor**	
Associate Publisher	Chris Patron	**Illustrators**
Scott Rogers		Michelle Galicia
	Copy Editor	Michael Mueller
Editorial Director	Lunaea Weatherstone	Kelly Stanton-Scott
Gareth Hancock		Lyssa Wald
	Proofreader	
Project Editor	Paul Tyler	**Series Cover Design**
Jody McKenzie		Ted Holladay
	Indexer	
	Irv Hershman	

This book was composed with Quark XPress™.

About the Authors

Louis R. Rossi is currently Director of CCPrep.com for Dice Incorporated. He is active in developing and maintaining different forms of training for CCPrep.com as well as teaching. Lou currently holds the CCNA, CCDA, CCDP, CCNP, and CCIE certifications. He is also a former Certified Cisco Systems Instructor (CCSI) and has taught hundreds of students to work with Cisco routers and switches.

Ronald Anthony is an instructor for CCPrep.com and teaches classes throughout the United States, including the CCNA and CCNP bootcamps. To date he has taught hundreds of students and has helped more than one hundred become CCNP certified. In addition to his CCNA, CCDA, CCNP, and CCDP certifications, he has an NCP, which is a security certification offered by Network Associates. Ron also teaches security classes, provides consulting for local businesses, and is currently working on his CCIE certification.

About the Technical Editor

Chris Patron is a freelance networking technologist, providing Cisco and Sniffer training and network consulting services. He started in the computing business 35 years ago, and has been an independent contractor for the past 24 years. He was certified as a Master CNE and Master CNI in 1996, a Certified Cisco Systems Instructor in 1997, and a Sniffer Certified Master in 2001. His specialties include ATM, Voice over IP and Wireless networks. He can be reached at cpatron@attglobal.net.

Dedication

This book is dedicated to the families and friends of the victims of September 11, 2001. Our hearts and prayers are with you.

Acknowledgments

I would like to thank all the instructors with whom I have taught in the past. Each and every one of them has taught me something new, and it is only with their help and support that this book is possible.

> Louis D. Rossi
> Steven Sowell
> Ron Anthony
> Rudy Koehle
> Chris Patron

—Louis R. Rossi

I would like to acknowledge all of those who have made this book possible:

At McGraw-Hill/Osborne, Jody McKenzie, Gareth Hancock, Jessica Wilson, and all the others, who showed great patience and were very detailed in their work to help create a CCNA book that will be beneficial to candidates attempting their CCNA certification.

Lou Rossi, Jr., the co-author of this book, who has been instrumental in moving my career forward and helping me do the things I have dreamed of.

My wife, Sandy, who runs the household and spends all of her efforts selflessly helping to care for and improve our wonderful family. Her commitment to our two children, Michael and Justin, as well as to me, has far exceeded the dedication of anyone I know. Without her, my accomplishments would remain only dreams, never becoming the reality she has made them.

My God, who has given me much prosperity by opening so many doors of opportunity. He allows me to live happily in spite of my failures and faults. He gives me freedom to make mistakes, so that I can accomplish projects without fear and worry.

—Ronald Anthony

Contents

Check-In

May I See Your Passport?

What do you mean you don't have a passport? Why, it's sitting right in your hands, even as you read! This book is your passport to a very special place. You're about to begin a journey, my friend, a journey towards that magical place called CERTIFICATION! You don't need a ticket, you don't need a suitcase—just snuggle up and read this passport—it's all you need to get there. Are you ready? Let's go!

Your Travel Agent—Mike Meyers

Hello! My name is Mike Meyers. I've written a number of popular certification books, and I'm the President of Total Seminars, LLC. On any given day, you may find me replacing a hard drive, setting up a Web site, or writing code. I love every aspect of this book you hold in your hands. It's part of a powerful new set of books called the Mike Meyers' Certification Passport series. Every book in this series combines easy readability with a condensed format—in other words, the kind of book I always wanted when I went for my certifications. Presenting this much information in an efficient *and* accessible format has been an enormous challenge, but I think we've achieved our goal, as I'm confident you'll agree.

I designed this series to do one thing and only one thing: give you only the information you need to achieve your certification. You won't find any fluff in here—the authors, Louis Rossi and Ron Anthony, have included nothing but the real nitty-gritty knowledge you need for this certification exam. Every page is packed with 100% pure concentrated certification knowledge! But never fear, we didn't forget to make the book readable as well. I hope you enjoy the casual, friendly style—I want you to feel as though the authors are speaking with you about the topics, not just spewing facts at you. Not only is this more fun, I believe it really helps you learn!

My personal email address is mikem@totalsem.com. Please feel free to contact me directly if you have any questions, complaints, or compliments.

Your Destination—Cisco CCNA 2.0 Certification

This book is your passport to the Cisco CCNA 2.0 exam (test number 640-507). The Cisco Certified Network Associate certification has become one of the most popular and valuable networking credentials available, and puts you on the road to more advanced Cisco certifications such as the CCNP, and ultimately the CCIE, the PhD of networking certifications. Exam 640-507 focuses on fundamental internetworking concepts such as cabling, protocols, the OSI model, and topologies as well as more advanced and Cisco specific topics like the VLANS, the Cisco IOS, access lists, ISDN, Frame Relay, and more.

Your Guides—Lou Rossi and Ron Anthony

Lou and Ron are both dedicated instructors who have taught thousands of students. They use their first-hand experience of what works and what doesn't work when teaching this material to enhance your learning experience. Ron comes from a background with Network Associates and has almost every Cisco certification in the Routing and Switching track. Ron is also preparing for his CCIE lab after having already passed the CCIE written exam.

Lou currently holds every Cisco Routing and Switching certification including the coveted CCIE. He taught Cisco Authorized classes for the world's largest Cisco Training Partners, and co-founded CCPrep.com with his father and brother. Today both Ron and Lou are dedicated instructors with CCPrep.com.

If you have any questions or comments feel free to contact Lou at lrossi@ccprep.com or Ron at ron677@earthlink.net.

Why the Travel Theme?

One of my favorite topics is the parallel between gaining a certification and taking a trip. All of the elements are the same: preparation, an itinerary, a route—even mishaps along the way. Let me show you how it all works.

This book is divided into twelve chapters. Each chapter begins with an "Itinerary," which maps out the objectives covered in that chapter, and an "ETA" to give you an idea of the time involved learning the objectives in that chapter. Each chapter is broken down according to actual exam objectives, arranged either according to official publications of the certifying body or, if that's not possible, according to our experts' take on the best way to organize the topics for maximum learning efficiency.

To further assist you in capturing all the key points, each chapter highlights important points and provides helpful information using these special features:

Exam Tip
Points out critical topics you're likely to see on the actual exam.

Travel Assistance
Shows you additional sources such as books and Web sites where you can find more information.

Local Lingo
Describes special terms in detail in a way you can easily understand.

Travel Advisory
Warns you about common pitfalls, misconceptions, and downright physical peril!

At the end of the chapter I provide two more handy tools. First, in the "Checkpoint" section, the authors summarize each objective covered in the chapter. This is a great way to reinforce what you've read. Finally, you can test yourself using the end-of-chapter questions, and of course check your understanding against the answers.

CHECKPOINT

Sounds great, but the fun doesn't stop there! After you've read the book, pull out the CD and take advantage of the free practice questions! Use the full practice exam to hone your skills, keeping the book handy to check answers.

If you want even more practice, log on to http://www.Osborne.com/Passport, and for a nominal fee you can get additional high-quality practice questions.

When you can nail the practice questions, you're ready to take the exam—go get certified!

The End of the Trail

The IT industry changes and grows constantly—and so should you. Finishing one certification is just a step in an ongoing process of gaining more and more certifications to match your constantly changing and growing skills. Read the Career Flight Path at the end of the book to understand where this certification fits into your personal certification goals. Remember, in the IT business, if you're not moving forward, you are way behind!

Good luck on your certification! Stay in touch!

Series Editor
Mike Meyers' Certification Passport

Basic Concepts, Network Operation, and Cabling

CHAPTER 1

	NEWBIE	SOME EXPERIENCE	VETERAN
ETA	5+ hours	3 hours	1 hour

1

To make a network run efficiently, there must be organization and coordination. There are millions of networks connected together to form the Internet. There are millions of unconnected networks used for educational, corporate, and other purposes. To organize this huge networking structure, models are developed, technical terms defined, and technology and protocols invented. There are basics that internetworking specialists must use as a starting point of reference. These basic models are put in place to make sense of the complexities involved in connecting users.

Objective 1.01   Internetworking Overview

In network design, there is a three-tier model to present a simplified way of looking at the general structure of internetworks. The three tiers are

- Core
- Distribution
- Access

These terms attempt to simplify how internetworks should be designed and structured. They provide structure that not only describes, but also logically assists in planning and maintaining an internetwork.

Local Lingo

Network, internetwork   The terms network and internetwork have two distinct meanings. Network is generally defined as a single routed subnet. Internetwork refers to the entire network. Many times the terms are used interchangeably to mean the entire network.

Core

The core is the backbone of an internetwork. It is what allows individual networks to pass traffic to other areas quickly. It is not enough to have a transit area to pass information from one place to another; it should do so as fast as possible. Anything that would hinder the quick delivery of information from one area of the internetwork to another should be eliminated. In an internetwork with well-defined core, distribution, and access layers, the core should be kept free of potential bottlenecks and failure points such as servers, routers, and slow protocols. Anything that would slow the speed of the core needs to be placed in a lower layer.

Distribution

The distribution layer is defined as the layer of policy. This is where departments and sections of your network are partitioned off so that there is structure, security, and routing, and an administrator can control and manage the internetwork. WAN connections from other sites are connected here, and VLANs and access controls are implemented. Think of the distribution layer as the layer that allows you to manage and implement policy in the internetwork. Everything flows from policy. Policy controls routing, placement of access lists, implementation of VLANs, and even the overall structure of the network.

Access

The access layer is where the user interfaces to the network. Whether by LAN or WAN connections, the user gains access here. For equipment, there are workgroup switches, access routers running technologies like ADSL, cable modems, ISDN, and asynchronous dialup. This area uses media types like Ethernet, Token Ring, or WAN media types as listed previously. Whereas the distribution layer uplinks to the core through 100 Mbps, Gigabit Ethernet, or ATM, the access layer uplinks to the distribution layer through Ethernet, Fast Ethernet, Token Ring, or WAN connections. Figure 1-1 shows the three well-defined tiers of a network.

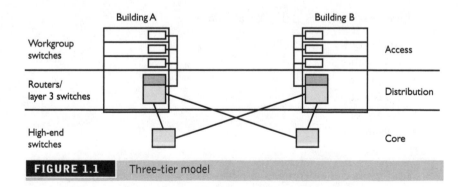

FIGURE 1.1   Three-tier model

OSI Structure and Definitions

Connecting users to accomplish tasks may seem simple on the surface—two users talking to one another. Implementation of this is much harder. From a human perspective, communication is simple, as sound is transmitted in certain patterns that another human listens to and interprets. However, if we begin to dissect the sum of what makes up human communication, there is great complexity. The functions of the brain, throat, ears, physical features, a common protocol (language) that has been learned, sound, and air all play a part. To break these down in further divisions allows for understanding of the parts and how they relate to the whole. The same is true with internetworking. The big picture is internetwork communication; internetwork models help present things in an organized manner.

We have seen the three-tier model of design; now let's focus on the Open Systems Interconnection (OSI) model. Where the three-tier model is concerned with the structure of building networks, the OSI is concerned with the communication that transverses that network. The OSI describes the protocols and functions necessary to pass information across network devices so that communication between end systems is accomplished. More specifically, the OSI is used to do the following:

- Simplify complex procedures into an easy-to-understand structure
- Allow vendors to interoperate
- Isolate problems from one layer to be passed to other areas
- Allow modular plug-and-play functionality
- Provide independence of each layer

There are seven layers of the OSI, as follows:

- Application
- Presentation
- Session
- Transport
- Network
- Data link
- Physical

These layers can be grouped into two main sections called the upper and lower layers. The upper layers refer to the application, presentation, and session, while the lower layers are the transport, network, data link, and physical. The data link is further subdivided into the Logical Link Control (LLC) and the Media Access Control (MAC).

Another way of dividing the model is the logical and the physical. This functional division describes the upper five layers as logical in nature and the lower two layers as physical in nature. As the model is explained, these two divisions will become apparent.

It is important to understand that the OSI is progressive in many ways. Intelligence varies between layers. Each layer progressing up the model is generally more intelligent than the layer below it, with greater capabilities and complexities. However, intelligence comes at a price—each layer progressing up the model is generally slower than the layer below it. The application layer has the most intelligence of the OSI, but it is also the slowest layer. The physical is the fastest layer, but has little intelligence.

The model is designed so that each layer communicates with the corresponding layer in the remote system. The application layer doesn't communicate with the presentation layer below it. It communicates with the application layer of the remote system. To accomplish this, headers are placed on the information as it progresses down the model. On the remote computer, the headers are stripped one by one as each layer recognizes and reads the header placed on the data from the respective layer in the remote system. This allows each layer to be independent of the layer above and below it to accomplish its tasks.

The basic building block of the OSI is the PDU, the protocol data unit. As the data is being passed from each layer, it is referred to as a PDU. When the information is passed from one layer to another, it is said that the PDU is passed to that layer. Each layer may add a header or a trailer to the PDU; this process is known as encapsulation. When the header is placed on the PDU, encapsulation means that the corresponding layer can only read the PDU in another system. The encapsulation process can be compared to mailing a Christmas gift to a friend. The gift might be a new shirt that is placed in a box, then wrapped and placed in a shipping box. The shirt, the box, the gift wrap, and the shipping box all may have a tag, which identifies each piece. It could be said that each piece is encapsulated within the other. The shirt when placed in the box is not seen and is referred to as a box. When the gift wrap is applied, it is called a gift, yet when it is placed in the shipping box, it is now a parcel. It is very similar with the OSI. Each layer encapsulates the PDU as it is moves down the model. As Figure 1-2 shows, while the PDU is at the application, presentation, or session layer, it is referred to as data. At the transport layer, though, it is known as a segment and the network layer encapsulation is referred to as a packet and the data link as a frame.

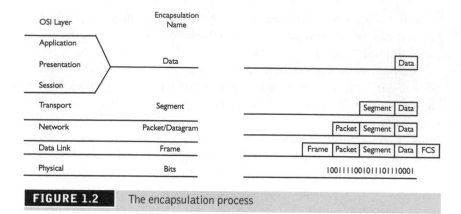

FIGURE 1.2   The encapsulation process

In the early days of networking before the Internet, the TCP/IP model described all these functions within five layers. TCP/IP is much like the OSI, except the single application layer in the TCP/IP model defines the top three layers of the OSI. The other four layers are the same as the lower four of the OSI. What is important about that model is the terminology it uses when describing the PDUs being passed between layers. The TCP/IP model uses the keywords data, segment, packet, frame, and bits to describe the encapsulation process. As was seen in Figure 1-2, the data is passed from the top of the model downward, and each of the lower layers encapsulates the data with a header. The data link layer adds a trailer known as the frame check sequence (FCS) as well. This encapsulation process is then reversed—that is, headers are stripped off as the PDU is passed up the model on the remote system.

The Seven OSI Layers

Each layer of the OSI is responsible for activities that take data and move it with the proper formatting and coordination, determining where it will be sent, setting up connections with remote hosts, and ensuring integrity. The process of how this is accomplished will be described as we look at the individual layers of the OSI, beginning at the top of the stack with Layer 7.

Application

The application is the layer of the user. This is where the user interfaces with the network. It is important to understand that some applications are not considered network applications, such as word processors, spreadsheet programs, and database programs. These applications do not require network connectivity to work. You can save each of these files on the computer's hard drive. On the other hand, there are applications that require the network to work. Without network connectivity, the application is useless. Examples of network applications and computer applications can be seen in Table 1-1. These applications are used constantly in today's internetworks.

Presentation

The presentation layer takes over when the data is passed down from the application. As the name would suggest, it is the job of the presentation layer to take the data and format it when passed to the remote user. The best term is code formatting. This layer puts the data in the form that will be required within the network communication process. Examples are ASCII, JPEG, TIFF, or even compression and/or encryption. Any manipulation of the data in terms of representation and formatting is done at this layer.

Session

Once the session layer takes over, it manages the inter-host communication. It keeps track of data from one application and keeps it separate so that the lower layers are able to distinguish what data is going to what host. Therefore, the session layer initiates, manages, and terminates data communication between hosts. This layer typically handles logins and session parameter negotiation.

Transport

The transport layer is responsible for achieving what the session later began. It sets up reliable and unreliable communication from end systems. This end-to-end communication is dependent upon ports used for a particular application. When

TABLE 1.1   Network Applications vs. PC Applications

Network Applications	PC Applications
E-mail	Spreadsheet
Remote access	Word processing
Network management	Database
File transfer	Presentation

HTTP data is sent down, the transport layer sets up communication from a source port on the local device to a destination port on the remote device. The transport layer is not concerned with the devices in between, only the end systems.

When it receives the data, it encapsulates this data in segments. The segments are created based on an agreed-upon segment size between the two end devices. This segment size is important for many reasons, such as reliable communication, flow control, and sequencing. The size of the segment is calculated by and communicated during the initial setup of the communication. With connection-oriented communication, there is communication between the two hosts at all times. It is because of this communication that each side knows what the other side is expecting.

Flow control is an important concept with segments because of the need to deliver the data without overwhelming the other end device. There are three basic forms of flow control at the transport layer:

- Buffering allows space for unprocessed data until it can be attended to by the system.
- Source-quench messaging is used to notify when the receiver has reached its limit of how much it can receive. When the receiver is being overwhelmed, it sends source-quench messages to stop the other side from sending data. Much like a traffic light, these ready/not ready messages allow the data to be sent in a measured amount without loss. However, if there is loss, there are retransmission messages that can notify the sender to resend a particular segment.
- Windowing is perhaps the most important form of flow control for TCP. It works by negotiating window sizes with the remote host. Think of the window as a buffer that constantly changes in size to allow more or less data to be received as necessary. It is the receiver that sets the window size. This number is used to tell the sender how much data the receiver can accept before the sender must stop sending and wait for an acknowledgment from the receiver.

Not only does flow control play a part, but reliability is also very important. The two sides need to be on the same page for reliable, connection-oriented communication. If something is sent but not received, this is damaging for communication. TCP deals with this by using acknowledgments for every communication. Acknowledgment is the most important part of reliable communication, because missing acknowledgments are a glaring light that means that something wasn't sent properly or there was a problem in transit.

Sequencing is used so that when segments are received out of order, they can be put back in the proper order. This will make it apparent if something is missing in the transfer. Say a computer sent three segments, all with sequence numbers, but when they were received, one was missing. The receiving computer would acknowledge the two received but not the third, and the transmitting station could then resend the missing segment.

Connection-oriented communication can be explained by using the analogy of a phone call. In a phone call between two people, there are the following three components:

- Call setup phase
- Data transfer phase
- Call termination phase

The call setup phase is when a person picks up the receiver, dials, and is answered on the remote end. The data transfer phase is when the person talks and the other person acknowledges and communicates in return. The termination phase is simply saying goodbye and hanging up. Connection-oriented protocols share in this behavior, having formal setup, transfer, and termination phases.

Connectionless communication is used when the protocol doesn't need to provide reliable segment delivery. Connectionless data transfer can be likened to a megaphone approach to communication. The words are sent out without checking to see if those around are hearing them. There is no concept of flow control, acknowledgment, and sequencing. These functions are left up to the session or application layer processes of the remote host to perform. A transport layer protocol such as UDP is not responsible for reliability; it is up to the application to provide reliable communication as necessary.

Network

The network layer of the OSI is used to set up paths to various locations. Path determination is a good way to explain routing. Routing is simply the determination of the next hop that should be taken en route to the destination network. Networks are defined with a network-addressing scheme such as IP or IPX addresses. These addresses are used to give a host a location and address. Network layer addresses are not used to communicate with as much as to determine where the host resides in the internetwork. The network layer has the following characteristics:

- **Two-part addresses containing host and network portions**   Typically, the first half is the network portion defining where hosts can reside, and the second half is the host portion itself.
- **Logical communication**   It is logical in that hosts don't communicate directly by network layer address. They provide for location and logical upper layer communication between hosts. Physical communication

never occurs by network layer address. Instead, a lower layer address is used for this purpose.

- **Flat or hierarchical in nature**   Flat means that there is little rhyme or reason in the relation of one address to another. There is only a comparison of network to host. IP is hierarchical, in that there are classes of addresses and, with the invention of the subnet mask, there are even more divisions in the class system of addressing.
- **Connectionless**   The network layer protocols IP and IPX are connectionless in that they provide best-effort delivery of packets to other devices.
- **Typically includes a time-to-live (TTL) field in headers**   This keeps packets caught in loops from being circulated forever. Each router hop decrements (IP) or increments (IPX) the TTL field by one.
- **Path selection**   This is accomplished with routing tables on the device. Network layer devices as well as most PCs have routing tables, also known as forwarding tables because they forward information based on interface and next-hop addresses toward the destination.
- **Unique addresses within the internetwork**   Two hosts cannot share the same network and host address in the internetwork. No matter how large the network, there cannot be any duplicates. Not only does IP reside at the network layer, but so does ICMP. ICMP is a messaging protocol used by *all* TCP/IP hosts. When TCP/IP is installed on a device, ICMP is running and ready to send messages as needed.

Data Link

The data link layer is broken into two parts: the Logical Link Control (LLC) and the Media Access Control (MAC). The division between these two sublayers represents a major division in the OSI. Everything above this division is logical in nature; everything below is physical. This layer provides for physical addressing of network devices, flow control, and error detection. The physical device's address must be known in order for communication between two devices to occur. This communication is always segment by segment. This is much different than what is defined at the transport layer. In the upper layers, communication is between end systems. At the data link layer, communication is between connected systems only. The addressing system at the data link is physical. For Ethernet and Token Ring, it is the MAC address. This address is also known as a burned-in address (BIA) and must be known between two systems before communication can take place. For WAN technologies like frame relay, the data link layer address is the DLCI; ISDN uses the TEI.

Characteristics of data link layer addressing are as follows:

- **Two-part 6-byte MAC address**   The first 3 bytes are known as the vendor code or the organizational unique identifier (OUI), and the last 3 bytes are the serial number. In an address like 0000.0c1f.2a4f, 0000.0c identifies the manufacturer of the network device as Cisco. The last half (1f.2a4f) is the serial number of the device as defined by Cisco.

- **Flat addressing space**   There is no routing or hierarchy in flat addressing space. Data link addresses don't indicate where a device is located; rather, it is the identification of the device used for local communication. Logical addresses are used for location. Physical addresses are used for direct communication and identification. The difference can be likened to an individual's house address and Social Security number. Network layer addressing is similar to a house address, which is logical and hierarchical, used for location of the person. Data link addresses, which reside at the data link layer, are more like a Social Security number—the address doesn't indicate a person's location.

- **Unique only on the segment on which they reside**   Because of the sheer number of devices manufactured, many times the MAC addresses are duplicated from older equipment to newer equipment. There is no problem with duplication as long as the duplicate MACs are not used on the same logical segment. As will be described later in the chapter, a logical segment consists of the devices called a network because they border a router interface.

- **Flow control and error detection**   Data link layer communication means two hosts on the same network communicating. Any time there is communication, there must be some type of flow control. Because of Layer 2 having less intelligence than the upper layers, there is error detection, not correction.

Exam Tip

While flow control is a description of the transport layer, the description topology and flow control are only possible at the data link layer.

Switches and bridges are examples of data link devices. A switch is the most popular Layer 2 device at the data link layer. Because switches and bridges are Layer 2, the only addressing they support is MAC addresses, not IP.

Physical

The physical layer is the layer of cabling, physical topology, and electrical, optical, and procedural standards. Cabling, transceivers, interfaces, hubs, and repeaters reside here. Some of the physical layer standards include the following:

- V.35
- EIA/TIA-449
- EIA/TIA-232
- HSSI

Note that topology is defined at both the physical and data link layers. When defined at the data link, it is referring to encapsulations such as Ethernet and Token Ring. Originally, Ethernet was defined in an industry agreement to run over a bus topology. When topology is mentioned at the physical layer, it is referring to the media over which the data link encapsulation runs. Frames are broken down into binary at the physical later to be sent across the wire. Depending on the technology and media, signaling types will vary, but all have the goal of signaling in such a way that patterns of binary 1s and 0s are understood by the other side.

Objective 1.03

Ethernet and Other Media Types

Media types are defined as encapsulations at Layer 2 running over a specified physical topology. This can lead to confusion because "media types" sounds as if it indicates only the physical medium. It does define physical media, but usually the emphasis is on the data link layer encapsulation.

Exam Tip

Media types indicate Layer 2 encapsulations used to transfer over a physical medium. Media is actually a plural for medium; however, at the data link layer, media types indicate topology. This is crucial because transparent switches and bridges don't translate between media types. Either a translational switch/bridge or a router must be used to change encapsulations. Transparent switches/bridges only forward, filter, and flood; they don't modify frames or translate between media types such as Ethernet and Token Ring.

Ethernet is defined by the IEEE standard 802.3. Originally intended to run over a bus topology at 10 Mbps half duplex, the standard has been adapted over time to allow for 10, 100 or 1000 Mbps using half or full duplex and a physical star topology in a logical bus topology. Figure 1-3 illustrates the difference between physical star and bus topologies.

So engrained was the concept of a bus topology with Ethernet, the term "wire" was used to indicate the medium to which every station was connected. On this wire, the IEEE defined Ethernet as a CSMA/CD technology denoting that Ethernet is contention-based. CSMA/CD stands for Carrier Sense Multiple Access Collision Detection. Because all stations shared the wire, there had to be a way of securing access to the medium. Ethernet implemented a listening mechanism so that stations could sense when the wire was available for transmission. The Ethernet station was required to sense the carrier—that is, it would listen to see if another station was transmitting on the wire. If there was traffic on the wire, the station would wait to send until it sensed that the transmission was over and the wire was free; then it would begin to send. Because the wire is made up of several stations (known as multiple access) listening and sending when able, collisions may occur. This made it mandatory for Ethernet to employ a collision detection mechanism. This mechanism defined a notification called a jam signal and a back-off interval so that sending stations would wait at random intervals before sending again.

Full/Half Duplex

Half duplex refers to bidirectional sending on the same wire, but not at the same time—that is, one direction at a time. Similar to a one-way bridge, half duplex Ethernet can transmit or receive, but not simultaneously. This means that half duplex is unable to make use of all wires simultaneously for data transfer. When a

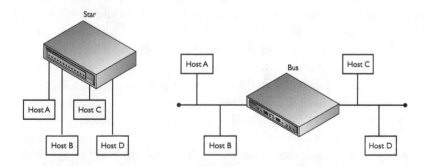

When connected to Layer 1 devices, Ethernet sees only 1 wire no matter how many physical wires are used.

FIGURE 1.3   Star and bus topologies

station sends, it must also listen and detect collisions. Because the shared wire means there is the possibility of a collision, a sending station must always be listening to detect a collision.

There are certain devices that demand half duplex mode be used. The most common is the hub. An eight-port hub may have eight separate stations plugged into it, but as far as Ethernet is concerned, it is a single wire. The hub can do nothing to divide the logical wire into separate collision domains. Thus, when a hub is used, half duplex must be employed. Repeaters also force a station into using half duplex. Any time two or more stations are contending for the wire, half duplex must be used.

In recent years there has been a move from shared to dedicated bandwidth. This change is referred to as microsegmentation. When stations share the wire, they can never make full use of it. Collisions inevitably waste bandwidth. Microsegmentation reduces contention so that stations enjoy increased bandwidth. When contention is removed, collision detection can be turned off and full usage of the media can be achieved. The advent of the switch allows for full duplex; however, even with a switch, there are three requirements:

- Point-to-point connection
- NIC support
- Full duplex turned on

Collision domains refer to shared media in which stations contend for access to the wire. When each station is placed on a separate logical wire, contention with other stations is removed and a separate collision domain is formed. In half duplex mode, the station must still contend for use of the wire with the switch, which may be trying to send data to the station. Reducing the size of collision domains in a network means reduced contention for the wire. Certain devices have the intelligence to segment the wire. Layer 1 devices such as hubs and repeaters cannot create new collision domains. Only devices that reside above Layer 1 can do this. The main two devices capable of segmenting collision domains are the switch and the bridge. Obviously, higher layer devices can do so also; the focus here is that Layer 2 devices have the intelligence to create separate wires. In fact, they do it naturally—just plug the device in and it is on its own logical wire. Every port on a switch is its own collision domain, and this is one of the reasons why some switches can support full duplex. Bridges are older devices that never developed many of the capabilities that a switch has. Therefore, bridges usually operate only at half duplex.

Once a switch is in place, all that is needed is an interface supporting full duplex plugged directly into it. Realize that a hub may be plugged into a switch port, so that many stations might be sharing the wire. In this case, there is no point-to-point connection and therefore half duplex must be employed. All the stations off the single switch port reside in the same collision domain.

10/100/1000 Mbps

Ethernet has been so developed that today, gigabit speeds are attainable, even using existing unshielded twisted-pair copper wiring. To do this, the signaling rate had to be increased. Fast Ethernet is 10 times faster than 10 Mbps Ethernet, therefore, the time slots had to be decreased by 10. This was not without a price. When using shared-media hubs, 100 Mbps operates poorly at best. Plug some stations into a hub and watch the collision light during data transfers. The light will be blinking constantly. Shrinking the time slots increases the chance of collisions on shared media. If 100 Mbps is chosen, use a switch. Hubs will only kill the improved performance that 100 Mbps was intended to have over 10 Mbps.

Objective 1.04

Network Devices and Relation Within the Networking Model

As described earlier, hubs and repeaters are Layer 1 devices. These devices have little intelligence and are used to amplify signals and add stations to the logical wire. Bridges have greater intelligence than their Layer 1 counterpart, a repeater, but they were never developed fully, because of the popularity of the switch. The reason for this popularity is speed. The bridge used software and CPU in order to forward frames between devices. This method of forwarding can be found in low-end routers as well. The CPU is interrupted repeatedly to make simple forwarding decisions.

The switch is far superior to a bridge. The main difference that separates the switch from the bridge is the ASIC. With the advent of ASICs, logic is programmed into chips so that decisions can be offloaded from the CPU and performed in hardware. This is what gives the switch the ability to forward data at "wire speed." Even though the bridge is at the same layer of the OSI, it cannot forward frames nearly as fast as a switch. The demands of modern networks are such that only the switch can satisfy the need for increased speed and flexibility. This is why the switch is the most popular Layer 2 device in the world. With the increase of speed, the switch has evolved so that it is much more capable than a bridge. New capabilities include VLANs, trunking, and low-latency forwarding mechanisms. These technologies offer superior control and scalability to existing networks.

As can be seen in Table 1-2, different terminology should be used when referring to the device's ports and what it is forwarding. The devices to focus on here are the repeater, hub, bridge, switch, and router. Higher layer switches are beyond the scope of this book.

TABLE 1.2 Terminology and Devices Used at the Lower Four Layers of the OSI

Layer	Device	Connection Type	Terminology
Transport	Layer 4 switch	Sockets	Segments
Network	Router, Layer 3 switch	Interface	Packets/Datagrams
Data link	Bridge, switch	Ports	Frames
Physical	Repeater, hub	Connectors	Bits

Collisions are not the only problem on a network. Often, it is necessary for a device to send a message to all other devices on the network. Essentially, the term "network" refers to the distance a broadcast travels; the network is known as a broadcast domain. The bridge/switch has the intelligence to segment collision domains, but cannot help with broadcasts. The bridge/switch floods broadcast and multicast frames out every port on the device.

Local Lingo

Broadcast, multicast, unicast A broadcast originates from a single host to every host in the network. A multicast originates from a single host to many hosts on the network. A unicast originates from a single host and is limited to a single other host. The following summarizes these terms: unicast, one to one; multicast, one to many; and broadcast, one to all.

The bridge/switch cannot filter broadcasts/multicasts because the frame is destined for all stations. Any time the destination is unknown, the bridge/switch must replicate the frame out to every port.

Routers reside at Layer 3 of the OSI and have more intelligence than a bridge/switch. The main capability they add over a switch is the ability to segment broadcast domains. A router divides networks, and a network is a broadcast domain, therefore the router prevents broadcasts from one network from passing to another network. This helps by saving bandwidth and CPU utilization that the broadcast/multicast would use on other segments.

The main problem with broadcasts is not bandwidth (although this can be a problem), it is that they are sent out to the local network and every host on that network must process them. In addition to its own MAC address, each host must also pay attention to the broadcast address FFFF.FFFF.FFFF, meaning everybody on the network. Destination MAC addresses that do not match the local host are dropped by the NIC without interrupting the CPU. A broadcast address means that this frame is intended for all hosts, and even if the host doesn't need the information contained in the broadcast, the CPU must be interrupted by the network interface and must process the frame. If there are many broadcasts crossing the network, the host's performance can be degraded, as it will be processing broadcast packets rather than doing other things the user needs the device to do.

> ### Exam Tip
>
> Broadcasts and multicasts are not forwarded by a router. Bridges and switches must replicate these frames on every port.

In addition to limiting broadcast/multicast, a router is able to naturally change between media types. Recall that a bridge/switch is not able to do this. In order for media type translation, many things must be changed within the frame. The most basic is that the frame encapsulation must be changed, which the bridge/switch cannot do. Translational bridges can do this, but performance suffers. Routers naturally translate media types because frames are read and the Layer 2 encapsulation is discarded by the data link layer on its way up the router's stack. When the router forwards the packet out an interface, it rebuilds a new frame to be sent out on that segment. Thus, media type translation is no problem—the frame is destroyed anyway and a new frame with the necessary encapsulation is created on the outgoing interface. This process is known as rewriting a frame.

What routers really do is connect broadcast domains to each other. A network address is defined for each domain and the router passes traffic from one broadcast domain to another. The IP address defines each individual network so that each device can be located and logical communication set up. Within each broadcast domain, the devices communicate physically with each other by MAC address. When a host needs to reach a host in a remote broadcast domain, it will send the message to a designated router and the router will be responsible for forwarding it to the destination. Many times the message will have to be forwarded over many networks to reach its ultimate destination. Within each of these hops, physical communication will have to be set up between devices. Whereas logical communication is end to end, physical communication is done by at least two devices (usually routers on the intermediate segments) on each routed network between the two end devices.

The penalty for the intelligence of the router is performance. The router is much slower than the typical switch. Most routers don't have ASICs and must make forwarding decisions with software and CPU. This can lead to bottlenecks within an internetwork. For all the benefits and intelligence a router brings, it can still be the device that slows down the network. Because of this, placement of routers and design of the network are very important. It is also why it was stated earlier that routers should be kept out of the core of the network if possible.

Objective 1.05 # Cabling the LAN and WAN

To set up a network, basic knowledge of wiring must be understood. LAN cabling, while different from WAN cabling, has many common elements. Both can be run over copper or fiber wiring and both make connections to repeaters, switches, and routers.

Connecting to the Cisco Device

Accessing a Cisco router/switch can be accomplished by direct cable connection through the console or auxiliary port located on the front of the device. The ports accept RJ-45 connectors and attach a computer's serial port to the console, or a DB25 is used to connect an external modem to the auxiliary port. Either connection requires a rollover cable. A rollover cable is so called because the pins are opposite each other from one end to the other as follows:

Pin 1-8
Pin 2-7
Pin 3-6
Pin 4-5
Pin 5-4
Pin 6-3
Pin 7-2
Pin 8-1

When connecting to the console, an application like Hyper Terminal (available with the Windows operating system) can be used. Simply use a rollover cable to connect the PC's serial port to the router's console port and set the following parameters under Properties for the serial connection.

9600 baud
8 bits
No parity
1 stop bit
No flow control

The console port doesn't support Ready To Send (RTS) or Clear To Send (CTS), which is used for flow control, so it should be turned off in the terminal program. By default, the console port operates at 9600 baud; it is not recommended that you change it.

Cisco provides cabling kits with the device to access the router properly. The router can also be accessed by Telnet.

Cabling the LAN

There are different cabling and signaling standards used for Ethernet. Table 1-3 displays these specifications.

Specifications such as 10BaseT should be understood in three parts. As can be seen following, the first section defines the speed (here 10 Mbps), and the second section refers to the signaling type, in this case baseband signaling. Finally, the last section is the cabling that is used. The *T* stands for twisted pair.

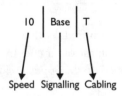

To connect end devices to their respective intermediate devices, different cabling is used depending on the topology. For Ethernet, the most common cabling is CAT 3 or CAT 5 unshielded twisted pair (UTP). When connecting devices, a straight-through cable is usually used. A straight-through cable is defined as a cable in which all the wires in the connector on one side match the wires in the connector on the other. Pin 1 on one side of the wire is connected to pin 1 on the other and so on. When connecting a PC to a switch or a hub, a straight-through connection is required. In terms of wiring, a router interface should be viewed like a host in that it requires a straight-through connection to the switch or hub. However, when connecting a switch to another switch or a host

TABLE 1.3	Cabling Specifications		
Description	**Topology**	**Media**	**Distance**
10Base2	Bus	Coax	185 meters
10BaseT	Star	UTP	100 meters
100BaseTX	Star	UTP	100 meters
100BaseFX	Point to point	Fiber	400 meters

Local Lingo

End device, intermediate device   An end device is a host that is the ultimate destination for logical communication. An intermediate device allows remote end devices to be logically connected. In a Telnet communication between two remote hosts, the two end devices communicate by passing the information through the intermediate devices. Examples of end devices are most often computers, while intermediate devices are typically routers and switches. However, in the case of Telnet and other applications, a router or a switch can be an end device. In this case, the devices used to connect these end hosts would be the intermediate devices.

---

to a host, a crossover cable is required. With a crossover cable, the TX and RX wires on one end are reversed on the other end. In particular for UTP (CAT 3 or 5), pins 1, 3 and 2, 6 are reversed on the opposite side as shown here.

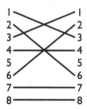

Cabling the WAN

When cabling a WAN connection, the most important thing to know is DCE and DTE. Typically, the router or PC is the DTE device, while the device that it plugs into for the WAN connectivity is DCE. DCE devices are important because they provide the clocking for the connection between the local device and the remote device. For frame relay, a CSU/DSU is used to supply the clock rate for the connection. With asynchronous communication, the modem does the clocking. In these examples, the CSU/DSU and the modem are considered DCE.

Local Lingo

DCE, DTE   Data circuit-terminating equipment and data terminal equipment, respectively.

Recall that the physical layer of the OSI defined connectors and cabling. The following physical layer specifications are used to connect a router to a CSU/DSU:

- V.35
- EIA/TIA 232
- EIA/TIA-449
- X.21
- EIA-530

The most common cable types for the CCNA material are the V.35 and EIA/TIA 232. V.35 is the faster, typically supporting clock rates of up to 2 Mbps, while EIA/TIA 232 supports up to 115 Kbps.

CHECKPOINT

✔ **Objective 1.01: Internetworking Overview**   Models help simplify and organize concepts in order to describe internetwork communication. The three-tier design model describes the core, distribution, and access areas within a network. The core is the backbone, the distribution implements policy, and the access is where the user interfaces with the network.

✔ **Objective 1.02: OSI Structure and Definitions**   The seven-layer OSI describes the actual process that a PDU goes through as it moves up and down the model. Each layer adds its requirements to the frame and passes it up or down to the next layer, and each layer communicates with its corresponding layer in the remote device. The model is progressive, so that intelligence is the greatest at the top; however, with more complexity, speed is diminished. Consequently, moving up usually means slower performance.

✔ **Objective 1.03: Ethernet and Other Media Types**   Ethernet is an encapsulation that works on several different media types, including UTP, coax, and fiber. Ethernet is the most common LAN encapsulation, and though conceived originally as 10 Mbps half duplex, today it supports gigabit speeds and full duplex.

✔ **Objective 1.04: Network Devices and Relation Within the Networking Model** Devices that help move information throughout the internetwork have evolved over time, allowing the network to run faster and more efficiently. The invention of the switch contributed much of the increase in speed because of the ASIC, which allowed forwarding decisions to be carried out with hardware. This is the reason some switches can run at wire speed. However, there are things the switch was unable to help with which the router is needed for. Switches cannot connect broadcast domains and move information between them. The router is the device that literally divides the internetwork into a collection of networks. It is the device used to set up logical communication by determining the path information takes to get to remote devices.

✔ **Objective 1.05: Cabling the LAN and WAN**   Finally, though the LAN and WAN have some similarities, there are many differences. Two important differences are the cables used to connect devices and the requirement for a device to supply clocking. The cabling for the direct connection to the router's console is rolled. For connecting Ethernet devices, most often the straight-through cable is used, unless it is host to host or switch to switch, in which case a crossover connection is necessary.

REVIEW QUESTIONS

1. The LLC and MAC sublayers are part of what OSI layer?

    A. Network
    B. Data link
    C. Hardware
    D. Physical
    E. Presentation

2. Which of the following is referred to as a best-effort protocol?

    A. IP
    B. FTP
    C. TCP
    D. NCP
    E. SPX

3. Which of the following descriptions best describes TCP windowing?

   A. The period in which routes are exchanged
   B. The number of seconds before the router disconnects
   C. How much data a receiving station can accept before an acknowledgment must be sent
   D. How large a TCP packet may be

4. Which of the following flow control methods is used by the transport layer?

   A. Read ready
   B. Gateway buffering
   C. Sequencing
   D. Delay
   E. Source-quench

5. What two layers of the OSI model support flow control and connection-oriented services?

   A. Presentation
   B. Session
   C. Transport
   D. Network
   E. Data link

6. What types of addresses are seen at the data link layer? (Choose two.)

   A. DLCI
   B. IP
   C. IPX
   D. MAC
   E. E-mail

7. A business has two buildings on the same campus. The computers within both buildings are on the same LAN; however, the network has been flooded with excessive broadcasts. What network device would you recommend to go between the two buildings?

   A. Switch
   B. Bridge
   C. Router
   D. Hub
   E. None of the above

8. Topology is defined at which layer of the OSI model?

   A. Physical
   B. Data link
   C. Network
   D. Transport

9. Which two devices are used to segment collision domains?

   A. Hub
   B. Repeater
   C. Switch
   D. Router
   E. Bridge

10. A company has two networks and on each network resides 40 stations. Each station is connected to a hub that is connected to a router interface, and the network administrator says that the hub collision light is continually on. What device would you replace the hub with to help this situation?

    A. Bridge
    B. Router
    C. Repeater
    D. Switch

REVIEW ANSWERS

1. **B** Layer 2 (data link) contains the LLC and MAC sublayers. The IEEE 802 committee subdivided the data link layer into two sublayers. The Logical Link Control (LLC) provides connectionless and/or connection-oriented services for high-level protocols at the data link layer. The Media Access Control (MAC) provides a unique address so that multiple devices can share the same medium and still identify each other.

2. **A** The Internet Protocol is referred to as a best-effort protocol because it simply receives data, applies the proper header information, and sends it along. IP, like most network layer protocols, is connectionless.

3. **C** A TCP window is the amount of outstanding data a sender can send on a particular connection before it gets an acknowledgment back from the receiver that it has received some data. For example, if a receiving host in a

TCP connection has specified a TCP window size of 64KB, the sender can only send 64KB of data and then it must stop and wait for an acknowledgment from the receiver that some or all of the data has been received. When the receiver acknowledges that all the data has been received, the sender is free to send another 64KB.

4.   **E**   The three flow controls mentioned at the transport layer are buffering, windowing, and source-quench messaging. Buffering stores the incoming segments for processing. Windowing is a dynamic method of flow control that changes based on receiver conditions. Source-quench messages are used to send a message to "back off" when segments are being sent too fast for the receiver to handle.

5.   **C** and **E**   The transport and data link layers both support connection-oriented and connectionless protocols and flow control. The difference is that the transport layer supports these for segments being sent end to end, and the data link layer supports them for frames as they are sent on the local network. The transport protocols deal with logical communication and the data link for physical communication.

6.   **A** and **D**   DLCI (data link connection identifiers) and MAC addresses both reside at the data link layer. MAC addresses are used in networks to establish communication between hosts. MAC addresses are physical, while IPX and IP addresses are logical. Logical addresses allow one host to find another, but all communication must be done physically. DLCIs are used in frame relay and are similar functionally to a MAC address; they identify the data link address of the frame relay connection.

7.   **C**   Of the devices listed, only a router will help the situation. Switches and bridges segment collisions but not broadcasts. Hubs are Layer 1 devices with no intelligence—hubs pass everything.

8.   **B**   Topology is defined at the data link layer. When we say "topology," we're most often referring to logical topology, which is the access method used and the encapsulation type. Because of the emphasis on the encapsulation rather than the physical cabling, it is defined at Layer 2. If the question had said "physical topology," the physical layer would have been correct.

9.   **C** and **E**   While the router will also do this, it does much more. The switch and the bridge are Layer 2, which is the layer at which wire segmentation

occurs. Therefore, they are the best answers. A hub and repeater cannot create collision domains, and all devices connected to them are on the same collision domain.

10. **D**   The switch is the appropriate device here because the problem is collisions. While the bridge and router segment collision domains, the switch is more capable than the bridge and faster than the router. The 40 stations don't even approach the maximum per network for TCP/IP or IPX, so a router is not necessary.

Introduction to the Cisco Internetwork Operating System

CHAPTER 2

	NEWBIE	SOME EXPERIENCE	VETERAN
ETA	5+ hours	3 hours	1 hour

27

Introduction to the Cisco Command Line Interface

Cisco prefers to be called a software company rather than a hardware company. One major reason for this is the Cisco command line interface, also known as the Cisco Internetwork Operating System (IOS). It is what Cisco is known for and is what makes their routers simpler to configure than other platforms. Once the IOS is learned on one platform, the same commands can be used to configure a different model of router or one of the many Catalyst switch platforms.

CLI Modes

The Cisco IOS is not displayed with a GUI; it is a CLI or command line interface. While Cisco does have GUI products to control routers and switches, the CLI is the focus for learning and managing the device. Cisco certification classes teach the CLI because it is the foundation for Cisco device configuration. It is hierarchical so that configuration commands are organized in various IOS modes. Since there are thousands of commands, organization of these commands is helpful for learning and configuring devices. When learning commands, you can logically associate them to what is being configured. As would be expected, IP addresses are configured under the interface's configuration mode, routing protocols under router configuration mode, and so on.

There are eight basic modes on a router, as follows:

- **Setup**　A series of prompts used to configure basic parameters on the router.
- **ROM monitor**　Similar to a BIOS prompt in Solaris, used to modify router behavior, including booting procedure, password recovery, and other system settings.
- **User exec**　Used for viewing settings on the router. Usually reserved for less-experienced technicians that need to perform basic router operations.
- **Privilege exec**　Used to access all configuration modes in the router. Without access to this mode, the technician is very limited in what can be configured on the router. Once access to this mode is achieved, the individual may configure anything on the router.
- **Global configuration**　Used to configure parameters that are to be applied to the router as a whole.

- **Interface configuration**   Used to configure interface parameters such as the IP address and clock rate of serial interfaces.
- **Router configuration**   Used to set up dynamic routing protocols on the router.
- **Line configuration**   Used to configure access to the console terminal, auxiliary terminal, asynchronous terminal, and Telnet lines.

Each of these modes has unique prompts to let you know which one is currently active. Each mode has different commands or procedures for accessing it, as can be seen in Table 2-1.

Most of the modes are used for configuration. Others, such as user exec, are used for displaying output only. The main configuration modes used for router commands follow the *<router name>*(*name of mode*)# format (see Table 2-3, later in this chapter). One of the most important modes, global configuration, will display a prompt that looks something like Router (config)# when the user enters the mode. Once the user is in a configuration mode, any other configuration mode can be entered without having to return to global configuration mode. Because all other modes are launched from global configuration, it is often thought that any other mode must be accessed from it. As shown in the code that follows, a user may enter global configuration mode, move to another mode, and without returning, move directly to still another mode. The following example illustrates what it looks like to connect to the router and move from the initial user exec mode through all other modes (other than setup and ROM monitor, which are illustrated later):

```
Rack-02-AS>
Rack-02-AS>enable
Password:
Rack-02-AS#configure terminal
Enter configuration commands, one per line.  End with CNTL/Z.
Rack-02-AS(config)#interface token 0
Rack-02-AS(config-if)#line vty 0 4
Rack-02-AS(config-line)#router rip
Rack-02-AS(config-router)#exit
Rack-02-AS(config)#exit
Rack-02-AS#
```

As shown, all configuration modes discussed are entered and accessed without returning to global configuration. Notice that **exit** is used to return to privilege exec mode. The CRTL-Z key sequence will return to privilege exec no matter what the current configuration mode. Use **exit** to move back from a specific

TABLE 2.1	IOS Command Modes		
Mode	**How to Access It**	**Prompt**	**Password Capable**
User exec	Press ENTER	>	Yes
Privilege exec	Type **enable**	#	Yes
Setup	Type **setup** or erase the saved configuration and reboot	[]	No
ROM monitor	Press CRTL and BREAK within 60 seconds of powering on the router	>	No
Global configuration	Type **configure terminal**	(config)#	No
Interface configuration	Type **interface ...** from any configuration mode	(config-if)#	No
Router configuration	Type **router ...** from any configuration mode	(config-router)#	No
Line configuration	Type **line ...** from any configuration mode	(config-line)#	No

configuration mode to global configuration mode; using **exit** again will return the prompt to privilege exec as displayed.

The prompt is not only important for configuring, it is important when booting a Cisco device. Sometimes prompts can be very confusing. The prompts used by user exec and ROM monitor both use > to indicate the respective mode. Usually, if ROM monitor mode is reached, there will be either rommon> or > by itself. When in user exec mode, the router by default will have the name "router" before the mode prompt and will look like this: router>. Using the **hostname** command as described later may change the prompt, which is the router name, and unless the administrator names the router rommon, a user should be able to distinguish between these two modes. ROM monitor mode allows an administrator to change the boot behavior of a Cisco router/switch.

The Boot Process of the Cisco Router/Switch

The Cisco router/switch has great flexibility in how it boots. The device can be interrupted to modify parameters, or it can be done after booting within the CLI. The device doesn't even have to store the IOS or the configuration file locally—they can be retrieved during the boot process by changing the configuration.

How the Router/Switch Boots by Default

Many things determine how a Cisco router/switch boots. By default, the router will boot with a screen similar to the one shown here:

```
System Bootstrap, Version 5.2(8a), RELEASE SOFTWARE
Copyright (c) 1986-1995 by cisco Systems
2500 processor with 16384 Kbytes of main memory
(output omitted)
Cisco Internetwork Operating System Software
IOS (tm) 2500 Software (C2500-JS-L), Version 11.2(22), RELEASE SOFTWARE (fc1)
Copyright (c) 1986-2000 by cisco Systems, Inc.
Compiled Mon 03-Apr-00 21:13 by htseng
Image text-base: 0x03040380, data-base: 0x00001000
```

```
cisco 2512 (68030) processor (revision E) with 16384K/2048K bytes of memory.
Processor board ID 01871656, with hardware revision 00000000
Bridging software.
SuperLAT software copyright 1990 by Meridian Technology Corp).
X.25 software, Version 2.0, NET2, BFE and GOSIP compliant.
TN3270 Emulation software.
1 Token Ring/IEEE 802.5 interface(s)
2 Serial network interface(s)
32K bytes of non-volatile configuration memory.
8192K bytes of processor board System flash (Read ONLY)


Press RETURN to get started!
```

Time should be spent learning how to read the bootup screen of the device. It displays the bootstrap version used to initially boot the device. The code image which is the IOS used for router/switch configuration is displayed with this line from the above output:

```
2500 Software (C2500-JS-L), Version 11.2(22)
```

Further down the output:

```
16384K/2048K bytes of memory
```

means that the device has 16 megabytes of memory installed. Also installed is a Token Ring interface and two serial interfaces. The interfaces are used for passing frames and packets across the device toward their destinations, which is the main purpose of any switch or router. The last two lines of the output show how much NVRAM (32K) and how much flash (8MB) are installed on the system. NVRAM is used to save the configuration so it isn't lost when the device is powered off. Flash is used to store the main IOS on the device. Both NVRAM and flash retain the information stored in them when the device is shut off. The contents of RAM are not retained. RAM is used for temporary information that is needed for quick retrieval and reference. The system processes, the current running configuration, and any table information run in RAM. When the device is powered off, the contents are flushed. Notice that the information above can be displayed after the router boots by using the command **show version**, as shown here:

```
Rack-02-AS#show version
Cisco Internetwork Operating System Software
IOS (tm) 2500 Software (C2500-JS-L), Version 11.2(22), RELEASE SOFTWARE (fc1)
Copyright (c) 1986-2001 by cisco Systems, Inc.
Compiled Fri 23-Feb-01 01:30 by kellythw
Image text-base: 0x0307D4D8, data-base: 0x00001000


System Bootstrap, Version 5.2(8a), RELEASE SOFTWARE
BOOTFLASH: 3000 Bootstrap Software (IGS-RXBOOT), Version 10.2(8a), RELEASE SOFTWARE (fc1)
Rack-02-AS uptime is 6 weeks, 1 day, 6 hours, 19 minutes
System returned to ROM by power-on
System image file is "flash:/c2500-jos56i-l.121-7.bin"


cisco 2512 (68030) processor (revision E) with 16384K/2048K bytes of memory.
Processor board ID 01871656, with hardware revision 00000000
Bridging software.
X.25 software, Version 3.0.0.
SuperLAT software (copyright 1990 by Meridian Technology Corp).
TN3270 Emulation software.
1 Token Ring/IEEE 802.5 interface(s)
2 Serial network interface(s)
32K bytes of non-volatile configuration memory.
8192K bytes of processor board System flash (Read ONLY)


Configuration register is 0x2102


Rack-02-AS#
```

Without observing the device boot, most of the information about the router's hardware and software installed can be accessed with the **show version** command.

Where the router boots is determined by several factors. When there is no saved configuration, the router will boot to setup mode. When the boot field in the configuration register is changed, boot behavior will change based on the parameters entered with the **config-register** command. The configuration register is a 16-bit field, and any modification to one of the first 4 bits may change the entire startup sequence of the device. Even if the configuration register remains the same, boot system commands entered in global configuration mode could alter the loading of one code image, so that another is used. The boot commands can be saved in NVRAM, a type of memory that stores configuration files, so that upon next restart, the router will execute these boot commands and load a code image as specified. Sometimes there might not be a valid image available to boot—maybe the flash memory has failed and the IOS stored in flash is inaccessible. If a PC operating system failed, the device would not boot, as it wouldn't make it past the ROM prompt. In order to prevent this from happening to a router or switch, Cisco built a smaller IOS into the ROM hardware chip, so that if need be the router will use this as a last resort.

Local Lingo

NVRAM   The memory used to store router configurations. Whenever **startup-config** is used in a command, it is indicating the contents of NVRAM. So in the command **show startup-config**, it displays the saved configuration in NVRAM.

Booting When There Is No Saved Configuration

If the startup configuration file is erased and the device rebooted, it is programmed to boot into setup mode. It doesn't matter why there is no saved configuration. It might have been erased or the device may be new and no configuration has been made on the device. In any case, the device will boot as normal except that instead of reaching user exec mode—the default mode the router boots to—it will enter setup mode, which is used for basic configuration of the device. Setup is a template presenting the user with a series of configuration questions so that the device can be easily and quickly configured. While convenient, this mode is for newbies. After some practice and instruction, the technician should ready the device from the other modes, so that setup mode is rarely used. The following is an example of setup mode:

```
Rack-02-AS#setup

        -- System Configuration Dialog --
Continue with configuration dialog? [yes/no]:  yes
```

At any point you may enter a question mark '?' for help.

Use ctrl-c to abort configuration dialog at any prompt.

Default settings are in square brackets '[]'.

Basic management setup configures only enough connectivity

for management of the system, extended setup will ask you

to configure each interface on the system

Would you like to enter basic management setup? [yes/no]: no

First, would you like to see the current interface summary? [yes]:

Interface	IP-Address	OK? Method Status	Protocol
Loopback9	1.1.1.1	YES manual up	up
Loopback10	unassigned	YES unset up	up
Serial0	unassigned	YES unset administratively down down	
Serial1	unassigned	YES unset administratively down down	
TokenRing0	140.10.42.10	YES manual up	up

Configuring global parameters:

  Enter host name [Rack-02-AS]:

  The enable secret is a password used to protect access to

  privileged EXEC and configuration modes. This password, after

  entered, becomes encrypted in the configuration.

  Enter enable secret: cisco

  The enable password is used when you do not specify an

  enable secret password, with some older software versions, and

  some boot images.

  Enter enable password [cisco]:

  The virtual terminal password is used to protect

  access to the router over a network interface.

  Enter virtual terminal password: cisco

  Configure SNMP Network Management? [no]:

  Configure LAT? [yes]: no

  Configure bridging? [no]:

  Configure AppleTalk? [no]:

  Configure DECnet? [no]:

  Configure IP? [yes]:

    Configure IGRP routing? [yes]:

      Your IGRP autonomous system number [1]:

  (Text Omitted)

Async lines accept incoming modems calls. If you will have

```
users dialing in via modems, configure these lines.
  Configure Async lines? [yes]: no
Configuring interface parameters:
Do you want to configure Serial0  interface? [no]:
Do you want to configure Serial1  interface? [no]:
Do you want to configure TokenRing0  interface? [yes]:
The following configuration command script was created:
Ouput Omitted
end
[0] Go to the IOS command prompt without saving this config.
[1] Return back to the setup without saving this config.
[2] Save this configuration to nvram and exit.
Enter your selection [2]:
```

Earlier it was said that if there is no saved configuration the router will boot to setup. Notice here that the command **setup** was invoked from privilege exec to enter the mode. Most of the items configured from this mode are

- Router name
- Passwords
- Routing protocols
- Interface's IP addresses

At the end, three options are given: go directly to a command prompt without saving, return to the beginning of setup mode if a mistake was made, or save the configuration and exit. Of course, if there is a saved configuration file, the router will not boot to this mode, it will only be accessible by typing setup.

Many times, it is necessary to alter the boot behavior of a router/switch. When upgrading the IOS or setting up more sophisticated options, the boot behavior can be changed as required.

Changing the Configuration Register to Modify Boot Behavior

The configuration register is a 16-bit field in which the bits may be manipulated to change the behavior of the network equipment. To understand basic booting of a router/switch, the configuration register must be explained.

Register Values Displayed in Hex

By default, a device such as a 2500 series router will boot the IOS loaded in flash because it has a configuration register value of 0x2102 or 0x0102 and no boot system commands in the saved configuration. Playing with either the register or the boot commands can radically affect the device. If, for instance, the register is changed to 0x2101, the router will boot to the built-in ROM IOS that is normally used for maintenance. Unlike computers or other manufactured devices, Cisco devices contain a mini-IOS that is stored permanently in the hardware ROM chip. When a device's IOS needs to be upgraded, this maintenance version aids as necessary. This small IOS is referred to as Rxboot or, more often, the subset IOS. Subset is a good way to refer to the code because it contains only enough commands to allow the device basic functionality until restored to a full IOS.

> ## Travel Advisory
>
> Be careful not to modify the configuration registers on production equipment until you have perfected the process under supervision and practiced on lab equipment.

The configuration register is always displayed in hex. Hex values are always indicated with a group of numbers that begin with 0x, which simply means that what follows is represented in hex. Because every two hex digits equal 1 byte of information, and there are 8 bits in a byte, the four hex digits of the configuration register equal 16 bits, as can be seen in Figure 2-1.

Bits	15	14	13	12	11	10	9	8	7	6	5	4	3	2	1	0
Hex bit values	8	4	2	1	8	4	2	1	8	4	2	1	8	4	2	1
Bit settings	0	0	1	0	0	0	0	1	0	0	0	0	0	0	1	0
Total bit value		2				1				0				2		

Hex description   0 X 2 1 0② Configuration register
                                    ↑Boot field

FIGURE 2.1   Configuration register bit meanings

In the figure, each four hex spaces have a division; this is because hex has a value range of 0–15. Because there is a need to represent all of these possible values with a single hex digit, anything above 9 in decimal requires that alphabetical letters be used when converting to hex, starting with the letter A, which represents the decimal value of 10. As shown in Table 2-2, the highest value of 15 is represented by F.

Try not to confuse bit values with the number of bits. While there are 16 bits in the configuration register, there are more than 65,000 possibilities. When converting from binary to hex, the 16 bits are sectioned off in groups of 4 bits; each section has 16 possibilities, represented as 0–F in hex. In Figure 2-1 the group to the farthest right, bits 0–3, represents the boot field. Because there are 4 bits, there are 16 possibilities. If the value of all the bits were set to 1 in this area, it would equal F, meaning that the router will look into the saved configuration and follow any boot commands present there when booting. If this group of bits equals 1 in value, the router/switch will boot to the subset IOS and ignore the operating system in flash. If the group is set to a value

TABLE 2.2	Decimal to Hex Conversion
Decimal	**Hex**
0	0
1	1
2	2
3	3
4	4
5	5
6	6
7	7
8	8
9	9
10	A
11	B
12	C
13	D
14	E
15	F

of 0, the router will not boot to any IOS. Instead, it will enter ROM monitor mode, which is like a BIOS prompt. This is illustrated in Table 2-3.

Some routers might begin with a configuration value of 0x0 instead of 0x2. The difference is that the 2 in the later value will cause the system to attempt to boot the IOS from a network TFTP server before looking at the local saved configuration file. A value of 0x0102 will cause the router to bypass network booting and boot from the saved configuration file on the local device.

Local Lingo

TFTP   Trivial File Transfer Protocol. This should not be confused with FTP. TFTP is a low-overhead protocol that allows many Cisco devices to boot from a network server. It may also be used to back up and restore both configurations and IOS files.

Exam Tip

Many times, hex doesn't display leading zeros. If the value directly after the 0x is 0, it might not be displayed. Documentation might not display leading zeros when displaying a hex value. If the configuration register is set to 0x0102, the documentation might display it as 0x102.

Components Used During Boot

A component that begins the boot process when the router or switch is first powered on is called the *bootstrap*. It is code built into the router/switch hardware and is used until the IOS is located. After the router locates and loads an IOS image that is used to continue the process, the bootstrap is relieved of its duty. POST

TABLE 2.3	Basic Configuration Register Values and Their Meanings
Boot Field Value	**Meaning**
0x2100	Boot to ROM monitor mode
0x2101	Boot to subset IOS
0x2102-F	Boot according to boot commands in saved configuration

(Power On Self Test), which is invoked by the bootstrap, is the process the router or switch goes through upon startup to check the device's hardware. It runs a series of tests that verifies if all the components are in working order. When it finds a problem, it will report the error onscreen. How severe the error is will determine if the device boots or not. As mentioned earlier, Cisco routers/switches have a mini-version of the IOS software built into their hardware. This is used if the router can't boot from anywhere else and is known as the subset IOS because of the limited commands supported. Finally, the code image is the router IOS, located in flash or loaded by using a TFTP server.

The router always attempts to find a usable IOS version to use when booting. If the router can't find a usable image, it will always boot from ROM. This is the last resort for the router. If the router boots to a full IOS, the prompt will look similar to the following:

```
Router>
```

If it can't find a full IOS code image, it will boot from ROM and the prompt will be similar to this one:

```
Router (boot)>
```

Both of the above prompts show that the router is in user exec mode; however, the additional (**boot**) reveals that the router for some unstated reason booted from ROM (Rxboot).

It might be necessary to modify boot commands rather than use the configuration register when altering the booting of the device. Whether it is required or just preferred, boot system commands may be used to boot the router/switch from a TFTP server, IOS stored in flash, or the subset ROM IOS.

Configuring Boot System Commands

Boot commands must be configured at global configuration mode, but are only used if the configuration register boot field is set to 2-F. The order in which the commands are entered will determine the order in which the system executes the commands. As with many other items on a Cisco router or switch, configuration files are read from the top down. The order of the boot commands in the configuration will determine the order they are implemented. Once a boot command is successfully executed, all other boot commands listed below it will be ignored.

In the router output that follows, a sample configuration shows how boot commands may be implemented to alter boot behavior. Here the system is to try to boot from a network TFTP server. If this fails, it is instructed to attempt the booting from the flash IOS. The last boot command, boot **system bootflash:**, is a newer way of referring to the ROM IOS. It replaces the older command **boot system rom**. The configuring of this last parameter is unnecessary because the device will boot from ROM any time it cannot load a full version of the IOS, with or without the command.

```
Rack-02-R6#show running-config
Building configuration...
Current configuration:
!
version 11.2
service timestamps debug uptime
service timestamps log uptime
no service password-encryption
no service udp-small-servers
no service tcp-small-servers
boot system tftp c2500-js-1.11-3.bin 172.16.5.1
boot system flash
boot system bootflash:
```

(Partial configuration listed.)

When the **boot system tftp** command is used, it should refer to an IOS file and the address of the TFTP server should be added as well. If there is no IP given for the TFTP server, the device will use a broadcast message to search for one.

In the absence of boot system commands, the system will follow the default behavior of booting from flash and then ROM.

Objective 2.03   # Configuration Using the CLI

Once the router is booted, user exec mode can be accessed by pressing the RETURN key. If there is a password configured, the user will be prompted for it. After the password is entered successfully, the prompt will have a > symbol next to the hostname of the router. At this prompt, type the command **enable** to enter privilege exec mode. Usually, there will be a password required, and after the password is entered, the prompt will change from > to # indicating the change in modes.

The command **show running-configuration** displays the current configuration on the router. To view the saved configuration, enter the **show startup-configuration** command. These two commands are the most basic for viewing the configuration loaded on a router or switch.

Global Configuration Mode

From privilege exec, all configuration modes are accessible. To go back to user mode, type **disable**, and the prompt will change back to >. By default, the hostname is "router," which is always displayed before the prompt for the mode the router is in. It can be changed with the **hostname** command from global configuration mode. To enter global configuration mode, type the command **configure terminal**. After the carriage return the prompt will change to "*<router name>* (config)#" to indicate the new mode. Entering the **hostname** command followed by the name intended for the router will change the name in the prompt. The **hostname** command is case sensitive, as shown here:

```
router(config)#hostname Rack-02-R6
Rack-02-R6(config)#
```

Travel Advisory

The hostname entered is case sensitive and should be entered exactly as documented. Configurations for dialup and other processes need to make use of the hostname of the device and must match exactly to function correctly.

To return from a configuration mode to the previous mode, use the command **exit.** This will move the user back one mode from the current mode. To move from any configuration mode to privilege exec, use CTRL-Z. This command sequence will not work from user exec or setup mode.

Interface Configuration Mode

To go to a specific configuration mode such as interface, line, or router configuration mode, the command **configure terminal** must be used. This command must be entered before any of the configuration modes can be used. To go to interface configuration mode from global configuration mode, enter the command **inter-face** followed by the interface intended. For example, to go to interface Ethernet 0 on the router, type **interface Ethernet 0** from the "Router (config)#" prompt. To go back to global configuration mode, type **exit**. Once in interface configuration mode, the prompt will change to "Router (config-if)#" and interface parameters such as IP address and clock rate can be entered.

```
Router (config)#interface serial 0
Router (config-if)#ip address 192.168.100.1 255.255.255.0
Router (config-if#clock rate 2000000
```

In this configuration, the IP address is set to the first host on the 192.168.100.0 network. The clock rate is placed on the interface if there is no external CSU/DSU, which is normally used to supply the clock rate for WAN connections. After these parameters are configured, the user should return to privilege exec mode and run the command **show interface**, as seen here:

```
Router (config-if)#CTRL z
Router #show interface serial 0
Serial0 is up, line protocol is up
  Hardware is HD64570
  Internet address is 192.168.100.1/24
  MTU 1500 bytes, BW 1544 Kbit, DLY 20000 usec, rely 255/255, load 1/255
  Encapsulation HDLC, loopback not set, keepalive set (10 sec)
  Last input 00:00:04, output 00:00:00, output hang never
  Last clearing of "show interface" counters never
  Input queue: 0/75/0 (size/max/drops); Total output drops: 0
  Queueing strategy: weighted fair
  Output queue: 0/1000/64/0 (size/max total/threshold/drops)
     Conversations  0/1/256 (active/max active/max total)
     Reserved Conversations 0/0 (allocated/max allocated)
  5 minute input rate 0 bits/sec, 0 packets/sec
  5 minute output rate 0 bits/sec, 0 packets/sec
     112578 packets input, 6216177 bytes, 0 no buffer
     Received 85095 broadcasts, 0 runts, 0 giants, 0 throttles
     0 input errors, 0 CRC, 0 frame, 0 overrun, 0 ignored, 0 abort
     112424 packets output, 6099468 bytes, 0 underruns
     0 output errors, 0 collisions, 1 interface resets
```

```
0 output buffer failures, 0 output buffers swapped out
2 carrier transitions
DCD=up  DSR=up  DTR=up  RTS=up  CTS=up
```

In the output, the IP address and the network mask should be verified and the interface display up and the line protocol up. The interface must have both the interface and the line protocol listed as up in order to be operational. The first part of the line, serial interface is up, refers to the interface receiving carrier signals from the cable being plugged in to another device. The second part of that line, line protocol is up, means it is receiving data link layer keepalives. Essentially, an interface and line protocol that are both up means that Layer 1 and Layer 2 connectivity has been achieved. While there still might be problems at either of these two layers, the basic signaling that the router requires at these layers is present.

Abbreviating Commands

Abbreviations are legal in the Cisco IOS; however, enough of the command must be typed in order for the device to recognize the command intended. Instead of typing every word fully in an example shown previously, the same could have been accomplished by typing the following:

```
Router (config)#int s0
Router (config-if)#ip add 192.168.100.1 255.255.255.0
Router (config-if#clock rat 2000000
```

As long as the IOS has enough to distinguish the command from another, the shortcut may be used. However, notice that the router couldn't decide which command was meant in the following example:

```
Rack-02-R6#cl set ?
% Ambiguous command: "cl set "
```

The router couldn't distinguish between the commands **clear** and **clock**. Using the question mark directly after the cl will show this.

```
R1#cl?
clear  clock
R1#cl
```

The Cisco IOS comes with an available help system, but typing "help" will not access it. Help is accessed by using the ? in conjunction with command words or sequences. It can also be used with no commands at all. Notice the difference— here it is used by itself:

```
Rack-02-R6#?
Exec commands:
  access-enable    Create a temporary Access-List entry
  access-template  Create a temporary Access-List entry
  bfe              For manual emergency modes setting
  clear            Reset functions
  clock            Manage the system clock
  configure        Enter configuration mode
  connect          Open a terminal connection
  copy             Copy configuration or image data
  debug            Debugging functions (see also 'undebug')
  disable          Turn off privileged commands
  disconnect       Disconnect an existing network connection
  enable           Turn on privileged commands
  erase            Erase flash or configuration memory
  exit             Exit from the EXEC
  help             Description of the interactive help system
  lat              Open a lat connection
  lock             Lock the terminal
  login            Log in as a particular user
  logout           Exit from the EXEC
  mrinfo           Request neighbor and version information from a multicast
                   router
 --More--
```

The question mark by itself shows the first word of the command for all the commands available in the mode. Going back to the previous example, the question mark could have been placed after the c in order to view all the commands that start with *c*, as shown here:

```
Rack-02-R6#c?
clear clock
```

If the question mark is placed one space after the **c**, notice the message:

```
Rack-02-AS#c ?
% Ambiguous command:   "c "
Rack-02-AS#c
```

When placed one space after the letter, the router interprets the user as asking for the next command in the sequence. Since the first command cannot be determined, it displays an error. After the message is displayed, the IOS returns what was typed on the next line. If a required word in the command sequence is left off, the router reacts differently:

```
Rack-02-AS#clock set
% Incomplete command.
Rack-02-AS#
```

The router displays the "% Incomplete" message because the time and date were not entered. Notice that after the error, the router does not return what was previously typed. The IOS punishes the user for not knowing the complete command by making them retype the command sequence again from scratch.

Exam Tip

It is important to be familiar with messages the router will display if a command is incomplete or causes an error message. The CCNA candidate should be able to predict which message an incomplete or wrong command sequence will display.

Symbols in the IOS

There are many other messages and symbols in the IOS that must be understood. When the question mark was entered earlier with no letters before it, it listed all the commands available. The message --More-- was listed at the bottom of the output. This tells the user that there is more text yet to be displayed. The key that is pressed at this point will determine how the remaining output is displayed. If the SPACE key is pressed, the next screen full of information is displayed. To see only the following line, press the ENTER key. If any other key is pressed, no more information will be displayed and the prompt will return.

When typing commands it is useful to pay attention to symbols such as brackets. The IOS uses [] with information inside to display a default choice. In the display of setup mode earlier in the chapter, the default answers are always depicted within the brackets. To take the defaults, all that is necessary is to press the RETURN key.

Setting a password on the system is one of the most basic tasks that needs to be performed to secure the router from unwanted access. Since a user can configure the router from the console, from the auxiliary, and through Telnet, all three modes will need to be password protected. In addition to these three modes, the enable password should be configured to protect privilege exec mode. This mode is the most important mode since it gives access to all configuration modes on the router and could be disastrous if accessed by an unauthorized person in a production network.

Line Configuration Mode

Lines on a Cisco router are used to configure terminal parameters such as login, passwords, baud, and flow control parameters. Think of a line as a way to access the routers/switches by an asynchronous terminal connection. The amount of lines and line numbering vary depending on model of router. On a typical 2500 series router, there are seven lines defined by default—one console, one auxiliary, and five Telnet lines called virtual terminals (VTY). Table 2-4 lists the seven lines and what they configure.

TABLE 2.4	Line Numbering on a 2500 Series Router	
Line Number	**Line Name**	**What Is Configured**
Line 0	line console 0	The console terminal
Line 1	line aux 0	The auxiliary terminal
Line 2	line vty 0	The first Telnet line
Line 3	line vty 1	The second Telnet line
Line 4	line vty 2	The third Telnet line
Line 5	line vty 3	The fourth Telnet line
Line 6	line vty 4	The fifth Telnet line

The status of the lines can be displayed with the command **show line** as shown here:

```
Rack-02-R6#show line
 Tty Typ    Tx/Rx     A Modem  Roty AccO AccI  Uses    Noise
 Overruns
*  0 CTY               -   -     -    -    -    0       0       0/0
   1 AUX   9600/9600   -   -     -               0       0       0/0
   2 VTY               -   -     -    -    -    0       0       0/0
   3 VTY               -   -     -    -    -    0       0       0/0
   4 VTY               -   -     -    -    -    0       0       0/0
   5 VTY               -   -     -    -    -    0       0       0/0
   6 VTY               -   -     -    -    -    0       0       0/0
Rack-02-R6#
```

In the above configuration, the * indicates the present lines in use. Here the CTY means console terminal and is the only line being used presently. As with most routers, line 1 is used for the auxiliary port, typically used to configure the device remotely using a modem. Lines 2–6 display the available Telnet lines on the device.

Setting Passwords

To configure a password on the console, enter the command **line 0** or **line console 0** from global configuration mode. Once on the line, enter the **login** command to let the router know that logging in with a password will be supported on the console, and then use the **password** command as follows:

```
Rack-02-R6#configure terminal
Enter configuration commands, one per line.  End with CNTL/Z.
Rack-02-R6(config)#line 0
Rack-02-R6(config-line)#login
Rack-02-R6(config-line)#password cisco
Rack-02-R6(config)#CTRL Z
Rack-02-R6#
23:28:32: %SYS-5-Crom console by console
Rack-02-R6#
```

To place a password on the auxiliary terminal, follow the same procedure, but change the line number, as shown here:

```
Rack-02-AS(config)#line aux 0
Rack-02-AS(config-line)#login
Rack-02-AS(config-line)#password cisco
Rack-02-AS(config-line)#
```

To set a password on the VTY lines, the procedure is nearly the same, though the login parameter isn't necessary on Telnet lines. To set the password, type in the line numbers from global configuration mode and then enter **password** followed by the password as shown here:

```
Rack-02-R6(config)#line vty 0 4
Rack-02-R6(config-line)#password cisco
Rack-02-R6(config-line)#^Z
Rack-02-R6#
```

Notice that all five Telnet lines are given a password in the example above. Line vty 0 4 means Telnet lines 0–4 (a space indicates the numbers in between).

Password protection for privilege exec mode cannot be done on a line configuration prompt. Instead, it is done from global configuration mode because the **enable password** command protects all the configuration modes. Supplying the correct password when connecting to the router from the console, aux, or Telnet will only gain access to user exec mode. If an enable password is configured, the user will have to type in the correct password after the **enable** command as indicated in the following:

```
Rack-02-R6 con0 is now available
Press RETURN to get started.
User Access Verification
Password: cisco
Rack-02-R6>enable
Password: CCNA
Rack-02-R6#
```

To set the enable password, move to global configuration mode and type **enable password** *ccna* (*ccna* being an example of a password). The trouble with the **enable password** command is that it is displayed in clear text within the configuration, so Cisco developed the **enable secret** command, which prevents the password from being displayed in clear text. Both commands are available on newer IOS versions and Cisco recommends that both be used. When both are used, different passwords should be used for the **enable password** and the **enable secret** commands. If they are the same, the clear text enable password will be a security hole, because anyone who sees the configuration will see the password. The reason for both being configured comes into play when the router must boot to the subset IOS. Many times the ROM IOS is an older version that may not understand the newer **enable secret** command. If only the **enable secret** is configured, the user won't be allowed to log in. If both are configured under normal conditions, the router will always prefer the enable secret and ignore the enable password. When booting to a later IOS, the enable password will be used only if the IOS version doesn't have an **enable secret** command configured. The following is an example of configuring both passwords:

```
Rack-02-AS#configure terminal
Enter configuration commands, one per line.  End with CNTL/Z.
Rack-02-AS(config)#enable secret ccie
Rack-02-AS(config)#enable password cisco
Rack-02-AS(config)#
```

Exam Tip

Make sure to learn the configuration mode in conjunction with the proper mode where the command is used. This will be helpful on the test if you know it, and will hurt if you don't.

Initiating, Suspending, and Ending Telnet Sessions

Earlier in the book, the process of hooking up a rollover cable and connecting a PC to the router/switch console was explained. Often, physical access to a device might not be readily available and it will be necessary to access the device through Telnet. Understanding how to suspend, resume, and disconnect Telnet sessions will be invaluable in a production network or lab.

When using Telnet to manage a remote router, the IOS gives the capability to suspend the Telnet session so that other Telnet sessions can be used without closing the previous ones. To Telnet, simply type the host name or IP address of the device from user or privilege exec modes—the **telnet** command is optional. After logging into the remote device, the session can be suspended by using what is known as the "escape sequence"—CTRL-SHIFT-^. This command sequence tells the local router to suspend the remote session, returning the user to the local router command prompt. At this point, another Telnet session can then be opened. Use the **show session** command to view all suspended terminal sessions on the router. To resume the last session initiated, simply press ENTER. To return to another session, type the number associated with the Telnet from the output of the **show session** command. The following output shows how a user with multiple open Telnet sessions suspends the third one and then returns to the first:

```
R3#CTRL-SHIFT-^(The sequence is not displayed but added to help clarify)
Rack-02-AS#
Rack-02-AS#show session
Conn Host            Address           Byte  Idle Conn Name
   1 r1               1.1.1.1            95  1w4d r1
   2 r2               1.1.1.1             4  3w2d r2
 * 3 r3               1.1.1.1             5  3w4d r3
Rack-02-AS#1
[Resuming connection 1 to r1 ... ]
R1#
```

The * next to the third session indicates that it is the active session. Though it could have been accessed again simply by pressing RETURN, instead "1" was entered and the first Telnet session resumed without closing any of the others. A Telnet session on the remote system can be ended by typing **exit** within Telnet. The session will end and the local router prompt will return. In the following output, a user Telnets to a remote router, logs in, and types **exit** to end the session, rather than suspending it:

```
Rack-02-R3#140.10.4.4
Trying 140.10.4.4 ... Open
User Access Verification
Password:
Rack-02-R4>en
Password:
Rack-02-R4#exit
[Connection to 140.10.4.4 closed by foreign host]
Rack-02-R3#
```

To end a session from the local router instead of the remote, use the command **disconnect** followed by the number of the session, as follows:

```
Rack-02-AS#disconnect 3
Closing connection to r3 [confirm]
Rack-02-AS#sh session
Conn Host            Address           Byte  Idle Conn Name
*  1 r1              1.1.1.1              0     0 r1
   2 r2              1.1.1.1              4  3w2d r2
   Rack-02-AS#
```

Using ping and traceroute to Check for Connectivity

If an IP address is entered and a system doesn't respond, there might be a connectivity problem. Two commands are commonly used to check for connectivity problems: **ping** and **traceroute**. **Ping** is used followed by the address or hostname in question. If connectivity exists, the ping will return exclamation marks denoting a successful ping. Five pings are sent out by default and if there is a failure on any one of the five, a period will be displayed after a two-second timeout interval expires. If all fail, it will take 10 seconds for all the pings to time out. If successful, five exclamation marks will return very quickly. Notice the two different results shown here:

```
Rack-02-R1#ping 192.86.2.2
Type escape sequence to abort.
Sending 5, 100-byte ICMP Echos to 192.86.2.2, timeout is 2 seconds:
 .....
Success rate is 0 percent (0/5)
Rack-02-R1#ping 140.10.5.5
Type escape sequence to abort.
Sending 5, 100-byte ICMP Echos to 140.10.5.5, timeout is 2 seconds:
 !!!!!
Success rate is 100 percent (5/5), round-trip min/avg/max = 4/4/8 ms
Rack-02-R1#
```

Traceroute is used to view the path that a packet uses to reach a destination device. Enter the command **traceroute** followed by the IP address or hostname of the remote device. The path between the local and remote hosts will be mapped out as follows:

```
Rack-02-R7#traceroute 198.133.219.25
Type escape sequence to abort.
Tracing the route to 198.133.219.25
 1 * * *
 2 151.164.162.66 [AS 600] 16 msec 20 msec 16 msec
 3 151.164.1.174 [AS 600] 20 msec 80 msec 16 msec
 4 151.164.240.234 [AS 600] 16 msec 20 msec 80 msec
 5 151.164.240.210 [AS 600] 16 msec 16 msec 84 msec
 6 151.164.241.161 [AS 600] 16 msec 20 msec 80 msec
 7 160.81.37.141 [AS 600] 20 msec 20 msec 20 msec
 8 144.232.11.249 [AS 600] 80 msec 24 msec 20 msec
 9 144.232.18.118 [AS 600] 88 msec 28 msec 32 msec
10 144.232.9.206 [AS 600] 60 msec 80 msec 64 msec
11 144.232.27.2 [AS 600] 64 msec 80 msec 64 msec
12 * * *
13 128.107.240.177 [AS 600] 64 msec 68 msec 64 msec
14 128.107.240.162 [AS 600] 72 msec 64 msec 80 msec
15 198.133.219.25 [AS 600] 68 msec * *
Rack-02-R7#
```

Viewing the path used to get to a remote host gives insight into how routing is working. Notice the * indicates timeouts which may be due to congestion or other problems that exist. This command can point out where the connectivity problems between the hosts exist. If the packet keeps moving back and forth between two IP addresses, this indicates a loop exists. If the packet is taken to a network not intended, this might mean there is a routing problem, often referred to as a "black hole." The times at the end of each line are used to show the average delay between routers by giving three samples. **Traceroute** measures each of these router hops three times, giving a good indication about the delay between each device.

Objective 2.04   Backup and Restoration of the IOS and Configurations

With most equipment, it is important to maintain backup copies of configuration files and of the operating system. The only thing worse than forgetting to back up files is not knowing how to make backups and restore them as needed.

Saving, Backing Up, and Restoring Configuration Files

The IOS **copy** command is used to save configuration files either locally or remotely to a network server. From privilege exec, use **copy** followed by the source file to the destination file. To save the current configuration, **copy running-config startup-config** is used. It means take the router configuration currently residing in RAM and save it to the startup configuration file stored in NVRAM. Information stored in nonvolatile RAM (NVRAM) is not lost when the router is turned off, unlike information stored in RAM.

Exam Tip

The source is the first parameter after the word copy when using the IOS **copy** command. After the source, the destination is entered, so that **copy run start** is understood as copy the (source) running configuration to (destination) startup-config, which means NVRAM.

Travel Advisory

Whenever something is copied to running-config, realize that the information will be merged. Copying to other places such as flash or startup will overwrite. Merging can lead to problems where there is information already in the present config that gets merged with the new config. So when restoring a configuration, it is recommended that you copy it using the **copy tftp startup-config** command and then reboot the device.

The main Cisco IOS is stored in flash memory and can be saved or moved just as the configuration can. The command **copy flash tftp** means take the IOS stored in flash and copy it to a TFTP server. Reversing the words flash and tftp will restore the image—**copy tftp flash** copies the IOS file on the TFTP server into flash memory on the router. The output that follows shows an IOS file being saved to a TFTP server.

```
Rack-02-R5#copy flash tftp
Source filename [cisco/igs-i-l_111-9.bin]?
Address or name of remote host []? 204.181.102.242
Destination filename [igs-i-l_111-9.bin]?
!!!!!!!!!!!!!!!!!!!!!!!!!!!!!!!!!!!!!!!!!!!!!!!!!!!!!!!!!!!!!!!!!!!!!!!!!!!!!
!!!!!!!!!!!!!!!!!!!!!!!!!!!!!!!!!!!!!!!!!!!!!!!!!!!!!!!!!!!!!!!!!!!!!!!!!!!!!
!!!!!!!!!!!!!!!!!!!!!!!!!!!!!!!!!!!!!!!!!!!!!!!!!!!!!!!!!!!!!!!!!!!!!!!!!!!!!
!!!!!!!!!!!!!!!!!!!!!!!!!!!!!!!!!!!!!!!!!!!!!!!!!!!!!!!!!!!!!!!!!!!!!!!!!!!!!
!!!!!!!!!!!!!!!!!!!!!!!!!!!!!!!!!!!!!!!!!!!!!!!!!!!!!!!!!!!!!!!!!!!!!!!!!!!!!
!!!!!!!!!!!!!!!!!!!!!!!!!!!!!!!!!!!!!!!!!!!!!!!!!!!!!!!!!!!!!!!!!!!!!!!!!!!!!
!!!!!!!!!!!!!!!!!!!!!!!!!!!!!!!!!!!!!!!!!!!!!!!!!!!!!!!!!!!!!!!!!!!!!!!!!!!!!
!!!!!!!!!!!!!!!!!!!!!!!!!!!!!!!!!!!!!!!!!!!!!!!!!!!!!!!!!!!!!!!!!!!!!!!!!!!!!
!!!!!!!!!!!!!!!!!!!!!!!!!!!!!!!!!!!!!!!!!!!!!!!!!!!!!!!!!!!!!!!!!!!!!!!!!!!!!
!!!!!!!!!!!!!!!!!!!!!!!!!!!!!!!!!!!!!!!!!!!!!!!!!!!!!!!!!!!!!!!!!!!!!!!!!!!!!
!!!!!!!!!!!!!!!!!!!!!!!!!!!!!!!!!!!!!!!!!!!!!!!!!!!!!!!!!!!!!!!!!!!!!!!!!!!!!
!!!!!!!!!!
3869420 bytes copied in 56.780 secs (69096 bytes/sec)
Rack-02-R5#
```

After the command is entered, the device prompts for specifics. The command **copy flash tftp** lets the router know that the IOS should be backed up to a TFTP server. The specifics such as the IP address of the TFTP server, the source filename, and the destination filename are requested with a series of prompts. If any of the information is entered incorrectly, an error will be displayed and the copy will fail, as displayed here:

```
Rack-02-R5#copy flash tftp
Source filename []? igs-i-l_111-9.bin
Address or name of remote host []? 204.181.102.242
Destination filename [igs-i-l_111-9.bin]?
%Error opening flash:igs-i-l_111-9.bin (No such file or directory)

Rack-02-R5#copy flash tftp
Source filename [igs-i-l_111-9.bin]? cisco/igs-i-l_111-9.bin
Address or name of remote host []? 204.181.102.242
Destination filename [igs-i-l_111-9.bin]?
TFTP: error code 1 received - File not found
```

```
Rack-02-R5#show flash
System flash directory:
File  Length   Name/status
  1   3869420  cisco/igs-i-l_111-9.bin
[3869484 bytes used, 324820 available, 4194304 total]
4096K bytes of processor board System flash (Read/Write)
Rack-02-R5#
```

In the first portion above, the error in the fifth line was caused by entering the wrong name for the IOS file stored in flash. The name "igs-i-l_111-9.bin" was mistyped. In the second portion, the name was corrected, but the TFTP server directory had the wrong permissions and it denied the copy. It is always good to run the **show flash** command before entering the copy to back it up. In the output of **show flash**, the name of the file that was incorrect should have been, "cisco/igs-i-l_111-9.bin." After displaying the contents of flash, highlight the name of the file, right-click and copy it. When the router prompts for the filename, paste it in.

The tricky part of the **copy** command is that the router determines what type of file to copy based on the source and destination provided. The command **copy startup-config tftp** tells the device to copy the saved configuration file to a TFTP server. The router interpreted the file to be a configuration file because configuration files are the only things saved in the startup configuration memory. If startup or running is part of the source or destination, the device assumes that it is a configuration file that needs to be copied. When start appears in the command, as in **copy start tftp**, the device knows that the startup configuration file is to be copied to a TFTP server. The router will then prompt for the specifics as shown here:

```
Rack-02-R5#copy start tftp
Address or name of remote host []? 204.181.102.242
Destination filename [startup-config]?
!!
2351 bytes copied in 0.280 secs
Rack-02-R5#
```

Notice the router prompts for the filename and the IP address or hostname of the TFTP server. For this copy to succeed, the TFTP server would have to be correctly configured prior to copying.

A Cisco device can be configured as a TFTP server to allow other devices to download the IOS that is stored in its flash. Obviously, there is no hard drive on

the router, so it cannot perform all the functions of a normal TFTP server. However, there might be times when setting this up can be useful in a network. To do so, from global configuration on the device that is acting as a TFTP server, enter the **tftp-server flash** command, as displayed in this output:

```
Rack-02-R5#show flash
System flash directory:
File  Length   Name/status
  1   3869420  cisco/igs-i-l_111-9.bin
[3869484 bytes used, 324820 available, 4194304 total]
4096K bytes of processor board System flash (Read/Write)
Rack-02-R5#config term
Enter configuration commands, one per line.  End with CNTL/Z.
Rack-02-R5(config)#tftp-server flash cisco/igs-i-l_111-9.bin
Rack-02-R5(config)#exit
Rack-02-R5#
```

It is best to view the filename first with the **show flash** command and then copy and paste when inputting the **tftp-server** command as above.

Other relevant commands used for the IOS are defined in Table 2-5.

TABLE 2.5	IOS Commands and Their Respective Meanings
Command	**Description**
show history	Shows the last ten commands entered.
show hosts	Displays the hostname table on a router/switch. It will display all hostnames configured on the system and the IP address(es) associated with each name.
show version	Displays IOS and ROM code information, memory installed, router uptime, and interfaces installed on the device. Useful for displaying basic system statistics and hardware configurations of the device. It also is a convenient method of verifying the status of the configuration register.
banner MOTD #	Command used to configure a "Message of the Day" on the router, which will be viewed when someone logs in. # can be substituted for any character referred to as the ending delimiter, which is used to end the message and return to the command prompt. Many administrators use this to display a warning that unauthorized access will be prosecuted.

CHECKPOINT

✔ **Objective 2.01: Introduction to the Cisco Command Line Interface**   The CLI is a text-based configuration program that allows a device such as a router or switch to be configured using a consistent interface. The CLI makes use of various modes to organize commands and secure the device. Knowing the various modes is critical in configuring Cisco devices.

✔ **Objective 2.02: The Boot Process of the Cisco Router/Switch**   Understanding the boot process means knowing what will happen depending if there is a saved configuration, the configuration register setting value or the if there are boot system commands configured.

✔ **Objective 2.03: Configuration Using the CLI**   Knowing how to move around the various modes and knowing which commands exist under each mode is critical in correctly setting up a router or switch. The line configuration modes present extra complexity and should have passwords configured for the console, auxiliary, and all VTYs.

✔ **Objective 2.04: Backup and Restoration of the IOS and Configurations** This section focused on how to use the **copy** command to back up and restore configurations and IOS versions on the router or switch. The **copy** command always specifies the source first followed by the destination intended.

REVIEW QUESTIONS

1. Given the following configuration, where will the router attempt to boot from first?

```
version 12.0
service timestamps debug uptime
service timestamps log uptime
no service password-encryption
!
hostname Rack-02-R1
boot system tftp 204.11.11.1 255.255.255.255
boot system flash
```

   A. Flash
   B. Bootflash
   C. ROM
   D. Rommon
   E. TFTP
   F. Cannot be determined

2. In initial configuration mode, what symbol indicates the default value?
   A. { }
   B. ( )
   C. [ ]
   D. < >
   E. # Value

3. Which of the following commands is used to configure clocking on a serial connection?

    A. (config)#clock rate 56
    B. (config)#clock rate 56000
    C. (config-if)#clock rate 56
    D. (config-if)#clock rate 56000

4. Which prompt presented here is not a valid configuration prompt?

    A. (config-if)#
    B. (config-line)#
    C. (config-router)#
    D. >

5. What is the configuration register setting if the device should boot from ROM?

    A. 0x0100
    B. 0x2100
    C. 0x0102
    D. 0x101

6. What type of memory is used to store the saved configuration file on a Cisco switch/router?

    A. NVRAM
    B. RAM
    C. Flash
    D. TFTP

7. What is the hex value of the binary output 00000001.00001111?

    A. 0x001F
    B. 0x0101
    C. 0x010F
    D. 0x101F

8. What is the command prompt for ROM monitor mode?

    A. router>
    B. router#
    C. router (rommon)
    D. >
    E. rommon#

REVIEW ANSWERS

1. **E** The configuration is processed in a top-down fashion so that this router will attempt to boot from the TFTP server 204.11.11.1 before going on to flash and then ROM.

2. **C** Notice that default answers are listed in brackets as shown by the following output:

```
         -- System Configuration Dialog --
At any point you may enter a question mark '?' for help.
Use ctrl-c to abort configuration dialog at any prompt.
Default settings are in square brackets '[]'.
Continue with configuration dialog? [yes/no]: yes
First, would you like to see the current interface summary? [yes]:
Interface          IP-Address       OK? Method Status        Protocol
Ethernet0          192.168.100.5    YES NVRAM  up            up
Ethernet1          204.181.102.254  YES NVRAM  up            up
Serial0            192.168.101.1    YES NVRAM  up            up
Serial1            192.168.102.1    YES NVRAM  up            up
```

3. **D** The "clock rate" command must be entered at the interface configuration prompt, and it specifies the clock rate in bits. Two of the incorrect answers used 56, which assumed 56K. This command requires all the zeros be typed out, so 56000 is correct.

4. **D** The prompt > is used with either user exec or ROM monitor mode. Neither mode is known as a configuration mode. User exec allows no configuration, while ROM monitor is more of a BIOS prompt, used to alter how the router will boot.

5. **D** Remember that many times the leading zeros are not displayed in hex. The hex value for the configuration register should be understood as 0x0101, which tells the router to boot to the subset IOS in ROM. The value 0x2101 is also valid. This value instructs the router to try to boot from the network before using boot commands; the former value does not.

6. **A** NVRAM (non-volatile RAM) is used to save the configuration because, unlike RAM, it is not erased when power is removed. Flash isn't erased when

power is removed, but it is used for IOS files, not configurations. TFTP is a protocol used to copy files.

7. **C** In order to display the 16 bits 00000001.00001111 in hex, divide the numbers in groups of four so that it is displayed as 0000 0001 0000 1111. Then add up the individual groups, remembering that each group has a bit value of 8 4 2 1 in this order. The first group is easy to add up since it is all zeros. Any answer that didn't start in 0x0 should be suspect right now. The second group has the 1 value turned on, so that the group equals 1. So far you have 0x01, which eliminates answers A and D. The third group is all zeros, so you have 0x010, which still allows for answers B and C. The last group has all bits turned on, and since you add the bit values of each bit in the group, you have 8+4+2+1, which equals 15. After consulting the hex chart from earlier in the chapter, you can see that 15 equals F.

8. **D** This is a tricky question because some routers/switches have rommon> as a prompt. Answer E was close, but not correct because of the # rather than the >. Other routers/switches use just the > by itself to indicate ROM monitor mode.

Managing and Updating Cisco Devices

ETA	NEWBIE	SOME EXPERIENCE	VETERAN
	4+ hours	2 hours	1 hour

In the previous chapter, we looked at basic commands for configuring and booting Cisco devices. This chapter will focus on the management features that the IOS offers. To begin with, CDP will be introduced and explained. Afterwards we will move to using CDP to help build a topology map of a network without having seen one in advance. We will then look at how to update the IOS and change the configuration register. The last part of the chapter presents a strategy for backing up IOS and configuration files.

Objective 3.01 Introduction to Cisco Discovery Protocol

CDP is a protocol and media-independent tool used to discover what Cisco devices are directly connected to the local device that is presently being accessed. CDP provides many different benefits that help in installation, discovery, and troubleshooting of networks. CDP can

- Discover directly connected Cisco devices
- Help troubleshoot Layer 2 connectivity issues
- Learn about the platform addressing, name, interface, and IOS of the remote device
- Run on most media types, such as Ethernet, frame relay, Token Ring, and FDDI

An experienced network technician can use CDP to skillfully move between Cisco devices for many situations. Suppose that a technician was called to an unfamiliar network and asked to troubleshoot a connectivity problem. The technician would probably ask for network documentation. What if there wasn't any or the documentation on hand was old and incomplete? If the network is operated using all Cisco equipment, the technician could log on to a router and document what interfaces and addressing were present, then Telnet to directly connected devices as identified by CDP. Once on the other device, the technician could document the interfaces and addressing for this device, use CDP again, and move to the next device, until a complete topology map was made. Without proper documentation, it is very difficult to troubleshoot a network. CDP allows the technician the ability to make a complete topology map or fill in the blanks of one that is incomplete.

CDP Frame Format

Cisco offers other GUI tools that allow this mapping to be done automatically; however, GUI tools aren't always available. At these times, CDP can be very handy. As stated above, CDP runs on most media types. This is important because of the amount of media types supported on Cisco equipment. LAN media types such as Ethernet, Token Ring, and FDDI support CDP by using the SNAP frame format. SNAP stands for SubNetwork Access Protocol and is unique from other frame types in that various media types implement this same frame type. Table 3-1 presents LAN frame encapsulations available for each media type. Notice that each media type has its own SNAP frame type.

Local Lingo

Frame type   Every LAN and WAN technology uses various frame types. A frame type is simply the format of the frame, the headers in the frame, and how many bytes each header is allocated for bits.

TABLE 3.1   LAN Frame Types

Media Type	Frame Encapsulation
Ethernet	Ethernet II
	Ethernet 802.2
	Ethernet 802.3
	Ethernet SNAP
Token Ring	SAP (default format)
	SNAP
FDDI	SAP
	FDDI raw
	SNAP

Because SNAP is used for each of these encapsulations, it is the best frame format for implementing CDP. The SNAP format is also supported by both ATM and Frame Relay, so that CDP may be used across both WAN and LAN connections.

Exam Tip
Knowing the information displayed by **show cdp neighbors** is foundational to understanding **CDP**.

CDP Operation

CDP operates at the data link layer of the OSI model. Because of this, a technician is provided clues as to Layer 2 operations between directly connected devices. If after issuing the command **show cdp neighbors** there are no neighboring devices listed, this might mean there is a Layer 1 or 2 connectivity issue. Beware, though—it could mean that CDP is not running on the other device. By default, CDP is enabled on Cisco equipment. It is designed to run on all Cisco equipment, including

- Hubs
- Switches
- Routers
- Access servers

CDP is on until someone turns it off. The command to turn the CDP process on is implemented at global configuration mode with the command **cdp run**. Since this is on by default when the device boots, it will multicast CDP advertisements every 60 seconds out every interface. If the interface is not configured, nothing, including CDP, will be sent or received on that interface. These advertisements are known as CDP hello packets.

Once a CDP advertisement is received from a remote device, an entry is added to the CDP table and CDP expects to receive another advertisement in 60 seconds. If the remote device doesn't send an advertisement within 180 seconds, which is known as the CDP hold time, it will remove the entry from the table, assuming that the device is no longer there. The timer always starts at 180 and counts down toward 0. If advertisements are being received as expected, this timer should never go much below 120 seconds. This is because advertisements should be received every 60 seconds, and when they arrive the timer will be reset to 180.

The first thing to do when checking to make sure that CDP is turned on is to issue the **show cdp** command from the privilege exec prompt, as follows:

```
Rack-02-R5#sh cdp
Global CDP information:
        Sending CDP packets every 60 seconds
        Sending a holdtime value of 180 seconds
Rack-02-R5#config term
Enter configuration commands, one per line.  End with CNTL/Z.
Rack-02-R5(config)#no cdp run
Rack-02-R5(config)#^Z
Rack-02-R5#show cdp
% CDP is not enabled
Rack-02-R5#
```

When the first **show cdp** was issued, CDP was running and the update and hold times were displayed. If CDP is turned off, the message "% CDP is not enabled" will be displayed when this command is entered.

While **show cdp** will show if CDP is enabled, it will not show the interfaces running it. CDP can be turned on globally and then manually turned off for certain interfaces. The command to shut off CDP on the interface is different than the command used to turn it on. To disable CDP on an interface, issue the **no cdp enable** command; to turn it on, use **cdp enable**. To verify that the intended interfaces are using CDP, issue the command **show cdp interface**, as shown here:

```
Rack-02-R5#sh cdp interface
Ethernet0 is up, line protocol is up
  Encapsulation ARPA
  Sending CDP packets every 60 seconds
  Holdtime is 180 seconds
Serial0 is up, line protocol is up
  Encapsulation HDLC
  Sending CDP packets every 60 seconds
  Holdtime is 180 seconds
Serial1 is administratively down, line protocol is down
  Encapsulation HDLC
  Sending CDP packets every 60 seconds
  Holdtime is 180 seconds
```

In this output, CDP is enabled on all interfaces; however, interface serial 1 has been shut down by an administrator. Therefore, while CDP is configured to run on all interfaces, serial 1 isn't sending or receiving CDP advertisements. After shutting down CDP on the Ethernet interface displayed above, **show cdp interface** returns this output:

```
Rack-02-R5(config)#int e0
Rack-02-R5(config-if)#no cdp enable
Rack-02-R5(config-if)#^Z
Rack-02-R5#show cdp interface
Serial0 is up, line protocol is up
  Encapsulation HDLC
  Sending CDP packets every 60 seconds
  Holdtime is 180 seconds
Serial1 is administratively down, line protocol is down
  Encapsulation HDLC
  Sending CDP packets every 60 seconds
  Holdtime is 180 seconds
```

Ethernet 0 is no longer listed as a CDP interface.

Sometimes it is important to disable CDP on an interface. If the interface is connected to an unsecured network, CDP should be disabled. If it is not, a device outside of your network may receive the advertisement and gain valuable information about the type of equipment to attack. Since CDP isn't routable, this is less likely, but always be cautious. The more likely place that CDP is a security hole is the internal networks within the company. If end stations are the only devices on the segment, shut off CDP on the connecting interface of the switch or router. Most network attacks come from internal employees or contractors. Leaving CDP running on end networks allows internal hackers to gather information about connected devices. Giving them the platform series and capabilities is a security hole because this information can help them compromise the device.

Exam Tip

Some devices do not support turning CDP on or off globally. For these devices, CDP is enabled or disabled by the **cdp enable** or **no cdp enable** command on an interface-by-interface basis. The 1900 switch doesn't support the global commands.

Using CDP to Build a Topology Map

Objective 3.02

O nce it has been determined that CDP is correctly configured and operating on the local device, **show cdp neighbors** can be used to see what devices are directly connected, as presented here:

```
Switch#show cdp neighbors
Capability Codes: R - Router, T - Trans Bridge, B - Source Route Bridge
                  S - Switch, H - Host, I - IGMP, r - Repeater


Device ID  Local Intrfce   Holdtme   Capability  Platform  Port ID
Rack-02-R7   Fas 0/18        122         R B        4500      Eth 1
Rack-02-R7   Fas 0/7         122         R B        4500      Fas 0
Rack-02-R6   Fas 0/19        149         R T        2500      Eth 0
Rack-02-R5   Fas 0/13        121         R         2500      Eth 0
Rack-02-R4   Fas 0/17        131         R T        2620      Fas 0/0
Switch#
```

The output above comes from a 2924 switch; notice that every router running CDP is listed. Table 3-2 lists the headings displayed with **show cdp neighbors** and their corresponding meaning.

In the preceding output, all the interfaces that the switch is receiving advertisements on are listed as Fast Ethernet interfaces. The routers attached have either Ethernet or Fast Ethernet interfaces. In addition, all the hold times are above 120 as they should be when the network is functioning correctly. The hostname of the remote device is given under the name heading. This is the actual name of the remote device displayed at its prompt, and as with all hostnames, they are case sensitive.

Exam Tip

It is important to know what type of information may be retrieved by using **show cdp neighbors** and **show cdp neighbors detail**.

TABLE 3.2	Description of show cdp neighbors
Heading	**Description**
Device ID	This is the hostname of the device to which your local device is connected.
Local Intrfce	The interface of the local device that received the remote device's CDP advertisement.
Holdtme	This is the amount in seconds before the entry is removed from the CDP table. This occurs if no hello is received within the 180-second holddown interval. This timer begins at 180 and counts down. Any value lower than 120 may indicate a connectivity or congestion problem.
Capability	This is explained in the top portion of the output which displays R = Router T = Transparent bridge B = Source route bridge S = Switch H = Host I = IGMP r = Repeater These may be combined, so R T means that it can function as a router or a transparent bridge.
Platform	Displays the model number of the remote device.
Port ID	The interface on the remote device that sent out the advertisement.

Notice that the **show cdp neighbors** command doesn't display the network address of the remote devices. To view this information, enter **show cdp neighbors detail**. This will give a couple of additional pieces of information. To save space, only the first portion of the output is displayed. This should be contrasted with **show cdp neighbors**, listed previously.

```
Switch#show cdp neighbors detail
-------------------------------
Device ID: Rack-02-R7
Entry address(es):
  IP address: 192.168.100.1
Platform: cisco 4500,  Capabilities: Router Source-Route-Bridge
Interface: FastEthernet0/18,  Port ID (outgoing port): Ethernet1
Holdtime : 159 sec

Version :
Cisco Internetwork Operating System Software
IOS (tm) 4500 Software (C4500-JS-M), Version 12.0(16), RELEASE SOFTWARE (fc2)
Copyright (c) 1986-2001 by cisco Systems, Inc.
Compiled Sat 03-Mar-01 02:01 by dchih
```

Two new pieces of information are learned by adding the keyword **detail** to the end of the command: the network addresses and IOS version are displayed. While it will show the network addresses configured on the remote device, it will not show any secondary addressing configured on the device. Only the primary network addresses are displayed. The addressing information can be used to connect to the device through Telnet. The IOS version is listed so that it can be verified without having to connect to the device and issue **show version**.

Displaying Specific CDP Entries

An alternate command that shows the same output is **show cdp entry**. With this command a specific device can be shown or * may be used to show all entries. When a single entry is to be viewed, the hostname can be entered at the end of the command. However, as stated earlier, these hostnames are case sensitive. If you don't enter it exactly as displayed, nothing will be displayed, as shown here:

```
Switch#show cdp entry rack-02-r7
Switch#
Switch#show cdp entry Rack-02-R7
-------------------------
Device ID: Rack-02-R7
```

```
Entry address(es):
  IP address: 192.168.100.1
Platform: cisco 4500,  Capabilities: Router Source-Route-Bridge
Interface: FastEthernet0/18,  Port ID (outgoing port): Ethernet1
Holdtime : 159 sec
Output omitted
```

The hostname rack-02-r7 didn't match the real hostname Rack-02-R7, so nothing was displayed. The IOS returned to the command prompt without displaying anything. When the capitalization was added as required, the correct output was shown.

As with the previous output, the IP address of the device is given. Using Telnet, the neighbor can be accessed and remotely controlled. In the following display, a Telnet session is initiated to 192.168.100.1, which was learned from the previous output. After logging in, **show ip interfaces brief** is executed, and every network address and interface is displayed:

```
Switch#telnet 192.168.100.1
Trying 192.168.100.1 ... Open
User Access Verification
Password:
Rack-02-R7>enable
Password:
Ethernet1          192.168.100.1   YES manual up              up
FastEthernet0      140.10.30.7     YES NVRAM  up              up
TokenRing1         140.10.43.7     YES manual up              up
```

After documenting these addresses, **show cdp neighbors** is once again entered:

```
Rack-02-R7#show cdp neigh
Capability Codes: R - Router, T - Trans Bridge, B - Source Route Bridge
                  S - Switch, H - Host, I - IGMP, r - Repeater
Device ID       Local Intrfce   Holdtme   Capability Platform  Port ID
Switch          Eth 1           163          S       WS-C2924C-Fas 0/18
Switch          Fas 0           163          S       WS-C2924C-Fas 0/7
Rack-02-R1      Tok 1           125          R B     4500       Tok 0
Rack-02-R7#
```

As shown here, a new device is revealed, Rack-02-R1. By issuing the **show cdp neigh entry Rack-02-R1** command, you can find its IP address, Telnet to it, and repeat the same process until the entire network is learned. Figure 3-1 shows what the topology map looks like to this point. Mapping out this entire network is beyond what we are trying to accomplish here, but how to use CDP to map out the network should be clear.

The IOS is constantly being updated with new features and bug fixes. On a large network, it can be a huge task to maintain the proper IOS versions for the equipment across the domain. At some point, in most networks, the IOS will have to be updated with a newer version.

Objective 3.03

Updating the IOS and Modifying the Configuration Register

W hen it becomes necessary to upgrade, Cisco has several methods for accomplishing this. In the previous chapter, the **copy** command was introduced. Now we want to expand on this command and show step by step how to upgrade

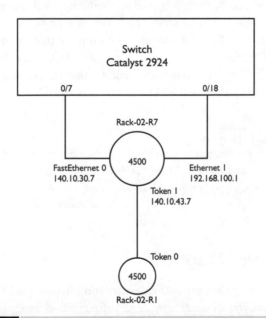

FIGURE 3.1   Topology map built by CDP

a router's IOS. For this section, let's assume that we have a router that is currently running Enterprise Version 12.0 of the IOS and a new feature in 12.1 needs to be implemented.

Travel Advisory

When upgrading the IOS software, be sure the system has enough flash memory installed to support the image. If there isn't enough, the copy will produce an error and end the process. Also, make sure there is enough RAM to load and run the new IOS.

The 12.0 version must first be acquired from Cisco's web site at http://www.cisco.com/, also known as Cisco Connection Online (CCO). All upgrades are obtained through a valid login with the proper authorization level. Just having a login to CCO isn't enough to download any IOS listed, though. You must be authorized to download the IOS by purchasing the software and rights to upgrades ahead of time. Cisco offers a matrix chart that can be easily used to obtain the correct version of the IOS. The file should be downloaded to a TFTP server that is able to serve the router or switch in need of upgrading. While many people prefer to use a Unix machine as a TFTP server, a small PC running Windows can be good enough to do the job. Cisco has a small TFTP program that can be downloaded from their site. The installation process is extremely easy; just double-click the executable file and it will install within a few seconds. After that, just copy the IOS versions to the proper directory of the TFTP installation and it is ready for use.

Travel Assistance

Many useful utilities such as TFTP Server and Config Maker can be downloaded from CCO at http://www.cisco.com/.

Error During Upgrade

On the router that is to be updated, make sure you can ping the TFTP server's IP address. If you can, you are ready to proceed. Before upgrading any IOS, it is always a good idea to perform a backup. Use the command **copy flash tftp** to back up the IOS version. As described in the previous chapter, the router will prompt you for the name of the file and the location of the TFTP server. While it is not necessary to change the configuration register value, if there are problems, it might be helpful to know how to make the change. When performing an upgrade, the router verifies that the file specified in the copy is on the TFTP server and accessible. If not, the process terminates with an error. When the copy process checks the file and verifies accessibility, it will begin the copy process. Depending on the IOS and platform currently running, this process might vary. Some of the later IOS versions will reboot the router before performing the copy process, while others will not reboot and will initiate the process right then. When the process runs, whether after rebooting or not, the first step will be to erase the current IOS in flash. Some routers can maintain multiple copies of IOS in their flash; however, here it assumed that there is only one and it will be replaced through the copy process.

If an error occurs after the first IOS is erased and the updated IOS fails, the router will boot to ROM. Recall from the previous chapter, whenever the device failed to load a full version of the IOS, it would load the ROM version as a last resort. The following is an example of a router's IOS being updated when a failure occurs resulting in the (boot)# prompt, indicating the ROM IOS has been loaded:

```
Source filename []? c2500-js-1.121-8.bin
Destination filename [c2500-js-1.121-8.bin]?
Accessing tftp://204.181.102.242/c2500-js-1.121-8.bin.
Erase flash: before copying? [confirm]

%SYS-4-CONFIG_NEWER: Configurations from version 12.1 may not be
correctly understood.
%FR-5-DLCICHANGE: Interface Serial0 - DLCI 104 state changed to ACTIVE
%FLH: c2500-js-1.121-8.bin from 204.181.102.242 to flash ...

System flash directory:
File  Length   Name/status
  1   14491400  /c2500-js-1.121-7.bin
[14491464 bytes used, 2285752 available, 16777216 total]
Accessing file 'c2500-js-1.121-8.bin' on 204.181.102.242...
Loading c2500-js-1.121-8.bin from 204.181.102.242
(via Ethernet0): ! [OK]

Erasing device...
eeeeeeeeeeeeeeeeeeeeeeeeeeeeeeeeeeeeeeeeeeeeeeeeeeeeeeeeeeeeeeeeeee
 ...erased
```

```
Loading c2500-js-1.121-8.bin .from 204.181.102.242 (via Ethernet0):
!!!!!!!!!!!!!!!!!!!!!!!!!!!!!!!!!!!!!!!!!!!!!!!!!!!!!!!!!!!!!!!!!!!!!!!!!!
!!!!!!!!!!! omitted text)
Loading c2500-js-1_121-8.bin ... [timed out]
 [failed]
 Cisco Internetwork Operating System Software
IOS (tm) 3000 Bootstrap Software (IGS-BOOT-R), Version 11.0(5),
RELEASE SOFTWARE (fc1)
Copyright (c) 1986-1996 by cisco Systems, Inc.
Compiled Tue 06-Feb-96 10:54 by hochan
Rack-02-R2(boot)>en
Password:
Rack-02-R2(boot)#
```

After finding this prompt, it is a good idea to view the output of the **show flash** command to see what the router displays about the file copy that failed:

```
Rack-02-R2(boot)#sh flash
System flash directory:
File  Length   Name/status
  1   7622144  /c2500-js-1.121-8.bin  [invalid checksum]
[7622208 bytes used, 9155008 available, 16777216 total]
16384K bytes of processor board System flash (Read/Write)
```

During the copy process, there was a failure so that not all the IOS was copied to flash. Any time the IOS to be loaded has an invalid checksum, the router will abort the loading of this IOS and attempt to boot somewhere else. If there is no other full IOS to boot to, the router boots to ROM as it did above.

There are many options to remedy this situation. The most obvious one is to attempt to copy another IOS to flash. Another option is to configure the router to load the IOS from a TFTP server. The latter option will be chosen so that it can be shown just how to do this.

Booting from Another Device

Sometimes it will be convenient to copy the IOS from another router using a compatible IOS. This can be very handy when a real TFTP server is not available. In fact, it can be configured so that a router upon booting copies and uses the IOS of another router. The steps to configure this will be presented in two parts. Part 1 is configured on the router acting as the TFTP server; part 2 is on the router that is receiving its IOS from the TFTP server while booting. Part 1 requires three steps:

1. On the TFTP router, view the IOS file in flash by using the **show flash** command.
2. Move to global configuration mode using **configure terminal** and enter the **tftp-server flash** [*name of the file in flash*] command.
3. Exit global configuration mode and verify the command is entered with **show run**. Save the configuration if this service is needed more than once. Use the command **copy running-config startup-config** to save the configuration.

On the router that is to boot from the TFTP server router, perform these three steps:

1. From privilege exec mode, go to global configuration by using **configure terminal**. Enter the command **boot system tftp** [*IP of TFTP server*] [*IOS filename to be loaded*].
2. Move back to privilege exec and **show run**, verifying that the command is entered correctly, the IP address is correct, and the filename is the one on the remote router.
3. Save the configuration, **copy run start**, and reboot the router by issuing the **reload** command.

After these steps are performed, the router should boot from the other router as shown here:

```
Rack-02-R2(boot)#reload
Proceed with reload? [confirm]
System Bootstrap, Version 11.0(5), SOFTWARE
Copyright (c) 1986-1994 by cisco Systems
2500 processor with 14336 Kbytes of main memory
%FR-5-DLCICHANGE: Interface Serial0 - DLCI 104 state changed to ACTIVE
Loading c2500-js-l_112-22.bin from 140.10.6.6 (via Ethernet0):
!!!!!!!!!!!!!!!!!!!!!!!!!!!!!!!!!!!!!!!!!!!!!!!!!!!!!!!!!!!!!!!!!!!!!!!!!!!!!!
(Text Omitted)
!!!!!!!!!!!!!!!!!!!!!!!!!!!!!!!!!!!!!!!!!!!!!!!!!!!!!!!!!!!!!!!!!!!!!!!!!
[OK - 8128764/13715514 bytes]
F3: 8029848+98884+316552 at 0x1000
```

```
(Text Omitted)
Press RETURN to get started!
Rack-02-R2>enable
Password:
(Text Omitted)
Rack-02-R2#
```

Every time this device is rebooted, it will go to the remote TFTP router to load its IOS. Due to circumstances, booting to an IOS from another router might be necessary.

Changing Configuration Register

When working with images in various networks, it is important to know how to change the configuration register values. There are times when the configuration register will need to be changed manually. Sometimes, an inexperienced technician may have changed it to an unintended setting and doesn't know what to do. The technician only knows that the router isn't booting correctly. There are two ways to change the configuration register: one is done when the device is booting, the other is done from global configuration mode.

Using ROM Monitor to Change the Register

The first method is to send a break signal within 60 seconds of the initial boot process. As pointed out in the previous chapter, this will interrupt the router and enter ROM monitor mode. Once in ROM monitor mode, the register value can be modified. On some routers, it is required that the configuration register utility be run. Below is an example of running "confreg" and changing the boot register to boot to the ROM IOS:

```
rommon 2 > confreg
    Configuration Summary
enabled are:
load rom after netboot fails
console baud: 9600
boot: image specified by the boot system commands
    or default to: cisco2-C2600
do you wish to change the configuration? y/n  [n]:  y
enable "diagnostic mode"? y/n  [n]:
```

```
enable  "use net in IP bcast address"? y/n  [n]:
disable "load rom after netboot fails"? y/n  [n]:
enable  "use all zero broadcast"? y/n  [n]:
enable  "break/abort has effect"? y/n  [n]:
enable  "ignore system config info"? y/n  [n]:
change console baud rate? y/n  [n]:
change the boot characteristics? y/n  [n]: y
enter to boot:
 0 = ROM Monitor
 1 = the boot helper image
 2-15 = boot system
    [2]: 1
    Configuration Summary
enabled are:
load rom after netboot fails
console baud: 9600
boot: the boot helper image
```

After displaying the current settings in the top portion of the display, the system prompts to see if some value should be changed. While many things can be changed here, the boot characteristics will be manipulated. Notice that the system is changed from booting to the boot commands to booting to ROM, called the "helper image" in the last line of the output. Entering the command **reset** will reboot the system and load the ROM IOS version.

On other versions of the IOS and/or router platform, there is no utility. Register values must be entered with the **o/r** command. This is typically the older IOS versions or platforms. The newer confreg utility is far easier to use. The following is an example of changing the register on an older 2500 series platform router so that it will boot to ROM:

```
System Bootstrap, Version 11.0(5), SOFTWARE
Copyright (c) 1986-1994 by cisco Systems
2500 processor with 14336 Kbytes of main memory
Abort at 0x10C51E8 (PC)
>o/r 0x2101
>i
System Bootstrap, Version 11.0(5), SOFTWARE
Copyright (c) 1986-1994 by cisco Systems
```

The **i** entered at the prompt stands for initialize and is used to boot the router/switch.

Sometimes, it may not be desired to have a device automatically reboot. It may be preferred for testing or other reasons that the system remains at the BIOS prompt (ROM Monitor). An administrator might want to manually boot the device so they are around while it is booting and can view the process as displayed here:

```
System Bootstrap, Version 11.0(5), SOFTWARE
Copyright (c) 1986-1994 by cisco Systems
2500 processor with 16384 Kbytes of main memory

Abort at 0x108FC26 (PC)
>o/r 0x0100
>i

System Bootstrap, Version 11.0(5), SOFTWARE
Copyright (c) 1986-1994 by cisco Systems
2500 processor with 16384 Kbytes of main memory
>
```

The router is booted using the i value, which sends it back to ROM. To now watch the boot process, the register should be changed and the i entered again.

Using the config-register Command to Change the Register

The configuration register may be changed within global configuration mode after the device has booted. To do so, move to global configuration mode and enter the **config-register** [*register value*] command. After modifying the register, the change can be put in effect by returning to privilege exec and issuing the **reload** command. It is not necessary to save when modifying the register since it isn't listed in the configuration. The command to view the configuration register is **show version**. In the router display that follows, the configuration register is changed to 0x0101 and then **show version** is entered to verify the modification before reloading:

```
Rack-02-R6(config)#config-register 0x101
Rack-02-R6(config)#^Z
Rack-02-R6#sh version
```

```
Cisco Internetwork Operating System Software
IOS (tm) 2500 Software (C2500-JS-L), Version 11.2(22), RELEASE SOFTWARE (fc1)
(Text Omitted)
2 Ethernet/IEEE 802.3 interface(s)
2 Serial network interface(s)
32K bytes of non-volatile configuration memory.
8192K bytes of processor board System flash (Read ONLY)
Configuration register is 0x2102 (will be 0x101 at next reload)
Rack-02-R6#reload
```

Now that you've seen how to manipulate the boot registers and use different boot methods, it might be helpful to talk about preventing bad situations where the router fails and there are no backups.

Objective 3.04 Backup Strategies

When working with intermediate devices such as hubs, switches, and routers, as pointed out in the previous chapter, it is important to know how to back things up. Without rehashing material already presented, this section will look briefly at methods for organizing and locating files when needed.

Documenting is one of the most important things that needs to be done from the time the equipment is installed, and it must be continually updated when there is any change. Documentation is your friend when there is a problem with the network. A diagram can be consulted to see if anything has been changed. Notes can be viewed to see if anything recently done might be conflicting with something that had been configured at an earlier time.

As valuable as documentation is, many times essential information is left out. Each router device may have a different IOS and will have a different configuration, yet too often this information isn't documented or the files themselves are not organized for easy retrieval. On a network server, every IOS version running and every configuration file needs to be stored. It is not recommended that the name of the IOS file be changed, so a folder with the device name might be used. Inside the folder might be the IOS as well as the present configuration file and all past configuration files that have been used on the device. When saving configuration files, they can be named to reflect which device they were used on. A consistent naming formula should be made beforehand so that whenever a change is made, the new file is stored on this server with the consistent naming convention.

In the following code sample, a configuration file is saved as a backup to a server. The naming convention "rack02-r6-10may2001" is used to illustrate what can be done, as shown in the output of **copy startup-config tftp**:

```
Rack-02-R6#copy startup-config tftp
Remote host []? 204.181.102.242
Name of configuration file to write [rack-02-r6-confg]? rack02-r6-10may2001
Write file rack02r6-10may2001 on host 204.181.102.242? [confirm]
Writing Rack02r6-10may2001 !! [OK]
Rack-02-R6#
```

The device used here is Rack02r6 and the date is May 10, 2001. Each time a change is made, a new file should be configured to the server following the convention agreed upon for the company. When there is a problem, the history of the configuration files may help in locating what the problem is.

CHECKPOINT

✔ **Objective 3.01: Introduction to Cisco Discovery Protocol** The CDP protocol is used to advertise device information to other directly attached devices. It operates by multicasting hello packets every 60 seconds, allowing remote devices to receive basic configuration/platform information about the device that is useful for documentation and troubleshooting.

✔ **Objective 3.02: Using CDP to Build a Topology Map** When documentation is incomplete or nonexistent, CDP can be used to fill in the gaps or develop a map of the entire internetwork. This can be done by Telnetting from device to device and documenting information from show commands along the way.

✔ **Objective 3.03: Updating the IOS and Modifying the Configuration Register** A router or switch will most likely need updating over time. By using a TFTP server, or another router/switch, the update can be copied to the device using various methods, such as the **copy** or **boot** system commands. When performing the upgrade, it might be necessary to change the configuration register from ROM monitor mode or from global configuration.

✔ **Objective 3.04: Backup Strategies** Many times, everything necessary to recover from a router/switch problem is not documented or organized properly. Using folders and file naming conventions can help in the process.

REVIEW QUESTIONS

1. What layer of the OSI does CDP operate at?

    A. Physical
    B. Data link
    C. Network
    D. Transport

2. What type of information does CDP display? (Choose three.)

    A. Configuration register
    B. Boot commands
    C. Name
    D. Platform
    E. Network address

3. How often is a CDP hello packet sent by default?

    A. 5 seconds
    B. 10 seconds
    C. 30 seconds
    D. 60 seconds
    E. 120 seconds
    F. 180 seconds

4. How long is the hold time for CDP?

    A. 5 seconds
    B. 10 seconds
    C. 30 seconds
    D. 60 seconds
    E. 180 seconds
    F. 240 seconds

5. Which of the following phrases best describes CDP? (Choose three.)

   A. CDP is used on Ethernet networks to display device information.
   B. CDP is a media-independent utility used to route network packets between Cisco-only devices.
   C. CDP is reserved for LAN topologies and may be helpful in learning about network-layer protocols running on directly connected devices.
   D. CDP is a Layer 2 protocol used to announce basic information to connected devices.
   E. CDP is a media-independent utility that requires a SNAP media type.
   F. CDP displays all network addresses in advertisements.

6. What type of addressing can be learned from CDP? (Choose two.)

   A. IP addresses
   B. MAC addresses
   C. DLCIs
   D. IPX addresses
   E. Data link addresses

7. Which command should be used to view information of all directly connected Cisco devices?

   A. show router
   B. show cdp
   C. show cdp neighbor
   D. show cdp entry
   E. show neighbor

8. Which piece of information cannot be learned by CDP?

   A. The router name
   B. The hostname
   C. The interface on the remote router that sent the update
   D. The local interface that received the advertisement
   E. The IOS of the remote device
   F. The configuration file on the remote device

9. What CDP command can be used to view a single device named Router1a?

   A. show cdp Router1A
   B. show cdp neighbor Router1A

    C. show cdp neighbors detail Router1A
    D. show cdp connected Router1a
    E. show cdp entry Router1a

10. Which of the following is the correct format for the **tftp-server** command?

    A. #tftp server flash 10.10.1.1 c2500-js-l.11-3.bin
    B. (config)#tftp-server flash 10.10.1.1 c2500-js-l.11-3.bin
    C. #tftp server flash c2500-js-l.11-3.bin 10.10.1.1
    D. (config)#tftp-server flash c2500-js-l.11-3.bin 10.10.1.1

REVIEW ANSWERS

1. **B** There is no network layer packet with CDP. CDP protocol information is encapsulated directly in the SNAP frame. Once the frame is stripped on the remote system, all that is left is the CDP information.

2. **C** **D** and **E** While the IOS can be seen in a **show cdp neighbor detail** display, the configuration register setting is not displayed. Configuration information outside of IP address is also not displayed.

3. **D** CDP hellos are multicast out all configured interfaces every 60 seconds by default. This can be changed with the **cdp timers** command from global configuration.

4. **E** The CDP hold time is a timer that starts at 180 seconds by default. It counts down toward 0. If it reaches 0, the CDP entry will be removed from the table. The hold time can be adjusted from global configuration mode with the **cdp holdtime** command.

5. **A** **D** and **E** CDP is used on Ethernet as well as most topologies. Make sure that you don't read too much into any one answer. The question didn't say *only* Ethernet networks. Answer D is a good general description of CDP, and answer E emphasizes that it works on all media that support the SNAP frame format. CDP has nothing to do with routing and works across WAN connections; these facts eliminate answers B and C.

6. **A** and **D** CDP operates at Layer 2, but isn't intended to provide data link layer information. The only addressing it displays is network layer. IP and IPX are addresses used at the network layer.

7. **C** There are only two valid IOS commands listed, B and C. However, **show cdp** will only show the settings for the update and hold timers. It will not show connected devices.

8. **F** Router name and hostname are the same thing. It is the first piece of information shown by **show cdp neighbors**. Both the local and remote interfaces are displayed so that the administrator knows what local interface received the update and what remote interface sent it. The IOS is displayed, but the name of the configuration file is not.

9. **E** The commands **show cdp neighbors** and **show cdp neighbors detail** do not show individual entries. There is no option to put a hostname at the end of these commands. If attempted, the router returns the following:

```
Rack-02-R4#show cdp neigh detail Rack-02-R6
    % Invalid input detected at '^' marker.
Rack-02-R4#
```

The '^' shows at what point the command was entered incorrectly. Notice that it was when a hostname was placed on the end. The only command that will do this is **show cdp entry** followed by the hostname. Remember that the hostname is case sensitive and must be entered exactly as CDP has it in its table.

10. **D** The **tftp-server** command must have the hyphen and be entered from global configuration mode as indicated by the (config)# prompt. This leaves answers B and D as the possibilities. The IOS filename must be entered before the IP address or the command will produce an error.

Catalyst 1900
Switch Operations

CHAPTER 4

	NEWBIE	SOME EXPERIENCE	VETERAN
ETA	8+ hours	3 hours	1 hour

87

Cisco's Catalyst 1900 switch is perhaps the most basic of the switching products available, and understanding its operation and configuration methods is required knowledge on the CCNA exam. In fact, the Catalyst 1900 is the *only* switch that is required knowledge on the CCNA exam. A Catalyst 1900 switch is like any other Ethernet switch except it does not have all the "bells and whistles" normally associated with Cisco's higher-numbered models. Regardless of the model number, the basic principles discussed in this chapter apply to all switches. A switch is merely a "turbocharged" transparent bridge. To understand a switch, you must first understand how a bridge works.

Objective 4.01 Three Functions of a Transparent Bridge

A transparent bridge is used primarily in Ethernet environments and is designed to be transparent to the end nodes, hence the name. There are three major functions of a transparent bridge:

- Learning
- Forwarding and filtering
- Avoiding loops

A transparent bridge performs all three functions concurrently while it is operational. Some definitions include a total of four functions, splitting forwarding and filtering into individual functions. Because Cisco considers them to be the same function, however, so will we.

Learning

A bridge must learn the destination MAC addresses so it can make accurate forwarding decisions. On an Ethernet physical segment, all stations see all frames transmitted on the segment. When a bridge is connected to a physical segment, it examines all the frames it sees. It reads the Source MAC Address field of the frame, and if it sees a frame coming from a node on a particular port, it assumes the station must reside on that port. The bridge will place this information in what is called a *bridge table*. The frame will perform the FCS before placing the entry in the bridge table, thereby eliminating erroneous entries. On a Catalyst switch, this table is called the *content addressable memory (CAM)*. A bridge table and CAM table are basically the same with some small differences which will be discussed later.

In Figure 4-1 there are four workstations, A, B, C, and D. There is also a bridge with two ports connected to two Ethernet segments. When workstation A transmits to workstation B, the frame traverses Ethernet segment 1 and is received by both the bridge and workstation B.

When the bridge receives the frame, it will learn that workstation A is on its port 1 since that is the port the frame was received on. It puts an entry into its bridge table recording the MAC address of workstation A as being on port 1, as in Figure 4-2.

Conversely, when workstation B responds to workstation A, the bridge will see a frame with workstation B's MAC address as the source, as in Figure 4-3.

The bridge will continuously learn. Entries will remain in the bridge table until no traffic is seen coming from that MAC address for five minutes. This time interval is configurable on almost all switches and bridges and is referred to as the *aging time*. Entries may also be manually entered into the bridge table, and these entries will not time out. Eventually all MAC addresses will be known by the bridge, assuming all stations are in use.

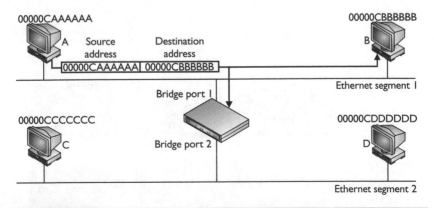

FIGURE 4.1   Workstation A transmits to workstation B.

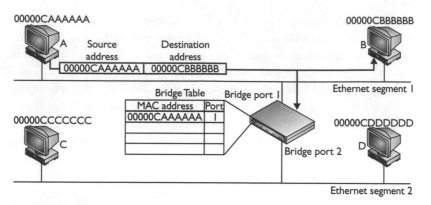

FIGURE 4.2   The bridge learns that workstation A is attached to port 1.

Forwarding and Filtering

The second major function of the switch is to forward and filter. Using the bridge table, a bridge will make a decision to forward or not forward (filter) a frame. This decision is made based on the destination MAC address in the frame header.

If workstation A were to transmit to workstation C, and workstation C had an entry in the bridge table, the bridge would forward the frame on to Ethernet segment 2, as shown in Figure 4-4.

If workstation A were to transmit to workstation B, forwarding of frames would be unnecessary since workstation B is on the same physical segment. Therefore the bridge would filter (not forward), as shown in Figure 4-5.

What happens if workstation A sends a frame to workstation C and the bridge does not have workstation C in the bridge table. In such a case, bridges will forward

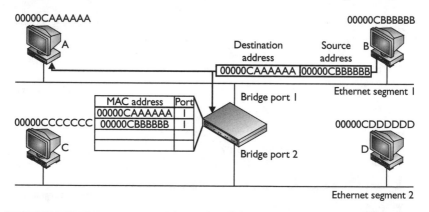

FIGURE 4.3   The bridge learns that workstation B is also attached to port 1.

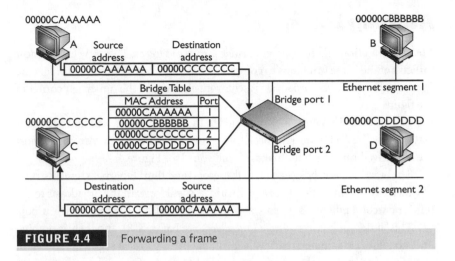

FIGURE 4.4 Forwarding a frame

frames destined for unknown destination MAC addresses to all ports except the port that originated the frame. The bridge behaves as a hub in this scenario to ensure that it is not preventing traffic from flowing.

A hub emulates an Ethernet segment by forwarding frames out to all ports except the port on which it was received. It is this behavior that makes it very similar to a switch in terms of broadcasts.

If the bridge were not to forward frames with unknown destination MAC addresses, workstation A would not have connectivity to workstation C until C transmitted a frame. This would be unacceptable. Bridges will also forward broadcasts and multicasts from all ports, much the same as frames with unknown destination ports.

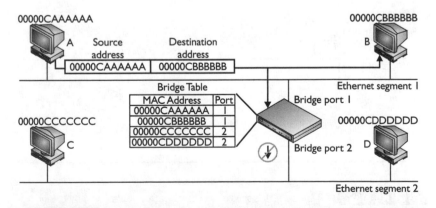

FIGURE 4.5 Filtering (not forwarding) a frame

Avoiding Loops

The final function of a transparent bridge is to avoid loops. This is by far the most difficult of the three functions to comprehend. In Figure 4-6, multiple bridges are used for redundancy. A broadcast is sent from a station in the upper-left corner of the figure.

Bridges X and Y, which are connected to the first segment, will see the broadcast. They will then forward the broadcast frame out all other ports except the port it was received on, which in this case is only one (see Figure 4-7).

The broadcast is propagated on to the second and third Ethernet segments, both of which have a connection to bridge Z. Bridge Z will forward the broadcasts to the third and second Ethernet segments, and hence the broadcasts become stuck in a loop.

This "little" problem is called a *bridge loop* (see Figure 4-8), and there is nothing little about it. This single broadcast will kill the three physical segments shown in Figure 4-6, and in the real world there might be hundreds of these physical segments.

Travel Advisory

Different versions of STP can cause bridge loops, which *kill* Ethernet physical segments. Be especially careful when using older switches such as Bay Networks. They have a tendency to use proprietary versions of STP that are not compatible with the IEEE version used with Cisco switches.

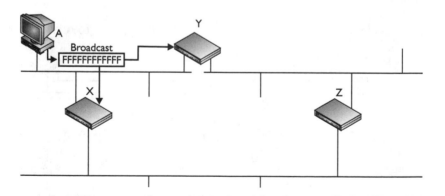

FIGURE 4.6   A broadcast is sent by workstation A and received by bridges X and Y.

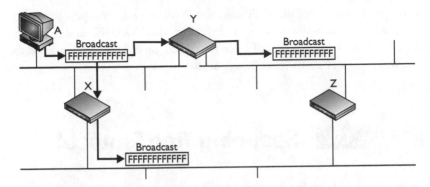

FIGURE 4.7 Bridges X and Y forward the broadcast frame out all ports.

This could lead to hours of downtime while an engineer tries to locate the loop. Once located, the simple solution would be to remove the offending connection.

The third major function of a bridge is to locate and eliminate the redundant connections like the one described in Figure 4-6. To do this a bridge must be aware of other bridges. The assumption that the source MAC address is located on the port it is received on does not work when there is more than one bridge. The protocol used by bridges to exchange information is called the *Spanning Tree Protocol* (STP).

There are several different versions of STP and they are not compatible with each other. It is important to verify that all bridges and switches use the same version of STP.

The two most commonly used STPs are DEC and IEEE. There are several other versions that are not very popular. It is important to verify that you are not

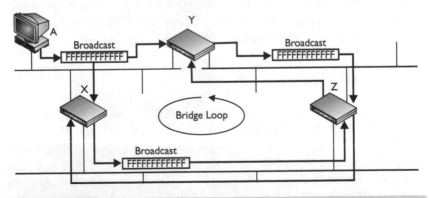

FIGURE 4.8 Bridge Z forwards both broadcasts.

using one of these rarely used STPs, as they could be a potential problem in the future. Most switches do not support anything other than DEC and IEEE. The Cisco Catalyst switch uses the IEEE version of STP on its Ethernet ports and the IBM version of STP on its Token Ring ports.

Objective 4.02   Spanning Tree Protocol

A bridge must transmit small packets out all ports to let other bridges know that it exists and can be a potential cause of bridge loops. These small packets are called *bridge protocol data units* (BPDUs). A Catalyst switch will send a BPDU out all of its active ports every two seconds. These BPDUs are received and the bridge uses a mathematical formula called the *spanning tree algorithm*. The spanning tree algorithm will let a bridge know when there is a loop and determine which of the redundant ports needs to be shut down. The process of shutting down a port is called *blocking*. A port that is blocking is still an active port—that is, it is still receiving and reading BPDUs. It will wait until a failure or topology change eliminates the loop. When this occurs, the port will start to forward frames since the loop is no longer present.

The purpose of the BPDUs and spanning tree is to create a "loopless" environment. A tree is free of loops naturally. A tree will have a root at the bottom of a trunk, the trunk will break into branches, and those branches will branch out into smaller branches and so on. A branch will never grow into another branch, thus it is a loopless environment.

The spanning tree algorithm can be complex, but understanding which ports go into the blocking state and why is important when troubleshooting bridge loops. As the name *spanning tree* indicates, the purpose of the protocol is to make the bridged network a tree, with all networks branches of the tree.

The Root Bridge

All trees have a root, and a spanning tree does too. It is a special bridge appropriately called the *root bridge*. All bridges are assigned a numerical value called *bridge priority*, and the bridge with the lowest priority is the root bridge. By default a Catalyst switch has a bridge priority of 32768. Therefore, if you only use Catalyst switches, all of your bridges have the lowest bridge priority—or the highest if you are a "glass is half full" kind of engineer. A tiebreaker must be used, and unlike the

NFL playoffs, a coin toss is not a good last resort considering most switches don't have a dime to their name. On a Catalyst switch, the lowest MAC address in the pool assigned to the supervisor engine will be used. This MAC address is commonly referred to as the *bridge ID*.

Local Lingo

Bridge ID   The bridge ID is really a combination of the bridge MAC address and the bridge priority—however, for the purposes of this discussion we equate the two.

The bridge ID is the tiebreaker: the lowest bridge ID will be the root bridge. Using the MAC address as the bridge ID will ensure that one and only one bridge will have the lowest value, due to the fact that MAC addresses are globally unique.

In Figure 4-9, you can see the same scenario discussed in the previous section. We have listed the bridge priority and the MAC address of the three bridges, X, Y, and Z. All the bridges used have the same bridge priority, therefore the tiebreaker will be the bridge ID. Bridge X has the lowest bridge ID and will be the root bridge. The root bridge is critical when determining the ports that will be forwarding and blocking.

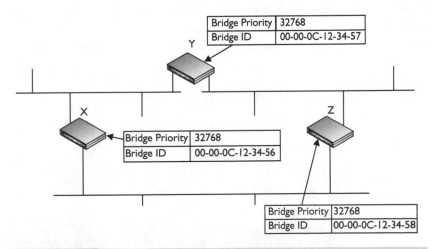

FIGURE 4.9   Bridge IDs and MAC addresses

Which Ports to Block

Using the BPDUs, the bridges must locate the loops and shut down or block on those ports that are causing a loop. There will always be two or more ports that are causing a loop, so which one should go into the blocking state? A decision must be made. *Port cost* is an arbitrary parameter that is assigned to ports in a bridged environment, usually by default and based on media rate. A Catalyst 1900 series switch will use the IEEE version of STP. The IEEE version of STP assigns port cost based on the media bandwidth. At first the IEEE used a simple calculation of 1000 Mbps divided by the bandwidth of the media. They realized this wasn't going to work as bandwidths increased. For example, a Gigabit Ethernet port would have a cost of 1, so what would 10 Gbps use? Fractions won't work! To resolve the problem, they came up with arbitrary port costs. Table 4-1 lists the old costs and the new costs.

Exam Tip

Remember that the CCNA 2.0 exam will only cover the Catalyst 1900, which will use the old costs.

A bridge will always look for the port that will lead to the root bridge in the cheapest way, similar to when you go to New York City. When traveling into the city from the airport, you could take a cab or a limousine service. The obvious choice is the cheapest method unless you are independently wealthy and like to spend money frivolously, which, if you are reading this book, you are probably not!

TABLE 4.1	Default Port Costs, Both the Old and New IEEE Defaults	
Media	**New Cost**	**Old Cost**
10 Mbps	100	100
100 Mbps	19	10
1 Gbps	4	1
10 Gbps	2	1

Everything is relative to the root bridge. As far as the bridge is concerned, it does not need more than one port that can lead to the root bridge. The port that is the closest or the "cheapest" to the root bridge is called the *root port*.

Referring back to the three bridge scenario (see Figure 4-10), you can see that the ports that are directly connected to the root bridge will be root ports since they are the "cheapest" of the two ports on bridges Y and Z. The root port will never be placed in the blocking state.

There is a loop in this situation, and one of the two ports on Y and Z, which lead to segment 3, must go into the blocking state to break the loop. To determine which one it will be requires an understanding of the *designated bridge*. The designated bridge on a segment is the bridge port that is closest to the root bridge on a physical segment. Remember that the root port is determined by looking at each non-root bridge. The designated bridge is determined by looking at each of the physical segments in the topology. Looking at segment 3 in Figure 4-10, there are two bridge ports to choose from. Both of these bridge ports are equally close to the root bridge. The tiebreaker will be a parameter called *port ID*, which is usually the MAC address of the port. There is a designated bridge on all physical segments. The designated bridge is the bridge advertising, via BPDUs, the lowest cost to the root. In the event of a tie, the port ID with the lowest MAC will be the designated bridge—and since the MAC address is globally unique, there will never be a tie.

If the cost of all ports in Figure 4-11 is the same, the port on segment 3 with the higher MAC address will be the port to enter the blocking state. In this case, bridge Y has a port ID of 00-00-0C-00-00-0A, which is higher than bridge Z's port ID, therefore bridge Y's port will enter the blocking state.

The designated bridge is determined by physical segment. The two physical segments that are directly connected to the root bridge will use the two ports of

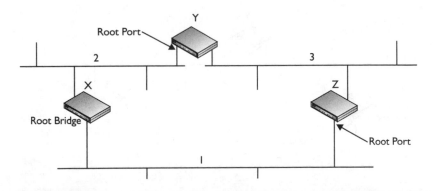

FIGURE 4.10 The root bridge and the corresponding root ports

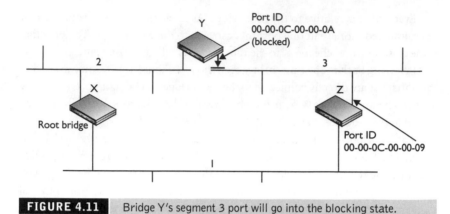

FIGURE 4.11   Bridge Y's segment 3 port will go into the blocking state.

the root bridge as the designated bridge. The root bridge will always be a designated bridge on all physical segments it is directly connected to.

A bridge will calculate which port is the root port and determine if any of its ports is the designated bridge of a physical segment. It will block on all other ports—in other words, if a port is not the root port or a designated bridge, it will block. In Figure 4-12, all the root ports and designated bridges are identified, leaving a single port to be blocked. Note that the root bridge will be the designated bridge on all of its ports and therefore will *never* block on any of its ports.

To further illustrate these concepts, let's look at a more complex environment, much like you would expect in the real world. Figure 4-13 is a network diagram with the workstations left out. As with all good network designs, there have been multiple cable runs for redundancy. There are four wiring closets in the building,

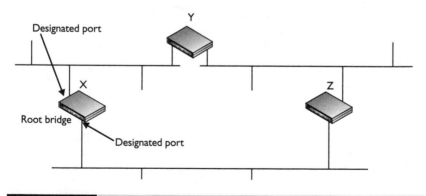

FIGURE 4.12   The root bridge's ports will always be designated bridges.

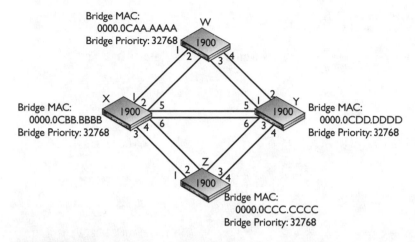

Bridge MAC:
0000.0CAA.AAAA
Bridge Priority: 32768

Bridge MAC:
0000.0CBB.BBBB
Bridge Priority: 32768

Bridge MAC:
0000.0CDD.DDDD
Bridge Priority: 32768

Bridge MAC:
0000.0CCC.CCCC
Bridge Priority: 32768

FIGURE 4.13 A sample network environment

each with a Catalyst 1900 switch. All connections are using 10 Mbps Ethernet ports. In the real world, you would probably find something a little more advanced than a 1900 because of the limited bandwidth of the 1900. It only has two ports that can support 100 Mbps.

All the bridge MAC addresses and bridge priorities have been listed. The bridge priority and port cost are left the same to illustrate situations in the real world. The port IDs can be found in Table 4-2. These parameters will often be left at the default.

It is important to look at each physical segment individually. To determine which ports will be forwarding and blocking, take the following steps.

Step 1: Determine the Root Bridge

The bridge with the lowest bridge priority will be the root bridge. If there is a tie, the bridge ID will be used as the tiebreaker. In Figure 4-14, all bridges have the same priority, therefore the bridge ID is used. Bridge W has the lowest bridge ID by virtue of its MAC address (0000.0CAA.AAAA), thus it is the root bridge.

Step 2: Determine the Designated Bridges

On a specific segment, the bridge port advertising the lowest cost to the root will be the designated bridge. In the event of a tie, the port ID is the tiebreaker.

Due to a switch's nature, each link listed is its own physical segment. The easiest physical segments to determine the designated bridges will be the physical segments

TABLE 4.2	Port IDs	
Bridge	**Port Number**	**Port ID**
W	1	0000.0C11.1111
W	2	0000.0C11.2222
W	3	0000.0C11.3333
W	4	0000.0C11.4444
X	1	0000.0C22.1111
X	2	0000.0C22.2222
X	3	0000.0C22.3333
X	4	0000.0C22.4444
X	5	0000.0C22.5555
X	6	0000.0C22.6666
Y	1	0000.0C33.1111
Y	2	0000.0C33.2222
Y	3	0000.0C33.3333
Y	4	0000.0C33.4444
Y	5	0000.0C33.5555
Y	6	0000.0C33.6666
Z	1	0000.0C44.1111
Z	2	0000.0C44.2222
Z	3	0000.0C44.3333
Z	4	0000.0C44.4444

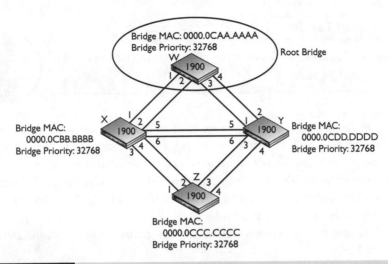

FIGURE 4.14   Determining the root bridge

directly connected to the root bridge. In Figure 4-15, all of the ports on the root bridge are designated bridges. The root bridge will obviously have the lowest cost to the root bridge.

The next physical segments from which the designated bridges can be easily derived are the segments between bridge Z and bridges X and Y. Clearly, the ports on X and Y are going to be the designated bridges as they are closest to the root bridge and therefore have the lower cost to the root.

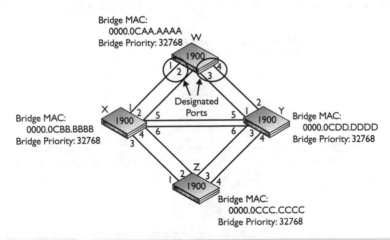

FIGURE 4.15   The root bridge's ports will all be designated ports.

> **Local Lingo**
>
> **Designated bridges**   Sometimes designated bridges are referred to
> as designated ports.

The last segments to examine are the two links between switches X and Y. Both ports are equally close to the root bridge so you must look to the bridge ID. On each of the segments, both ports are equally close to the root bridge, therefore you must go to the tiebreaker. In this case, the tiebreaker is the bridge ID, because bridge X's ports are advertising a lower bridge ID than bridge Y. Bridge X's ports 5 and 6 will become designated bridges.

You now have determined all of the designated bridges, as indicated in Figure 4-16.

Step 3: Determine the Root Ports

The port closest to the root bridge is the root port. Of course it is not necessary to determine the root port on the root bridge; however, there are several candidates on each of the other switches.

Bridge X has two ports that are equally close to the root bridge, ports 1 and 2. Only one port may be the root port. The first tiebreaker is the bridge ID being advertised by the other end of ports 1 and 2—in other words, ports 1 and 2 of bridge W. Since both ports are connected to the same switch, you must look to the next tiebreaker.

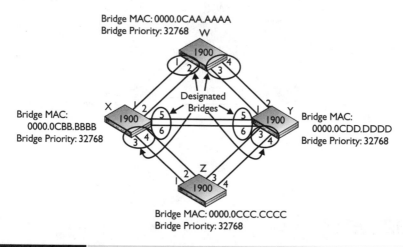

FIGURE 4.16   All designated bridges

Port cost is the next tiebreaker, but since both ports are 10 Mbps ports, the costs are also the same.

Next is *port priority*, an administrative value that can be set to fine-tune the topology determined by STP without changing the entire topology. You could adjust the port cost from its defaults, but this could affect the entire topology since it could alter the cost back to the root.

The final tiebreaker is the port ID, which is derived from the MAC address assigned to each port. In a typical environment, the MAC address assigned to a switch port would correspond to the port number in some way. For instance, on a Catalyst 1900 switch, the port's MAC address comes from a pool of addresses, and the lowest MAC address is assigned to the lowest numbered port and then assigned numerically from that point. Therefore on bridge X, port 1 will have a lower port ID than port 2 and will become the root port. Similarly on bridge Y, port 1 will have a lower port ID than port 2 and will also become a root port. Finally, bridge Z will follow the same parameters and thus have its port 1 become the root port. Table 4-2 lists the MAC addresses to further illustrate the concept. Bridge X, Y, and Z ports 1 all have the lowest MAC address on their respective switch. Figure 4-17 illustrates all the root ports and designated bridges; notice that all root ports are ports 1.

Step 4: Determine Which Ports Will Be Forwarding

All root ports and designated bridges will forward, so this step is very simple: all ports identified in Figure 4-17 will be forwarding.

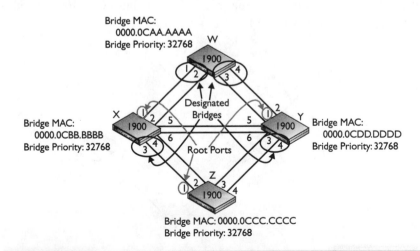

FIGURE 4.17 All root ports and designated ports

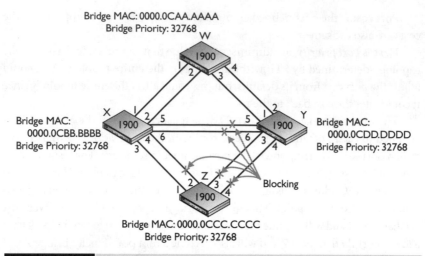

FIGURE 4.18 Final topology

Step 5: Determine Which Ports Will Be Blocking

The final step is to simply set all ports to blocking other than ports that are the designated bridge or root ports. This leaves the topology shown in Figure 4-18.

After you remove those blocked ports, you can see the spanning tree. Bridge W is the root and forwards on all of its ports, creating a sort of bush, not really a tree. Most of its branches are off the bridge X side. When you think of a tree, there is only one trunk, but with spanning tree it's more of an oleander or rhododendron. Figure 4-19 illustrates a somewhat pitiful plant but a very effective bridge topology. Whatever it is, it works.

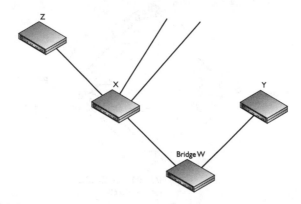

FIGURE 4.19 A simplified look at the topology

Spanning Tree Port States

One thing to consider when working in a switched/bridged environment is the fact that the Spanning Tree Protocol (STP) must determine the ports that are blocking and forwarding. This takes time, and the ports involved will go through several states before they end up in their final state.

When a bridge or switch has a port become active—the link light turns on—it goes through several states before it actually begins forwarding or blocking. A port first enters the listening state, when it listens for BPDUs. It reads these BPDUs to determine its root port and the designated bridges. If it has been determined that a port needs to be placed in the blocking mode, it enters that state when listening mode is complete. If it is determined that the port should be in the forwarding state, the port enters an intermediate state called learning. It is called the learning state because the port will be examining source MAC addresses and placing entries in the bridge table. Once learning is complete, forwarding will begin (see Figure 4-20). If there is a change in the link state or spanning tree topology, the spanning tree states are cycled. This may cause short periods of downtime on the network. Because of this, we recommend not making substantial changes to a bridged environment during mission-critical times of the day.

> **Exam Tip**
>
> It is important to understand that there *will* be a delay in forwarding frames when a switch port comes up.

While a bridge or switch port is in the listening and learning states, it is *not* forwarding. This can be a source of great problems when using switched Ethernet to the desktop. When workstations are plugged directly into a switch port, the link

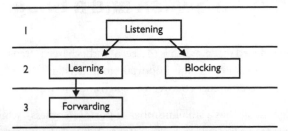

FIGURE 4.20   Spanning tree port states

state will change whenever the machine is power cycled. When a user comes into the office in the morning and turns his workstation on, the switch port must go through the spanning tree states. These states can take a minute or more depending on the switch settings. The NOS client software that is running on the workstation may have problems with this delay in connectivity. Once the machine loads the client software—Novell DOS or Windows Requester or Windows NT client—the workstation will look for a server. If no server is found, the workstation will often not have connectivity to the resources it needs, rendering the user unable to work (assuming he actually does work in the first place). This can be fixed by simply rebooting the workstation, but this is usually not an acceptable solution, especially to the user. A configurable parameter called *forward delay* will set the amount of time a port will be in the listening and learning states. Listening state and learning state will each be half of the forward delay time. This is not a parameter that we would recommend changing—these times are for the entire switch or bridge and when changed will affect the entire switch. This would include ports that may need to spend the whole minute to accurately calculate whether or not its ports belong in the forwarding state or blocking state.

On a Catalyst switch, a port can be configured to enter the forwarding state immediately to ensure connectivity to servers. This will not affect other ports on the switch. This will also not turn off the Spanning Tree Protocol. Engineers often refer to this as turning off spanning tree, but rather, you are simply allowing the switch to forward while it goes through the learning and listening states. We will revisit this subject when we get to configurations.

The spanning tree disabled state is when a port is administratively shut down. In this state, a port will not listen for BPDUs, forward frames, or learn MAC addresses. A disabled port must be reenabled manually. It will then go through the normal cycling of states described earlier.

Objective 4.03

The Difference Between a Switch and a Bridge

Earlier we mentioned that a switch is merely a "turbocharged" transparent bridge. In preparing for your exam, it is important to understand these differences. In general, there are two differences between a switch and a transparent bridge:

- A bridge usually has a small number of ports (16 or less), while a switch can have many. For example, the Catalyst 1900 can have up to a total of 26 ports.

- A bridge is generally slower than a switch. This is due to the architecture of the switch. A switch is primarily hardware based while a bridge is software based.

A third difference, which we mention really as a caveat because it is not standard, is the fact that a Catalyst switch can have more than one instance of the STP. This will be discussed in much greater depth in Chapter 6.

Frame Forwarding Methods of the Catalyst 1900 Switch

One of the reasons why a switch is faster than a bridge is in the frame forwarding methods of the switch. In general, a frame may be forwarded in one of two ways: *store-and-forward* and *cut-through*. There is also a third method developed by Cisco and supported on the Catalyst 1900 switch, called *fragment-free*.

Store-and-Forward

When a bridge receives a frame, the entire frame is received before it is forwarded to the destination port, regardless of the frame size. Store-and-forward frame forwarding will have different latencies based on the size of the frame. The smaller the frame, the smaller the latency, and the larger the frame, the larger the latency. This can be a disadvantage in networks where very large frames are common.

One advantage, however, is the capability of the bridge or switch to perform a cyclical redundancy check (CRC). This allows the bridge or switch to determine if the frame has any errors and, if it does, discard it. In an environment where there are many collisions or unreliable cabling, store-and-forward frame forwarding can save processing power and bandwidth by discarding these errored frames.

An understanding of bridging and frame architecture tells you that the bridge could start forwarding the frame after the first 6 bytes of the frame are received.

Cut-Through

As mentioned in the previous section, a bridge or switch only needs the first 6 bytes of the frame to make a forwarding decision. Cut-through switching allows the switch to start forwarding the frame before it is completely received. This can dramatically decrease the latency and forwarding rates depending on the frame size.

Cut-through switching is not dependent on the frame size like store-and-forward. Frame forwarding takes place immediately after the first 6 bytes, and therefore regardless of the frame size latency will remain constant.

A disadvantage with cut-through switching is the fact that the CRC cannot be checked as in store-and-forward. Although the switch will actually read the CRC to know whether to put the source MAC address in its forwarding table, the switch cannot stop the frame. It is going to be forwarded regardless of whether it is errored. This can cause unnecessary bandwidth utilization and consumed processing on all switches forwarding the frame.

Fragment-Free

One of the most common errors found on Ethernet networks is called a *runt*. A runt, as its name would imply, is a frame that is smaller than the minimum frame size. These frames are likely created by a collision. With fragment-free switching, this runt will not be forwarded, while with cut-through switching the frame will be forwarded. Fragment-free switches, unfortunately, *do* forward legal-sized frames that have CRCs. If you use store-and-forward, you will have the increased latency, while if you use cut-through you will have runts running around like an out-of-control nursery school.

Fragment-free is a happy medium developed by Cisco. Rather than forwarding the frame immediately after the first 6 bytes, the switch waits until 64 bytes have been received before forwarding. This ensures that the frame is not smaller than the minimum frame size and thus is not a runt. The latency is increased, but only slightly and not nearly to the degree that store-and-forward yields. At the same time, those pesky runts are kept out of your network infrastructure.

Objective 4.05

The Cisco Catalyst 1900 Series of Switches

On the CCNA exam, a basic understanding of the Catalyst 1900 series of switches is required. In this section, we will give a brief overview of the 1900 and discuss its operating system.

Understanding Cisco IOS Device Operation

It is important to remember that a Cisco IOS Device is like any other computer product. It has memory, a processor, and a backplane on which data will traverse. The Catalyst 1900 is no different. It has RAM for storage of its programs, NVRAM

Travel Advisory

Although this is required material for the exam, it should be noted that the Catalyst 1900 operating system is mostly unique to the Catalyst 1900 and 2820 series of switches. Commands and configurations discussed in this section will most likely *not* work on other Catalyst switches.

for storage of its configuration file, and of course a main processor to handle the forwarding and filtering of the frames as well as run the overall operating system.

Like the Cisco IOS–based routers, a Catalyst 1900 has two main modes of operation: user mode and privileged mode. From user mode, you can view the current status of the many processes running on the router as well as perform basic testing with tools such as Telnet and Ping. From privileged mode, the switch may be configured and advanced debugging can take place.

One difference between the 1900 and other Cisco IOS devices is the presence of a menu system. Originally the 1900 did not have Cisco IOS and used a menu-driven interface. This interface is still present in the latest versions and is one of the options when the switch is booted, as seen below:

```
Catalyst 1900 Management Console
Copyright (c) Cisco Systems, Inc.  1993-1998
All rights reserved.
Enterprise Edition Software
Ethernet Address:      00-D0-D3-71-80-00
PCA Number:            73-3121-01
PCA Serial Number:     FAB032531RW
Model Number:          WS-C1924-EN
System Serial Number:  FAB0327V0PK
Power Supply S/N:      PHI031403J4
PCB Serial Number:     FAB032531RW,73-3121-04
------------------------------------------------
1 user(s) now active on Management Console.
        User Interface Menu
    [M] Menus
    [K] Command Line
    [I] IP Configuration
Enter Selection:
```

Option K will take you to the Cisco IOS command line interface (CLI), while you can use M or I to configure the switch using the older menu interface.

> ### Exam Tip
>
> Although we have mentioned the menu system in this book, please be aware that it will most likely not be testable material. The exam will be more interested in your knowledge of Cisco IOS.

There is yet another way to configure the Catalyst 1900. Cisco IOS also has a HTTP interface which allows you to configure the switch via a normal web browser. Of course for this to take place the switch must be configured with an IP address on its management interface. By default the management interface has an IP address of 0.0.0.0 which is, of course, invalid. In the coming sections, we will look at configuring parameters such as these.

Different Methods of Configuring a Cisco 1900 Switch

As mentioned earlier there are three ways in which the Catalyst 1900 may be configured:

- Through the menu interface
- Through the Cisco IOS CLI
- Through the HTTP interface

You will be expected to know the Cisco IOS CLI commands. One of the great features of Cisco products is that they all use pretty much the same operating system. The CLI for the 1900 is very similar to that of the router.

The Catalyst 1900 LEDs

Before you can begin to configure the switch you must first assemble all the necessary cables and parts. Although the Catalyst 1900 does not require assembly, you must be sure to connect the power cable and the patch cords to the patch panel. If the switch needs to be configured, you will need to connect the console cable for access to the configuration interfaces.

Once powered on, the 1900 will go through its POST tests before eventually loading its operating system and forwarding traffic. An easy way to follow the switch through this process is to monitor its LEDs. Unlike Cisco IOS–based routers (most of them, anyway), the Catalyst 1900 LEDs are very informative. The LEDs are multicolored, allowing even more information to be interpreted.

On the front of the switch to the right you will find two LEDs with the words System and RPS. The System LED indicates whether the system is functioning properly. If the LED is green, the switch is loaded and operating properly. If it is amber (not red), the switch has had a malfunction or may still be booting. The RPS LED indicates whether there is a functioning redundant power supply attached. The indicators are as follows:

- When there is no RPS, the LED is off.
- When the RPS is attached and functioning, the LED is green.
- When the LED is amber, the RPS is installed but not functioning properly.
- When the LED is flashing green, the RPS is installed but the switch is running off the internal power supply.

There are also LEDs above each of the Ethernet ports on the front of the switch. These LEDs, by default, will indicate the link status—in other words, whether the port is attached to a valid, running network node. When the port LEDs are configured to display port status (indicated by STAT on the switch), the following applies:

- If the LED is green, the link is present.
- If the LED is flashing green, traffic is flowing on this port.
- If the LED is alternating between green and amber, there is a problem with the link.
- If the LED is amber, the port is not forwarding, possibly due to STP shutting it down.

The LEDs above the port can also be configured to display switch utilization and whether the ports are operating in full duplex. Just below the System and RPS LEDs is a button that can alternate the modes of the port LEDs. The modes are STAT (the default), UTL (the backplane utilization), and FDUP (whether the port is operating in full duplex mode).

The UTL mode will turn all the port LEDs into one long measuring bar, lit from left to right. The number of LEDs that are lit indicate the amount of backplane utilization, as shown here:

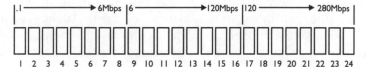

The FDUP mode is actually very funny. You will notice that a 1900 switch can only have two ports that can be in full duplex mode, therefore if you are in this mode all LEDs except for the two ports to the right will be off. The two ports will be green if they are indeed in full duplex mode.

Starting a Catalyst 1900

To have a firm grasp of the basics of the LEDs, it is important to understand what the switch will normally do at startup. If there are any problems, you can quickly identify them.

When the switch is booted, all the port LEDs and the System and RPS LEDs are green. There is one port LED that is off; you will notice that this "off" LED will actually count down. In other words, if port 9's LED is off, in a couple of seconds it will come on and port 8's LED will turn off. This is the switch's way of letting you know that it is counting down. When it reaches 1, that indicates the switch is just a second away from being ready to forward frames.

Each of the LEDs that were off during the countdown indicates a POST test that is being performed (see Table 4-3).

It should be noted that if any of the LEDs are lit during the POST test, the switch will not function. The exceptions are LEDs 1, 2, 4, and 5, which indicate non-fatal errors. For more information, see the documentation that came with your switch or visit the Cisco Connection Online web site at http://www.cisco.com/.

Connecting to and Configuring the Catalyst 1900

Once the switch has been booted and all the cables have been connected, the switch now needs to be configured. When you first configure the switch, this must be done through the console port. Like most all Cisco devices, connection can be made easily with the provided *rollover cable*. The rollover cable is so named because the pins are reversed as if the wires were completely rolled over. Pin 1 on one side corresponds to pin 8 on the other. These cables are fairly commonplace in Cisco environments, and every new Cisco device ships with one.

The default settings of the console port are 9800 Baud, 8, None, and 1 Stop Bit. These can be accessed using any terminal program.

As mentioned earlier, in this book we'll be discussing the CLI (option K). All parameters configured through the CLI can also be configured through the menu system (option M). For those of you wondering what the IP configuration option is, don't worry—it's just an extension of the menu system. For whatever reason it

TABLE 4.3	Catalyst 1900 Fault LEDs
Port Number	**Device Being Tested**
16x	ECU DRAM
15x – 13x	Not used (for future development, presumably)
12x	Forwarding engine
11x	Forwarding engine's SRAM
10x	Packet DRAM
9x	ISLT ASIC
8x	Port control status
7x	System timer interrupt
6x	CAM SRAM
5x	Real-time clock
4x	Console port
3x	CAM
2x	BIA (burned-in address)
1x	Port loopback

On the 1912, the Ax port is used in place of 16x because the 1912 only has 12 ports.

appears as an option off the main screen. But remember, for this book and the CCNA exam be sure to learn the CLI and not the menu.

Using the Command Line Interface and Configuration Modes

Once you enter the CLI by pressing **K**, you will see the following prompt:

```
Enter Selection:  K
     CLI session with the switch is open.
     To end the CLI session, enter [Exit].

>
```

The > prompt indicates that you are in user mode. This mode will allow you to view parameters but not make any changes. Of course, all the features of Cisco IOS still apply—most importantly, the context-sensitive help. Recall from earlier that the ? key can be pressed at any time to indicate what commands are available or the possible endings to the beginning of a command you have typed. Note that you do not need to press RETURN after pressing ?; help automatically appears.

When you type ? at the prompt, a list of available commands are displayed:

```
>?
Exec commands:
  enable     Turn on privileged commands
  exit       Exit from the EXEC
  help       Description of the interactive help system
  ping       Send echo messages
  session    Tunnel to module
  show       Show running system information
  terminal   Set terminal line parameters
>
```

Not a whole lot of choices from user mode, but look what happens when you go from user mode to privileged mode by entering **enable**:

```
#?
Exec commands:
  clear            Reset functions
  configure        Enter configuration mode
  copy             Copy configuration or firmware
  delete           Reset configuration
  disable          Turn off privileged commands
  enable           Turn on privileged commands
  exit             Exit from the EXEC
  help             Description of the interactive help system
  menu             Enter menu interface
  ping             Send echo messages
  reload           Halt and perform warm start
  session          Tunnel to module
  show             Show running system information
  terminal         Set terminal line parameters
  vlan-membership  VLAN membership configuration
#
```

There are now many more commands.

Local Lingo

Enable and disable On any Cisco IOS device, the **enable** command can be used to enter privileged mode and the **disable** command can be used to reenter user mode. Most commonly, **enable** is shortened to **en**.

While in privileged mode, you can configure the switch as well as perform any of the commands that were available while in user mode.

Viewing Switch Parameters

When you first get into a brand-new switch it is a good idea to document the version of code running on the switch. To view the current version of IOS on the switch, use the **show version** command or the abbreviated **sh ver**, as shown here:

```
#sh ver
Cisco Catalyst 1900/2820 Enterprise Edition Software
Version V8.01.02
Copyright (c) Cisco Systems, Inc.  1993-1998
 uptime is 0day(s) 01hour(s) 35minute(s) 57second(s)
cisco Catalyst 1900 (486sxl) processor with 2048K/1024K bytes of memory
Hardware board revision is 5
Upgrade Status: No upgrade currently in progress.
Config File Status: No configuration upload/download is in progress
27 Fixed Ethernet/IEEE 802.3 interface(s)
Base Ethernet Address: 00-D0-D3-71-80-00
#
```

This is a little different than what we saw with the router. The version number is in the 8s while most router IOSs are in the 12s. You can gather a great deal of information from the **show version** output, as shown in Table 4-4.

After documenting the switch's operating system, it may be a good idea to verify that all the ports that are in use are currently active. A switch does not need to be configured to begin forwarding frames. That is why you can verify that the ports have come up before actually configuring the switch.

TABLE 4.4	The show version Command Explained
Parameter	**What It Means**
Version V8.01.02	The 1900/2820 Enterprise Version of software being used.
uptime is 0day(s) 01hour(s) 35minute(s) 57second(s)	How long the router has been running.
cisco Catalyst 1900 (486sxl) processor	The model of router and the processor it was built with.
with 2048K/1024K bytes of memory	The amount of total memory/shared memory. The shared memory is that area of memory set aside for packets to be stored.
27 Fixed Ethernet/ IEEE 802.3 interface(s)	The number of interfaces on this particular 1900.
Base Ethernet Address: 00-D0-D3-71-80-00	The MAC address the switch will use. This address is necessary if it will be automatically obtaining an IP address from a BootP server.

You can obtain copious amounts of information pertaining to the port using the **show interface** command. The command can be used by itself or a specific port can be specified. The port numbering begins at 0/1, and all ports are referred to as **ethernet** ports except the Fast Ethernet ports, which are referred to as **fast ethernet** ports. For example, to view parameters about the 12th port from the right (numbering begins on the right and works to the left when looking at the front of the switch; the numbers are printed clearly on the front), you would use the following command:

```
#show interface ethernet 0/12
Ethernet 0/12 is Suspended-no-linkbeat
Hardware is Built-in 10Base-T
Address is 00D0.D371.800C
MTU 1500 bytes, BW 10000 Kbits
802.1d STP State:  Forwarding     Forward Transitions:  1
```

```
Port monitoring: Disabled
Unknown unicast flooding: Enabled
Unregistered multicast flooding: Enabled
Description:
Duplex setting: Half duplex
Back pressure: Disabled
--More--
      Receive Statistics                    Transmit Statistics
----------------------------------   ----------------------------------
Total good frames            0   Total frames                   0
Total octets                 0   Total octets                   0
Broadcast/multicast frames   0   Broadcast/multicast frames     0
Broadcast/multicast octets   0   Broadcast/multicast octets     0
Good frames forwarded        0   Deferrals                      0
Frames filtered              0   Single collisions              0
Runt frames                  0   Multiple collisions            0
No buffer discards           0   Excessive collisions           0
                                 Queue full discards            0
Errors:                          Errors:
  FCS errors                 0     Late collisions              0
  Alignment errors           0     Excessive deferrals          0
  Giant frames               0     Jabber errors                0
  Address violations         0     Other transmit errors        0
#
```

If you were to leave **ethernet 0/12** off the command, you would see this out-put for every port. For simplicity, we will leave it to your imagination to see all the ports listed. Table 4-5 outlines some of the important statistics found in the **show interface** command.

Travel Advisory

The Catalyst 1900 IOS is unlike router IOS. It is not necessary to save the configuration file to NVRAM. This can be very dangerous because unless you document your changes you may have a difficult time restoring the previous configuration file.

TABLE 4.5	Some show interface Output Explained
Parameter	**What It Means**
Ethernet 0/12 is Suspended-no-linkbeat	This port currently is not connected to anything (there is no link).
Address is 00D0.D371.800C	The MAC address of the port.
MTU 1500 bytes	The maximum frame that can be transmitted (maximum transmit unit).
BW 10000 Kbits	The bandwidth of the port in Kbps.
802.1d STP State: Forwarding	The STP port state.
Duplex setting: Half duplex	The current duplex setting.

After checking your interfaces, you can check to see the default configuration file using the **show running-config** command. This will display the active configuration file. Just like any other Cisco device, the 1900 has an active and an initial configuration file.

The following is the output seen from a new Catalyst 1900 switch:

```
#show running-config
Building configuration...
Current configuration:
!
<Text Omitted>

!
interface Ethernet 0/1
!
interface Ethernet 0/2
!
interface Ethernet 0/3
!
<text ommitted>
!
interface Ethernet 0/23
```

```
!
interface Ethernet 0/24
!
interface Ethernet 0/25
!
interface FastEthernet 0/26
!
!
!
interface FastEthernet 0/27
!
!
!
line console
end
#
```

The default configuration will list all the interfaces the switch has—and that is about it, not very exciting. In the next section, we will spice it up a bit.

Configuring the Switch from the Command Line

In the previous section, you saw a very blank configuration for a Cisco Catalyst 1900 switch. To configure the switch, you must add the appropriate commands to the configuration file.

To manage and configure the switch remotely, the switch must have an IP address. To configure the switch with an IP address, you must add the command **ip address** *<IP address to be used> <subnet mask>*. To add this command to the active configuration file, the command must be entered in global configuration mode. If you were to type this command from the # prompt, the switch would return an error. It is like editing a text file from DOS. You just don't type and hope that it gets added to the file. You first open a text editor. The Cisco IOS device's text editor is global configuration mode. To enter global configuration mode, use the **configure terminal** command, which can be shortened to **conf t**.

```
#conf t
Enter configuration commands, one per line.  End with CNTL/Z
(config)#
```

Notice that the prompt has changed to (config)# to indicate that you are now in global configuration mode. At this point, you can add commands to the configuration file.

```
#conf t
Enter configuration commands, one per line.  End with CNTL/Z
(config)#ip address 172.16.1.1 255.255.255.0
(config)#
```

We have set the IP address of the switch to 172.16.1.1 with a subnet mask of 255.255.255.0. To exit from global configuration mode, you can use the command **exit**, or the keystrokes CTRL-C or CTRL-Z.

Now when the **show running-config** command (shortened to **sh ru**) is executed, the configuration is displayed:

```
#sh ru
Building configuration...
Current configuration:
!
<text omitted>
ip address 172.16.1.1 255.255.255.0
!
interface Ethernet 0/1
!
interface Ethernet 0/2
```

Another possible way of verifying the IP address on the switch is using the **show ip** command from privileged mode:

```
#sh ip
IP Address: 172.16.1.1
Subnet Mask: 255.255.255.0
Default Gateway: 0.0.0.0
Management VLAN:  1
Domain name:
Name server 1: 0.0.0.0
Name server 2: 0.0.0.0
HTTP server : Enabled
```

```
HTTP port :  80
RIP : Enabled
#
```

The IP address and subnet mask configured earlier are verified with the **show ip** command.

Many of the general Cisco IOS commands covered earlier can be used as well. For example, to configure the hostname of the switch, the **hostname** command can be used from global configuration mode:

```
#conf t
Enter configuration commands, one per line.  End with CNTL/Z
(config)#hostname C1900-1
C1900-1(config)#
C1900-1#
```

Many of the commands learned earlier can also be used on the 1900. In Chapter 5, we will examine more complex configurations of the 1900.

CHECKPOINT

✔ **Objective 4.01: Three Functions of a Transparent Bridge**   A switch is simply a complex transparent bridge with many ports and more advanced frame forwarding technology. To understand a switch you must first understand the transparent bridge. There are three main functions of the transparent bridge:
- Learning
- Forwarding and filtering
- Loop avoidance

✔ **Objective 4.02: Spanning Tree Protocol**   The third function of the transparent bridge is to prevent bridge loops to prevent broadcast storms. These broadcast storms can bring down a network. To accomplish loop avoidance, the switch uses a protocol called the Spanning Tree Protocol (STP). STP will allow switches to learn of loops and to block traffic on those ports causing the loops.

✔ **Objective 4.03: The Difference Between a Switch and a Bridge**   A switch is merely a bridge with three main distinctions:
- A switch will typically have many ports while a bridge will have few.

- A switch will generally use technology much more sophisticated than a bridge when forwarding frames, thus making it faster.
- A switch can forward frames before they are completely received on the incoming port, while a bridge must wait until the entire frame has been received before forwarding.

✔ **Objective 4.04: Frame Forwarding Methods of the Catalyst 1900 Switch**
The Catalyst 1900 switch has three frame forwarding methods:

- **Store-and-Forward** The frame must be completely received before being forwarded out the destination port. A frame check sum is performed ensuring that no errored frames are forwarded.
- **Cut-Through** In this case the switch will forward the frame as soon as the destination MAC address is read and a destination port is determined. This will reduce the latency, but the switch will be unable to stop errored frames from being forwarded.
- **Fragment-Free or Modified Cut-Through** Like cut-through the switch will not receive the entire frame before forwarding, but unlike cut-through it will wait until the first 64 bytes of the frame have been received before forwarding to ensure that the frame is not a runt.

✔ **Objective 4.05: The Cisco Catalyst 1900 Series of Switches** The Cisco Catalyst 1900 series of switches is a Cisco IOS device that can be configured easily through a command line interface, a menu system, or an HTTP configuration utility. Although it is a Cisco IOS device, some of its commands and operations are unique to the 1900.

REVIEW QUESTIONS

1. At what layer of the OSI model does switching occur?
    A. Layer 1 (Physical)
    B. Layer 2 (Data Link)
    C. Layer 3 (Network)
    D. Layer 4 (Transport)
    E. B and C

2. Which of the following is *not* a function of a transparent bridge?
    A. Loop avoidance
    B. Spanning Tree Protocol
    C. Forwarding
    D. Filtering
    E. Learning

3. Bridges forward frames by reading which of the following frame fields?

   A. Source MAC address
   B. Destination MAC address
   C. Source IP address
   D. Destination IP address
   E. The type code

4. Where do switches place frames that have invalid frame check sums when the switch is in fragment-free mode?

   A. The switch does not forward the frame.
   B. The switch fixes the FCS and forwards the frame to its destination.
   C. The switch forwards the frame.
   D. The switch informs the sender using an ICMP message and discards the frame.
   E. The switch discards the frame but forwards the data.

5. Which of the following statements regarding latency and frame forwarding methods is true?

   A. When using fragment-free frame forwarding, there is less latency, and all frames with invalid FCSs are discarded.
   B. When using store-and-forward frame forwarding, there is less latency, high frame forwarding rates, and error checking.
   C. When using cut-through frame forwarding, there is less latency, high frame forwarding rates, and error checking.
   D. When using fragment-free frame forwarding, there is low latency and some degree of error checking.
   E. When using cut-through frame forwarding, there is high latency, high frame forwarding rates, and no error checking.

6. In a Cisco Catalyst switch environment, the root bridge will be which of the following?

   A. The switch with the lowest MAC address.
   B. The switch with the lowest bridge priority.
   C. The switch with the highest MAC address.
   D. The switch with the lowest bridge.
   E. The router will always be the root bridge.

7. Which of the following procedures will take you to the CLI of a Catalyst 1900?

   A. Pressing K.
   B. Pressing L.
   C. Pressing C.
   D. Pressing M.
   E. Nothing is required; the Catalyst 1900 boots right to the CLI.

8. A Catalyst 1900 series switch is a Layer 2 device, so why does it need an IP address?

   A. The switch needs an IP address so it can read the IP headers for its learning operation.
   B. The switch needs an IP address because Cisco requirements say so.
   C. The switch needs an IP address for remote management and possibly SNMP.
   D. The switch does not need an IP address and there is no command to configure it with an IP address.
   E. The IP address allows the switch to build routing tables to back up the router.

REVIEW ANSWERS

1. **B** Switching and bridging both occur at Layer 2. They use the Layer 2 MAC address to make their forwarding decisions, unlike a router, which is a Layer 3 device making its forwarding decisions based on the IP, IPX, Appletalk (and so on) address.

2. **B** All of the answers are valid functions of a transparent bridge except the Spanning Tree Protocol. The Spanning Tree Protocol is part of the loop avoidance function. Some people might argue that forwarding and filtering are not valid because they are both part of the same function. However, the questions *always* call for the best answer, and clearly the correct answer is STP.

3. **B** Bridges read the destination MAC address when making their forwarding decisions. As indicated in the previous answer, all other answers are invalid.

4. **C** Switches in fragment-free mode forward frames that are at least 64 bytes long, therefore eliminating runts on your network. Fragment-free cannot check the FCS, however, and therefore has no way to filter the frame or perform any of the other possible scenarios listed.

5. **D** Fragment-free or modified cut-through allows frames to be forwarded without having to completely receive the frame. Unlike cut-through, it does not forward the frame until it is at least 64 bytes in length, thus making sure it is not a runt.

6. **D** The root bridge is the bridge with the lowest bridge ID. The bridge ID is a combination of the bridge priority and bridge MAC address. The bridge priority makes up the high order bits, and thus the switch with the lowest bridge ID becomes the root bridge.

7. **A** In Cisco's great wisdom, they chose to use the letter *k* to indicate kommand line interface. (We're joking, but it is easy to remember it this way.)

8. **C** A switch is configured with an IP address for remote management or possibly SNMP management through Cisco Works. Although a switch does not require an IP address, there is indeed a command to configure it.

Virtual Local Area Networks (VLANs)

	NEWBIE	SOME EXPERIENCE	EXPERT
ETA	6+ hours	2.5 hours	1 hour

With the growing number of users on a network comes the challenge of management, so it is not surprising that VLANs have become a popular feature of switches. VLANs ease the administrative duties of a network engineer. A VLAN will give an administrator the ability to remove the physical restrictions of the past and control a user's Layer 3 network address regardless of his or her physical location.

Other advantages of VLANs include enhanced security features, easier to control broadcasts, and the ability to distribute traffic. Cisco Catalyst switches have the capability to perform numerous features to enhance and ease the implementation of VLANs.

The use of trunking allows multiple VLANs to share the same cable, which makes it easy to have VLANs span large areas when necessary. Cisco has also implemented the trunking feature into many of its routing products, resulting in many helpful and interesting network designs.

Objective 5.01   Virtual Local Area Networks (VLANs)

A VLAN can be defined in two words: broadcast domain. As we discussed in Chapter 1, a broadcast domain is a Layer 3 network. A switch defines a VLAN and the switch's ports will have membership in one of the defined VLANs. For example, in Figure 5-1 a switch has ports defined in two VLANs, Accounting and Management.

In Figure 5-1, ports 1 through 12 have been assigned to the Accounting VLAN, and ports 13 through 24 have been assigned to the Management VLAN. The switch will not allow broadcasts to flow between VLANs, thus logically segmenting the network.

If station A were to send a broadcast, all stations on the Accounting VLAN would receive it; however, the switch would not forward the broadcast to any of the Management VLAN ports (see Figure 5-2). In fact, a switch will not forward a frame from one VLAN to another unless it is a multilayer switch, which will be discussed when you're further in your CCNP studies. A switch can logically segment, but in the real world it is ludicrous to use a switch without a router as a device to logically segment, as traffic will never be allowed to pass between VLANs. This is a very unlikely scenario and is pointless to discuss.

The stations in the Accounting VLAN will be in a completely different broadcast domain than the Management VLAN's users and therefore will be in an entirely different IP subnet. In Figure 5-3, the Accounting VLAN is assigned the

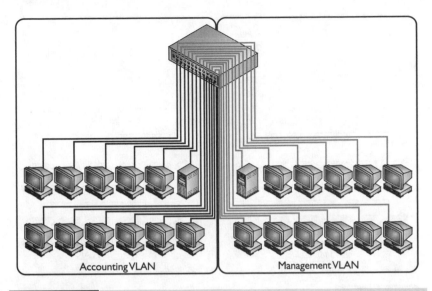

FIGURE 5.1   A simple two-VLAN design

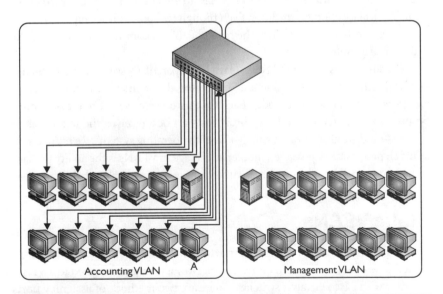

FIGURE 5.2   Broadcasts are kept within all ports in their VLAN.

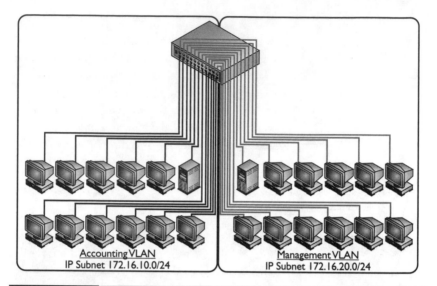

Accounting VLAN
IP Subnet 172.16.10.0/24

Management VLAN
IP Subnet 172.16.20.0/24

FIGURE 5.3   IP subnet assignments for the two VLANs

IP subnet 172.16.10.0/24 and the Management VLAN is assigned the IP subnet 172.16.20.0/24. Traffic from one VLAN has no effect on the other, regardless of their physical location on the floor. Even though two ports physically reside right next to each other on the switch, they are not able to communicate without the presence of a router.

The advantages to using VLANs are readily apparent. By segmenting the broadcast traffic, smaller broadcast domains are created, thus reducing traffic on the wire and processor utilization on nodes. Each time a node receives a broadcast, it must be processed, therefore the fewer broadcasts a node receives the less it has to process—and we all know that with Microsoft's operating systems, we need to save as much processing as possible. Another advantage to VLANs is the ability to make moves, adds, and changes to stations without always having to alter their IP address.

Static VLANs

Cisco's implementation of VLANs is port-centric. The port that a node is connected to will define the VLAN it resides in. How a port gets assigned to a VLAN can vary with Cisco Catalyst switches. There are two methods of assigning ports to VLANs, static and dynamic.

The static VLAN procedure is to administratively assign a port to a VLAN. An engineer determines which ports he or she would like on a particular VLAN and statically maps that VLAN to a port. For example, in Figure 5-1 the Accounting VLAN was defined to be any node connected to ports 1 through 12. An engineer would enter the appropriate commands from the command line interface (CLI) of the switch, a SNMP management station, or Cisco's software management tool CiscoWorks for Switched Internetworks (CWSI) to assign ports 1 through 12 to the Accounting VLAN. This method can be very time consuming, as the engineer has to manually enter the commands necessary to map the ports to their appropriate VLANs. It is, however, the most common method of assigning a port to a VLAN.

Dynamic VLANs

Dynamic VLAN configuration is when the port decides for itself what VLAN it belongs in. No, this is not *The Terminator* or *The Forbin Project* becoming nonfiction, but rather a simple mapping that occurs based on a database created by an engineer. When a port that is assigned to be a dynamic VLAN port becomes active, the switch caches the source MAC address of the first frame. It then makes a request to an external server called a VLAN management policy server (VMPS) that contains a text file with MAC address to VLAN mappings. The switch downloads this file and examines it for the source MAC address it has cached for the port in question. If the MAC address is found in the table, the port is assigned to the listed VLAN. If the MAC address is not in the table, the switch uses the default VLAN if defined. In the event that the MAC address is not listed in the table and there is no default VLAN, the port does not become active. This can be a very good method of security.

On the surface, dynamic VLANs appear to be advantageous, but the building of the database can be a painstaking and tortuous feat. If a network has thousands of workstations, there will be a lot of typing. Assuming that you could survive the process, there are still issues with dynamic VLANs. Keeping the database current can become an ongoing time-consuming process. Currently the Catalyst 1900 can have its ports assigned via dynamic VLANs, but it is unable to be a VMPS. The VMPS must be an external Catalyst switch such as a 5000 or 6000.

Objective 5.02 # Trunking

An individual switch defines VLANs. How can you extend VLANs beyond a single switch? For example, in Figure 5-4 there are nodes on the first and second floor that are part of the Accounting department and the Management department. This organization would like its Layer 3 addressing scheme to mirror

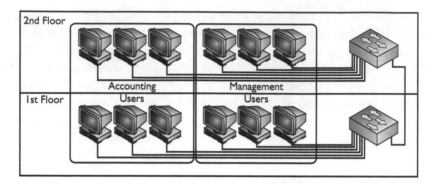

FIGURE 5.4   Accounting and Management users spread across two floors

its organization, not its physical configuration. How can the nodes on both floors participate in the same VLAN?

The physical connection between the two switches could be assigned to the Accounting VLAN, but this would limit traffic between the floors to the Accounting VLAN. A second connection could be made between the switches and placed in the Management VLAN, but this could be costly, especially when there are more than two VLANs. Trunking allows multiple VLAN traffic to flow across a single physical connection. If the connection between the two switches in Figure 5-4 was made a trunk connection, both VLANs could communicate across the same physical link. This is accomplished by using a tag.

Each frame that is transmitted across a trunk line is tagged with the VLAN ID. A Catalyst switch identifies each VLAN with a unique number. If the Accounting VLAN is assigned the VLAN number 100, all frames that traverse the trunk line for the Accounting VLAN are tagged with the VLAN number 100, as shown in Figure 5-5.

When the second-floor switch receives the frame over the trunk, it reads the tag and learns that the frame is destined for the Accounting VLAN. Broadcasts are propagated across trunk lines—this is very important because a VLAN is a broadcast domain. With broadcasts being propagated across the trunk in the appropriate VLAN, the broadcast domain can be extended across multiple switches. The switches keep broadcasts in the appropriate VLANs by reading the tag on the frames that come across the trunks.

In Figure 5-6, a network is made up of six floors with users in the Accounting department dispersed on all six floors. With trunking, all the Accounting users can be placed in the same broadcast domain or VLAN.

All Accounting nodes will be connected to a port in VLAN 100, regardless of which floor they reside on. This will allow all the Accounting users to be in the same IP subnet and see traffic from one another without having to go through a

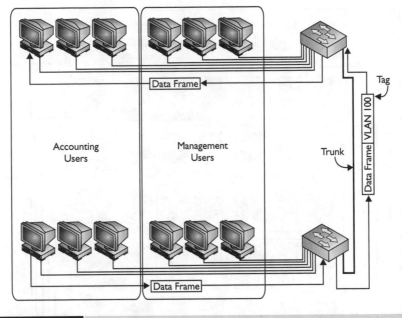

FIGURE 5.5   Frame tagging

router. Frames are being tagged and untagged only on the trunks and are completely invisible to the end nodes. It should also be noted that in Figure 5-6, through the use of VLANs, the servers have all been strategically located together, yet can remain in the broadcast domains of their respective users.

All VLAN traffic will travel across the trunk if necessary, ensuring that other VLANs will have connectivity across the entire network, as in Figure 5-7.

This organization has assigned their logical addresses according to the departments within the organization, regardless of their physical location. Engineers were unable to easily separate the logical addressing scheme from their physical configuration before trunking.

Cisco's Inter-Switch Link (ISL)

The Catalyst 1900 switch is an Ethernet switch. When trunking over Ethernet, Cisco switches have two possible trunking methods:

- Inter-Switch Link
- IEEE 802.1Q

The Inter-Switch Link (ISL) tag is a Cisco proprietary tag used over most Fast Ethernet trunks and is the only trunking method supported on the Catalyst 1900.

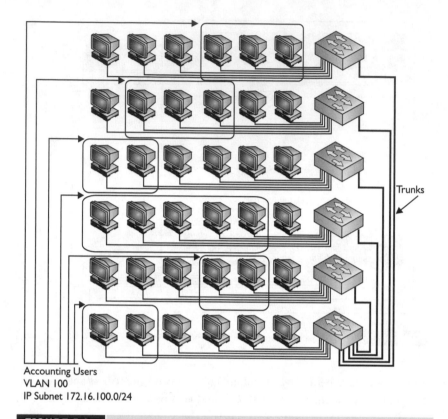

Trunks

Accounting Users
VLAN 100
IP Subnet 172.16.100.0/24

FIGURE 5.6 The Accounting VLAN

The IEEE 802.1Q tag is a standard tag that is supported by some of the Cisco Catalyst switches but not all (consult the Cisco Connection Online web site for your model number switch). For this reason, we will only be discussing ISL. Trunking is performed by application-specific integrated circuits (ASICs) built into each port on the switch. Trunking is hardware based, thus having little effect on the latency.

ISL tags can be performed on various devices, not just switches. They can be performed on any device that has only one physical interface but requires access to multiple VLANs, such as a corporate e-mail server. Rather than having traffic routed from all VLANs to the one VLAN where the e-mail server resides, have the e-mail server use an intelligent ISL-aware NIC which will allow the server to trunk to the switch, as shown in Figure 5-8.

A router may also have an ISL connection to a switch so it can simultaneously, through a single interface, route traffic to and from multiple VLANs.

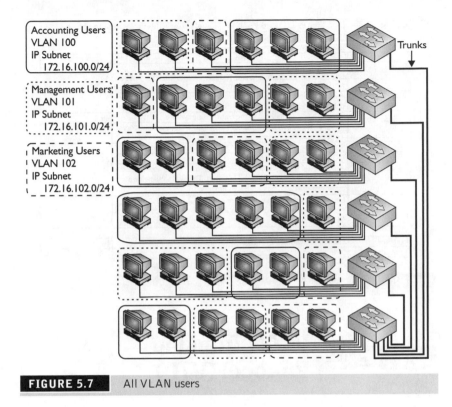

Accounting Users
VLAN 100
IP Subnet
172.16.100.0/24

Management Users
VLAN 101
IP Subnet
172.16.101.0/24

Marketing Users
VLAN 102
IP Subnet
172.16.102.0/24

Trunks

FIGURE 5.7   All VLAN users

The ISL tag contains several fields, not just the VLAN field. You can see them all listed in Figure 5-9.

The most important field in this header is the VLAN field. It is this field that identifies which VLAN the encapsulated frame belongs to. It is important to remember that non-Cisco routers do not have the ability to read the ISL tag.

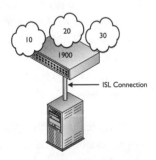

10   20   30

1900

ISL Connection

FIGURE 5.8   An ISL connection to a server

| Destination MAC ||| Source MAC | Length | AAAA03 || VLAN || Index | Res | Encapsulated Frame | FCS |

| | Type || User | | | HSA || BPDU | | | | |

Field	Description	# of bits
Destination MAC	A multicast address that is destined for trunk ports.	40
Type	Identifies the encapsulated frame [Ethernet-0000, Token Ring-0001, FDDI-0010, ATM-0011]	4
User	A possible addition to the Type field, in Ethernet it can be used to define priorities.	4
Source MAC	The Source MAC address of the transmitting switch.	48
Length	Identifies the length of the frame excluding the Destination Address, Type, User, Source Address, Length, and FCS fields.	16
AAAA03	This is the standard IEEE 802.2 Logical Link Control header.	24
HSA	Identifies the Vendor code or OUI of the source station.	24
VLAN	A 15 bit field used to identify the VLAN of the encapsulated frame, currently only the lower 10 bits are used. This will provide for a maximum of 1024 possible VLAN numbers.	15
BPDU	Identifies whether or not the encapsulated frame is a BPDU. If set, could also identify that encapsulated frame as a Cisco Discovery Packet.	1
Index	Used for diagnostic purposes.	16
Reserved	Used for additional information.	16
Total Bits		208 bits or 26 bytes

FIGURE 5.9   The ISL tag

Objective 5.03
VLAN Trunking Protocol (VTP)

There are two steps to creating and implementing VLANs:

1. Create the VLAN.
2. Assign the appropriate ports to the VLAN.

A switch has a list of VLANs that it knows exist and has its ports assigned to some or all of the VLANs in the list. VLANs that have ports assigned to them are said to be active VLANs on the switch that ports are assigned. It is possible for a switch to have VLANs in its VLAN list and *not* have ports assigned to them. These VLANs are often referred to as transit VLANs. A transit VLAN is known to the switch, but has no ports assigned to it so that VLAN traffic can pass through a switch's trunk ports.

In Figure 5-10, switch B has no ports assigned to VLAN 20, but it appears in the VLAN list. Switch B must know about VLAN 20 to properly recognize traffic coming from switches A and C that are tagged VLAN 20. Switch B will only forward these frames out its trunk ports since it has no ports assigned to VLAN 20. VLAN 20 is said to be a transit VLAN on switch B.

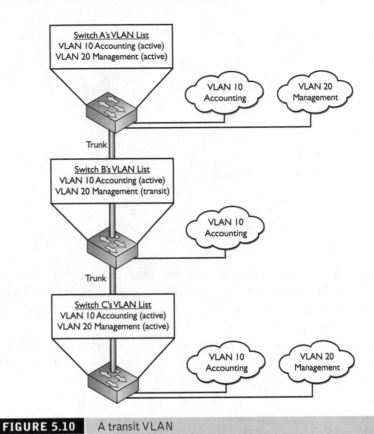

Switch A's VLAN List
VLAN 10 Accounting (active)
VLAN 20 Management (active)

VLAN 10
Accounting

VLAN 20
Management

Trunk

Switch B's VLAN List
VLAN 10 Accounting (active)
VLAN 20 Management (transit)

VLAN 10
Accounting

Trunk

Switch C's VLAN List
VLAN 10 Accounting (active)
VLAN 20 Management (active)

VLAN 10
Accounting

VLAN 20
Management

FIGURE 5.10   A transit VLAN

When VLANs are configured on a Catalyst switch, there are several parameters that may be defined. The VLAN number is the parameter to uniquely identify the broadcast domain. The VLAN name is an optional parameter for documentation purposes. All ports that are to be in the same broadcast domain will be assigned to the same VLAN number; the switch does not assign ports based on VLAN name. When VLANs span multiple switches, it is helpful to have these parameters consistent. The VLAN Trunking Protocol (VTP) is a protocol to exchange information about VLANs between switches to keep VLANs consistent. It is a Layer 2 protocol that runs on the trunk ports—for example, if two switches are configured to trunk. Switch A has two VLANs: VLAN 10, named Accounting, and VLAN 20, named Management. Switch B has the same two VLAN numbers but different names: VLAN 10 is named Management and VLAN 20 is named Accounting as shown here (perhaps due to a configuration error on someone's part).

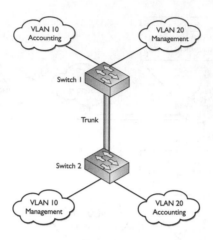

This is not a large issue, but it could lead to further configuration errors and lengthy troubleshooting in the future. Remember, documentation is very important for troubleshooting and future configurations. By naming a VLAN you are creating documentation.

VTP is a protocol that runs over *only* trunk lines to exchange information about VLANs between switches to ensure that VLANs are consistent. The problem is automatically corrected by a VTP update, as shown here.

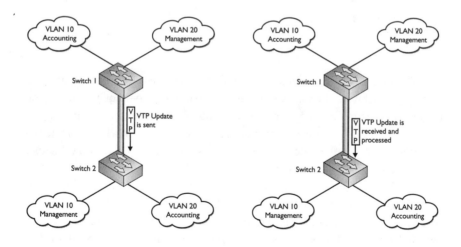

When the VTP update is sent by switch 1 to switch 2, switch 2 changes its VLAN configuration to match that of switch 1. This will ensure that VLANs are kept consistent.

Without VTP, an engineer would have to physically go to each switch's CLI and configure a new VLAN on all switches. With VTP, new VLAN data will be automatically propagated out all trunk lines, making it unnecessary to create VLANs on multiple switches.

VTP Modes

A switch can be in one of three VTP modes:

- Server (default)
- Client
- Transparent

A switch in the VTP server mode, which is the default, sends updates out all of its trunk ports, reads and learns from the updates it receives on its trunk ports, and can have VLANs configured on its CLI. It also stores all VLAN information in its non-volatile RAM (NVRAM). If the switch is rebooted, it will not have to wait to be updated of the current VLANs.

A switch in the VTP client mode sends updates out all of its trunk ports, reads and learns from the updates it receives on its trunk ports, and *cannot* have VLANs configured on its CLI. This mode is ideal for a switch that may be in a remote wiring closet where major configuration changes, such as adding or deleting VLANs, are unwise due to the inability to judge the impact of those changes.

Travel Advisory

Client mode switches do not store VLAN information in NVRAM and are thus reliant on the VTP servers when first booted. With no connectivity, a Client switch will not be able to maintain its VLANs and will have its ports disabled if not in VLAN 1.

A switch in the VTP transparent mode does not listen to VTP updates received on its trunk ports, but forwards any updates it receives from another switch in its management domain.

If you refer back to the example where we had misconfigured VLANs, you may be asking which switch was considered right when trunking was configured and VTP updates began. In the illustrations, switch 1 was overwriting switch 2, but how? Perhaps switch 1 was configured as a VTP server and switch 2 was configured as a VTP client? You would think so, but the VTP mode has nothing to do with which switch will take precedence in the event of a conflict. It is a parameter called the *config revision number*. This number is simply a value that is incremented every time a VLAN is added, deleted, or modified in the VTP domain. The VTP domain is simply the group of switches that are trunked together and exchanging VTP updates. All switches in the VTP domain synchronize to the latest config revision number—that is, the highest number.

Travel Advisory

The switch with the highest config revision number may not be the switch that you would like to have precedence. An example would be a switch that has been in the lab and has had many VLANs configured and reconfigured and deleted. This switch will have a very high config revision number, but when put into production you don't want it to overwrite the other production switches. On the Catalyst 1900 there is a convenient command that can be entered in privileged mode, **delete vtp**. This command resets the config revision number, ensuring that you don't overwrite the current VLANs.

VTP Pruning

VTP pruning is a feature of VTP that reduces unnecessary traffic on trunk lines. To get a better understanding of what unnecessary traffic is, we use the example illustrated in Figure 5-11.

Switch A receives a broadcast from a VLAN 20 port, which it then forwards out all VLAN 20 ports and all trunk ports—in this case, the trunk port to switch B. Switch B does the same, forwarding the broadcast out all VLAN 20 ports and all trunk ports (except the trunk port it was received on). Switch C repeats the same process, except it has no ports in VLAN 20, therefore it only forwards frames to all trunk ports which will be the trunk port to switch D. When switch D receives the broadcast for VLAN 20, it discards the broadcast due to the fact it has no ports in VLAN 20 or trunk ports other than the one the broadcast was received on.

The broadcast traffic coming from switch B to switch C and then from switch C to switch D is unnecessary. VTP pruning is the ability of the switch to *not* forward the unnecessary traffic. By exchanging information about active VLANs, switches can determine whether or not traffic is necessary. With VTP pruning enabled, the unnecessary traffic would not be forwarded in this example.

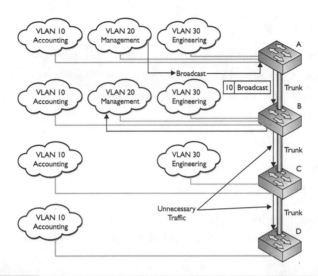

FIGURE 5.11 Unnecessary broadcast traffic

The only exception to VTP Pruning is VLAN 1. Due to administrative traffic (such as CDP and VTP traffic) that must flow across trunks on VLAN 1, VLAN 1 traffic will never be pruned.

Objective 5.04 Creating and Configuring VLANs on a Catalyst 1900

The Catalyst 1900 with Enterprise Edition software is a robust and feature-rich switch. Almost all of the features discussed above are available on the 1900. Although there are several ways to configure the 1900, as discussed in Chapter 4, in the final objective of this chapter, we will examine how to configure these features through the Cisco IOS command line interface.

Creating the VTP Domain

In order to create VLANs on a switch, the switch must first be assigned to a VTP domain.

By default the VTP domain name is not set, the VTP mode is server, and VTP pruning is disabled. All of these parameters can be set from global configuration using the command **vtp** as follows:

Local Lingo

VTP domain   VTP domain is another name for the management domain. Management domain is the most commonly used reference to a group of switches all sharing the same config revision number by virtue of their VTP updates traveling across their trunks.

```
1924EN(config)#vtp <server|transparent|client> pruning <enable|disable>
1924EN(config)#vtp domain <vtp domain name>
```

The default settings will be used if any of the parameters are not specified. To verify the configurations the command **show vtp** is used as follows:

```
190024EN#sh vtp
    VTP version: 1
    Configuration revision: 0
    Maximum VLANs supported locally: 1005
    Number of existing VLANs: 5
    VTP domain name       :
    VTP password          :
    VTP operating mode    : Server
    VTP pruning mode      : Disabled
    VTP traps generation  : Enabled
    Configuration last modified by: 0.0.0.0 at 00-00-0000 00:00:00
190024EN#conf t
Enter configuration commands, one per line.  End with CNTL/Z
190024EN(config)#vtp server pruning enable
190024EN(config)#vtp domain ccprep
190024EN(config)#
190024EN#sh vtp
    VTP version: 1
    Configuration revision: 1
    Maximum VLANs supported locally: 1005
    Number of existing VLANs: 5
    VTP domain name       : ccprep
    VTP password          :
    VTP operating mode    : Server
```

```
VTP pruning mode       : Enabled
VTP traps generation   : Enabled
Configuration last modified by: 172.16.1.1 at 00-00-0000 00:00:00
190024EN#
```

The last parameter, **Configuration last modified by:**, does not list the station that last made a configuration change to the switch; rather, it is the last switch that sent a VTP update. Since this 1900 is the only switch on our network, it is listing itself as the last updater.

By default, a switch will exchange VTP updates with any switch that it trunks. This can be a security hazard, and for this reason VTP domains can be made secure with a password. All switches that want to exchange VTP updates will need to be configured with the *exact* same password, and yes, they are case sensitive. To assign a VTP password to a Catalyst 1900, use the following command:

```
1924EN(config)#vtp password <password>
```

Creating VLANs

With the VTP domain settings out of the way, the VLANs can now be created. By default there are several VLANs preconfigured on the switch. Of these, only VLAN 1 will be discussed. The others are seldom used—and almost never used with the 1900—but do not try to remove them. They cannot be deleted or modified.

> ### Exam Tip
>
> A VTP client switch cannot have VLANs configured from its command line interface. The VTP client switch must receive updates from VTP server switches.

To create a VLAN on the 1900, use the following command:

```
1924EN(config)#vlan <vlan#> name <vlan name>
```

The VLAN name is optional, but the VLAN number is not. The very least that you must specify is a number. Any VLANs created can be verified using the **show vlan** command as in the following example:

```
1924EN(config)#vlan 10 name Accounting
1924EN(config)#vlan 20 name Management
1924EN(config)#vlan 30 name Engineering
1924EN(config)#vlan 40 name Human-Resources
1924EN(config)#vlan 50 name Recreation
1924EN(config)#
1924EN#sh vlan
```

VLAN	Name	Status	Ports
1	default	Enabled	1-24, AUI, A, B
10	Accounting	Enabled	
20	Management	Enabled	
30	Engineering	Enabled	
40	Human-Resources	Enabled	
50	Recreation	Enabled	
1002	fddi-default	Suspended	
1003	token-ring-defau	Suspended	
1004	fddinet-default	Suspended	
1005	trnet-default	Suspended	

VLAN	Type	SAID	MTU	Parent	RingNo	BridgeNo	Stp	Trans1	Trans2
1	**Ethernet**	**100001**	**1500**	**0**	**0**	**0**	**Unkn**	**1002**	**1003**
10	Ethernet	100010	1500	0	1	1	Unkn	0	0
20	Ethernet	100020	1500	0	1	1	Unkn	0	0
30	Ethernet	100030	1500	0	1	1	Unkn	0	0

```
--More--
```

VLAN	Type	SAID	MTU	Parent	RingNo	BridgeNo	Stp	Trans1	Trans2
40	Ethernet	100040	1500	0	1	1	Unkn	0	0
50	Ethernet	100050	1500	0	1	1	Unkn	0	0
1002	**FDDI**	**101002**	**1500**	**0**	**0**	**0**	**Unkn**	**1**	**1003**
1003	**Token-Ring**	**101003**	**1500**	**1005**	**1**	**0**	**Unkn**	**1**	**1002**
1004	**FDDI-Net**	**101004**	**1500**	**0**	**0**	**1**	**IEEE**	**0**	**0**
1005	**Token-Ring-Net**	**101005**	**1500**	**0**	**0**	**1**	**IEEE**	**0**	**0**

```
1924EN#
```

As you can see in the **show vlan** command, there are quite a few default VLANs, all having to deal with other topologies. The important parameters of this command are the non-default VLANs, which we have placed in bold. You will also notice that we have not placed any ports in these VLANs…yet.

Assigning Ports to a VLAN

On the Catalyst 1900, the ports are referenced and configured using a similar procedure to that of the router. However, the 1900 port numbers have a slot number even though there are no slots! For example, in Figure 5-12 we see the port numbering used on the Catalyst 1924EN.

The ports all begin with 0/. We don't know why, they just do! The Fast Ethernet ports are listed as Fast Ethernet 0/26 and Fast Ethernet 0/27. In case you are wondering, Ethernet 0/25 is the AUI port on the back. These ports may be assigned to any VLAN known to the switch (those displayed using **show vlan**). To assign them to a VLAN, the following command is used in interface configuration mode:

```
190024EN(config-if)#vlan-membership static <vlan number>
```

Note that you may specify "dynamic" instead of "static" when using dynamic VLANs.

For example, to configure a 1900 with ports 1–5 in VLAN 10, 6–10 in VLAN 20, 11–15 in VLAN 30, and 16–20 in VLAN 40, the following commands would be issued:

```
1924EN#conf t
Enter configuration commands, one per line.  End with CNTL/Z
1924EN(config)#interface ethernet 0/1
1924EN(config-if)#vlan-membership static 10
```

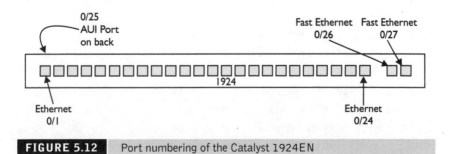

FIGURE 5.12 Port numbering of the Catalyst 1924EN

```
1924EN(config-if)#interface ethernet 0/2
1924EN(config-if)#vlan-membership static 10
1924EN(config-if)#interface ethernet 0/3
1924EN(config-if)#vlan-membership static 10
1924EN(config-if)#interface ethernet 0/4
1924EN(config-if)#vlan-membership static 10
1924EN(config-if)#interface ethernet 0/5
1924EN(config-if)#vlan-membership static 10
1924EN(config-if)#interface ethernet 0/6
1924EN(config-if)#vlan-membership static 20
1924EN(config-if)#interface ethernet 0/7
1924EN(config-if)#vlan-membership static 20
1924EN(config-if)#interface ethernet 0/8
1924EN(config-if)#vlan-membership static 20
1924EN(config-if)#interface ethernet 0/8
1924EN(config-if)#vlan-membership static 20
1924EN(config-if)#interface ethernet 0/10
1924EN(config-if)#vlan-membership static 20
1924EN(config-if)#interface ethernet 0/11
1924EN(config-if)#vlan-membership static 30
1924EN(config-if)#interface ethernet 0/12
1924EN(config-if)#vlan-membership static 30
1924EN(config-if)#interface ethernet 0/13
1924EN(config-if)#vlan-membership static 30
1924EN(config-if)#interface ethernet 0/14
1924EN(config-if)#vlan-membership static 30
1924EN(config-if)#interface ethernet 0/15
1924EN(config-if)#vlan-membership static 30
1924EN(config-if)#interface ethernet 0/16
1924EN(config-if)#vlan-membership static 40
1924EN(config-if)#interface ethernet 0/17
1924EN(config-if)#vlan-membership static 40
1924EN(config-if)#interface ethernet 0/18
1924EN(config-if)#vlan-membership static 40
1924EN(config-if)#interface ethernet 0/19
1924EN(config-if)#vlan-membership static 40
```

```
1924EN(config-if)#interface ethernet 0/20
1924EN(config-if)#vlan-membership static 40
1924EN(config-if)#
1924EN#
```

This is not a lot of fun. And you'd better be familiar with the use of the up arrow on the keyboard. Of course, remember that there are other configuration alternatives for the 1900. To verify these settings, you once again use the **show vlan** command:

```
1924EN#show vlan

VLAN Name                  Status     Ports
---------------------      --------   -----
1    default               Enabled    21-24, AUI, A, B
10   Accounting            Enabled    1-5
20   Management            Enabled    6-10
30   Engineering           Enabled    11-15
40   Human-Resources       Enabled    16-20
50   Recreation            Enabled
1002 fddi-default          Suspended
1003 token-ring-defau      Suspended
1004 fddinet-default       Suspended
1005 trnet-default         Suspended
---------------------      --------   -----
```

As you can see, the **show vlan** command which we have truncated lists not only the VLANs known to the switch, but also the ports assigned. A similar display can be found using the command **show vlan-membership**, as follows:

```
1924EN#sh vlan-membership
 Port  VLAN   Membership Type      Port  VLAN   Membership Type
 ----------------------------      ----------------------------
  1     10       Static             13    30       Static
  2     10       Static             14    30       Static
  3     10       Static             15    30       Static
  4     10       Static             16    40       Static
  5     10       Static             17    40       Static
```

6	20	Static		18	40	Static
7	20	Static		19	40	Static
8	20	Static		20	40	Static
9	20	Static		21	1	Static
10	20	Static		22	1	Static
11	30	Static		23	1	Static
12	30	Static		24	1	Static
				AUI	1	Static
A	1	Static				
B	1	Static				

```
1924EN#
```

This provides a slightly cleaner screen to read, in some people's opinion. Either command will provide the port VLAN assignments.

Configuring Trunking

The two Fast Ethernet ports on the switch are the only ports that may be configured to trunk with other switches, and they will only support the ISL Tag Trunking method. To configure these ports as trunks, use the following command in interface configuration mode:

```
1924EN(config-if)#trunk <on|off|desirable|auto|nonegotiate>
```

The switch can use a protocol called the Dynamic Inter-Switch Link (DISL) or what we like to call Diesel. DISL allows the switch to negotiate with the other side of the link to determine if the sides want to trunk or not. Table 5-1 explains the different settings available.

The settings of the trunk can be verified with the **show trunk a** command for interface Fast Ethernet 0/26 and **show trunk b** for interface Fast Ethernet 0/27. An example is shown here:

```
1924EN(config-if)#trunk nonegotiate
1924EN(config-if)#
1924EN#sh trunk a
DISL state: Nonegotiate, Trunking: Off, Encapsulation type: Unknown
1924EN#
```

TABLE 5.1	Trunk Settings Explained
Setting	**Description**
On	The port will always trunk and will let the other side know that it must trunk.
Off	The port will never trunk and will use DISL to let the other side know that it cannot trunk.
Auto	The port will do whatever the other side wants.
Desirable	This will cause the port to want to trunk as opposed to doing whatever the other side wants.
Nonegotiate	The port will trunk, no ifs, ands, or buts about it. It will also not use DISL to tell the other side that it is trunking.

The **Trunking** parameter is **Off** because the link is not currently connected. However, if connected, the link would trunk and wouldn't negotiate with the other side, it would just trunk.

Viewing Spanning Tree Protocol Parameters and Settings

In Chapter 4, we gave a detailed explanation of how bridging and switching work. In that chapter, you learned that the Spanning Tree Protocol is used to control loops. On the 1900, the Spanning Tree Protocol is used and its parameters can be viewed with the **show spantree** command. The following is a partial listing of its output:

```
1924EN#show spantree
VLAN1 is executing the IEEE compatible Spanning Tree Protocol
   Bridge Identifier has priority 32768, address 00D0.D371.8000
   Configured hello time 2, max age 20, forward delay 15
   Current root has priority 32768, address 00D0.D371.8000
   Root port is N/A, cost of root path is 0
```

```
     Topology change flag not set, detected flag not set
     Topology changes 0, last topology change occured 0d00h00m00s ago
     Times:  hold 1, topology change 8960
             hello 2, max age 20, forward delay 15
     Timers: hello 2, topology change 35, notification 2
Port Ethernet 0/21 of VLAN1 is Forwarding
   Port path cost 100, Port priority 128
   Designated root has priority 32768, address 00D0.D371.8000
   Designated bridge has priority 32768, address 00D0.D371.8000
   Designated port is Ethernet 0/21, path cost 0
   Timers: message age 20, forward delay 15, hold 1
Port Ethernet 0/22 of VLAN1 is Forwarding
   Port path cost 100, Port priority 128
   Designated root has priority 32768, address 00D0.D371.8000
   Designated bridge has priority 32768, address 00D0.D371.8000
   Designated port is Ethernet 0/22, path cost 0
   Timers: message age 20, forward delay 15, hold 1
VLAN10 is executing the IEEE compatible Spanning Tree Protocol
   Bridge Identifier has priority 32768, address 00D0.D371.8001
   Configured hello time 2, max age 20, forward delay 15
   Current root has priority 32768, address 00D0.D371.8001
   Root port is N/A, cost of root path is 0
   Topology change flag not set, detected flag not set
   Topology changes 0, last topology change occured 0d00h00m00s ago
   Times:  hold 1, topology change 8960
           hello 2, max age 20, forward delay 15
   Timers: hello 2, topology change 35, notification 2
Port Ethernet 0/1 of VLAN10 is Forwarding
   Port path cost 100, Port priority 128
   Designated root has priority 32768, address 00D0.D371.8001
   Designated bridge has priority 32768, address 00D0.D371.8001
   Designated port is Ethernet 0/1, path cost 0
   Timers: message age 20, forward delay 15, hold 1
```

This command is perfect when troubleshooting bridge loops or connectivity issues where the Spanning Tree Protocol is the likely cause.

CHECKPOINT

✔ **Objective 5.01: Virtual Local Area Networks (VLANs)** A VLAN is a broadcast domain defined by ports on a switch. The switch controls broadcasts, but does not allow traffic to pass between broadcast domains. To pass traffic between VLANs, a router must be employed. A Cisco Catalyst switch uses a port-centric method of defining VLANs—that is, the port defines the VLAN.

✔ **Objective 5.02: Trunking** The ability to pass multiple VLAN traffic across a connection is called trunking. The Catalyst 1900 with the Enterprise Edition of software supports trunking on its two Fast Ethernet ports. The 1900 uses Cisco's proprietary tagging method, the Inter-Switch Link (ISL). Although there are other methods available on other switches, the 1900 only supports ISL.

✔ **Objective 5.03: VLAN Trunking Protocol (VTP)** The VLAN Trunking Protocol (VTP) is used to maintain a consistent VLAN configuration across the VTP domain. A VTP domain is a group of switches that are all trunked together and are passing VTP updates to one another. All switches in the VTP domain will have the same config revision number. In the event of a conflict, the switch with the highest config revision number will be assumed to have the latest VLAN configuration.

✔ **Objective 5.04: Creating and Configuring VLANs on a Catalyst 1900** The Catalyst 1900 offers many different configuration options and features. In this chapter, we reviewed many commands that can be used to create VLANs, assign ports to VLANs, configure trunking, and verify all of these settings.

REVIEW QUESTIONS

1. Which of the following statements best describes a VLAN?

   A. A collection of nodes that share the same physical wire.

   B. A collection of nodes that can receive each other's broadcasts but are most likely connected to different switch ports.

   C. A collision domain.

   D. A procedure to tag frames as they traverse trunks.

   E. An imaginary LAN.

2. Which of the following is a valid advantage of using VLANs?

   A. Easy to make moves, adds, and changes.
   B. Controls broadcasts more easily.
   C. Allows organizations to group users by department rather than physical location.
   D. Reduces bandwidth consumption by broadcasts.
   E. All of the above.

3. Which of the following best describes a "dynamic VLAN"?

   A. Dynamic VLAN is used to describe a VLAN that constantly changes.
   B. Dynamic VLAN is used to describe when VLAN ports are assigned by a central database that can be created by the administrator.
   C. Dynamic VLAN is used to describe when VLAN ports are assigned manually by an administrator.
   D. Dynamic VLAN is used to describe a VLAN that can scale to large geographic areas.
   E. Dynamic VLAN is not a term used by Cisco Systems to describe its ever-changing switching product line.

4. What is meant by the term "trunk" as it relates to switching?

   A. The ability of a switch to forward frames with unknown destination addresses.
   B. The ability of a switch to extend VLANs across multiple switches, thus allowing groups of users in different physical locations to all be part of the same VLAN.
   C. The ability of a switch to extend VLANs across multiple routers, thus allowing users to be in the same VLAN even though they are separated by many routers.
   D. The ability of a switch to dynamically create VLANs to handle bandwidth overloads.
   E. The ability of the switch to pack up and leave at the drop of a hat without having to pack long.

5. Which of the following devices can be connected to a switch via an ISL trunk?

   A. Another Cisco switch.
   B. A Cisco router.
   C. A server using an ISL compatible NIC.
   D. Both A and C.
   E. All of the above.

6. When using a Catalyst 1900 configured in VTP client mode, which of the following is true?

   A. The switch will not advertise VTP updates.
   B. The switch will learn VLANs through VTP updates and save them to NVRAM.
   C. The switch will *not* allow any VLANs to be created on itself by an administrator.
   D. The switch will *not* learn VLANs through VTP.
   E. The switch will advertise VTP updates with a lower priority than a VTP server.

7. What is the default VTP mode of a Catalyst 1900?

   A. Server.
   B. Client.
   C. Transparent.
   D. Configuration.
   E. There is no default VTP mode.

8. Which of the following commands will display the Spanning Tree Protocol settings?

   A. show spam
   B. show spanning
   C. show spantree
   D. show STP
   E. The Catalyst 1900 does not support the Spanning Tree Protocol.

REVIEW ANSWERS

1. **B** A VLAN is a broadcast domain or, in other words, a collection of nodes that can receive each other's broadcasts. The other distractors are all invalid.

2. **E** All of the answers listed are advantages to using VLANs.

3. **B** Dynamic VLAN is the advanced process of having the switch figure out what port a VLAN should be assigned by going to a central database that is created by the administrator.

4. **B** Trunking allows VLANs to span multiple switches, which allows users separated by physical location to be part of the same logical group. All other answers sound nice, but are completely wrong.

5. **E** All of the devices listed can be connected to a switch using an ISL trunk.

6. **C** A VTP client will *not* allow any VLANs to be created by an administrator that is connected to the switch. It can only learn about VLANs through VTP updates that are sourced from a VTP server. These VLANs will *not* be stored to NVRAM, thus making the switch reliant on a VTP server every time it boots.

7. **A** For all Catalyst switches regardless of model number, the default VTP mode is server.

8. **C** The **show spantree** command will display all of the spanning tree settings.

Overview of the TCP/IP Protocol Stack

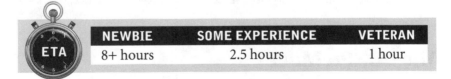

	NEWBIE	SOME EXPERIENCE	VETERAN
ETA	8+ hours	2.5 hours	1 hour

Since the beginning of the "network revolution," one protocol has stood above the rest: the Internet Protocol. As a matter of fact, you could really call IP the first protocol to be widely used. It is funny to hear novices remark that Novell's IPX is old and outdated and everyone should switch to IP. This is, of course, completely false. IP has been around much longer. It is true that much advancement has been made with the protocol, but the basic concepts remain.

TCP/IP was developed by the Defense Advanced Research Projects Agency (DARPA) in the late 1960s. It is interesting to note that many have speculated that TCP/IP was developed because of the threat of nuclear war. Although it is true that DARPA's creation was the result of the launching of Sputnik by the Soviets, we have never seen any evidence that TCP/IP was developed primarily for the purpose of maintaining communications during a nuclear war.

Another interesting note regarding DARPA is that they have changed their name several times. DARPA changed their name to the Advanced Research Projects Agency (ARPA) and then back to DARPA. When you're conversing with other computer geeks, don't be alarmed if they criticize you for using DARPA when they expected ARPA or vice versa. In the real world, the terms are used interchangeably.

TCP/IP is a collection of protocols that many applications rely on. It is the process behind the scenes of many network operating systems (NOSs). Both Novell's NetWare and Microsoft's NT and 2000 software use this protocol by default in their latest releases. Undoubtedly you've heard of IP addresses, but addressing is only a small part of what the protocol suite has to offer.

Introduction to the Protocol Stack

The TCP/IP suite was built around the DARPA model of communications, which was the precursor to the OSI model. It was very similar, as can be seen in Figure 6-1.

The DARPA Model

The DARPA model has some attractive features, such as grouping the application, presentation, and session layers of the OSI model into a single layer called *application*. This makes it easier to remember, and it also makes more sense from a network engineer's standpoint, because rarely is it important for us to distinguish among the top three layers of the OSI model.

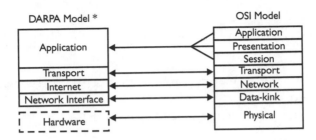

*Taken from Douglad E. Conner's "Internetworking with TCP/IP"

FIGURE 6.1 The DARPA communications model as it compares to the OSI model

You will also note that the data link and physical layers of the OSI model are grouped into a single layer called *network interface*. Douglas Comer, in his book *Internetworking with TCP/IP*, also makes reference to a pseudo-layer called "hardware" which is indicated in Figure 6-1. If you want to be precise about it, there are really only four layers in the DARPA model. (Again, this may come in handy for those water cooler discussions.)

Local Lingo

DARPA model The DARPA model is also sometimes referred to as the TCP/IP model or Department of Defense model. All the terms refer to the same four-layer model.

The Application Layer

The application layer, as its name implies, encompasses all the TCP/IP applications. Cisco devices use several TCP/IP applications, and it is important to understand what they are. It is also important to remember that there are *many* applications that have been developed for TCP/IP and we will only be discussing a few. They are as follows:

- File transfer
  - TFTP (Trivial File Transfer Protocol)
  - FTP (File Transfer Protocol)
  - NFS (Network File System)

- E-mail
  - SMTP (Simple Mail Transfer Protocol)
- Remote login
  - Telnet (for remote command line interface [CLI] access, used on Cisco devices)
  - rlogin (most commonly used on Unix hosts)
- Management
  - DNS (Domain Name System used for name management)
  - SNMP (Simple Network Management Protocol used for network device management)

Exam Tip

Telnet and TFTP are the two applications most commonly used with Cisco devices.

These so-called applications aren't necessarily the names of the retail products you would install on a PC. For instance, Netscape Mail uses SMTP, but so does Microsoft Outlook. The application front end may not be named after the protocol at the application layer it uses.

Objective 6.02   The DARPA Transport Layer

With all these applications, the protocol suite must now offer transport layer services. In other words, the data coming from these applications must be encapsulated into segments at Layer 4 of the OSI model or Layer 3 of the DARPA model. The Layer 4 protocols that are most commonly used are the Transmission Control Protocol (TCP) and the User Datagram Protocol (UDP). TCP provides reliable, connection-oriented, flow-controlled service, and UDP provides connectionless service.

Depending on the application, one or the other of these protocols may be used. For example, FTP uses TCP, while TFTP uses UDP. This would explain the name Trivial File Transfer Protocol. Although you would hardly expect the data to be trivial, it is merely an indication that TFTP uses a connectionless Layer 4 protocol. But remember, just because connectionless data flow is occurring at Layer 4, that does *not* mean that connection-oriented service is not occurring at another layer of the OSI model, such as in the application itself, which would be the application layer.

Transmission Control Protocol (TCP)

As mentioned previously, TCP is the Layer 4 protocol that will provide reliable, connection-oriented service for the upper layer applications that require it. FTP is just one example of an application that uses TCP as its Layer 4 transport. Other examples include Telnet, rlogin, SMTP, and HTTP.

This application data is broken up into segments and given a Layer 4 header. The TCP header has several fields to ensure proper data delivery, as seen in Figure 6-2.

Table 6-1 lists a brief description of each header, but the headers that are key are the Port Number, Sequence Number, and Acknowledgment Number fields. These are the fields that will be used when troubleshooting.

The Sequence and Acknowledgment Fields

With TCP sessions it is very important that each segment be identified with a sequence number so the receiving station can place the segments in the proper order when the data is received. It is also important that the sending station know which segments have been received and which haven't. The Sequence and Acknowledgment fields ensure segments are not lost or sent to the application out of order.

The *sequence number* identifies the octet number of the first byte of data in the TCP payload of this packet. When a TCP session is established between two hosts, it is the sequence number that indicates just how much data has been sent and in what order it needs to be. In Figure 6-3, the data from the sender is broken into 8-bit words and numbered starting at 1. In the real world, this number is actually created using a complex process beyond the scope of this CCNA book (or any CCIE book for that matter!). The number itself is not important; rather, it is the relation it has to the other sequence numbers. Figure 6-3 illustrates 80 bytes of data being

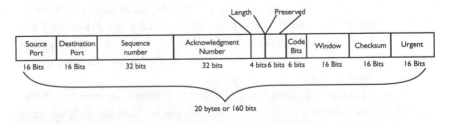

FIGURE 6.2   The TCP header

TABLE 6.1	The TCP Header Fields
Field	**Description**
Source Port	The application process where the data is sourced.
Destination Port	The application process the data is being sent.
Sequence Number	A number used to identify the order in which segments are being sent.
Acknowledgment Number	A number indicating which segments have been received and which segment is expected next.
Length (a.k.a. Data Offset)	The length of the header in 32-bit words.
Reserved	These bits are not used and are always 0.
Code Bits	For setup and teardown of sessions. It will also indicate if the Urgent and Acknowledgment fields are being used.
Window	Indicates how many bytes of data the receiver is willing to accept.
Checksum	Validates the integrity of not only the data, but also the header.
Urgent	When used (see Code Bits), indicates the end of the portion of data considered urgent.
Options	There is an optional field for options. If options are used, the field is 32 bits.

sent to a receiver. Notice that the sequence number begins at 1 and counts to 10. The total segment length is 100 bytes (20 for the TCP header plus 80 bytes of data).

Typically 80 bytes of data will be sent as one segment, but what happens when there are 8000 bytes of data? Clearly, you cannot put all the data in a single segment—it would be much too large.

The segment size will depend on a value called *maximum segment size* (MSS). The MSS is an announced value by both stations in a TCP session. This is beyond the scope of a CCNA candidate, however.

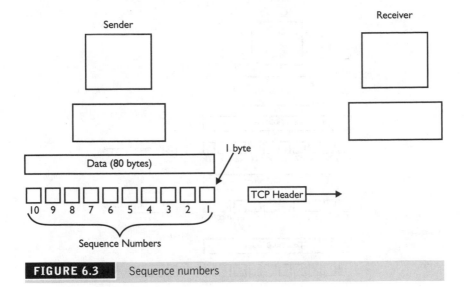

FIGURE 6.3   Sequence numbers

For the sake of argument, let's assume that the sender will transmit segments with a maximum of 1000 bytes of data. A simple calculation tells us this will take eight segments, as indicated in Figure 6-4.

Each segment will send out 1000 bytes, and the sequence number will increase in increments of 1000.

The acknowledgment number lets the sender know that the receiver has received and processed all octets with a sequence number less than the value of the acknowledgment number. The acknowledgment number also indicates the next expected octet. Going back to our 8000 bytes of data example, take a look at Figure 6-5.

We have left off all fields in the TCP header except for the sequence number of the sending station and the acknowledgment number of the receiving station, so you can see exactly how the exchange takes place. Notice that the receiver uses an acknowledgment number that identifies which segment it expects to receive next.

TCP sessions are bidirectional, therefore a sequence number and acknowledgment number must be established in the reverse direction.

Local Lingo

Expectational   The TCP flow of data is sometimes referred to as *expectational* due to the fact that the acknowledgment number refers to the sequence number the receiver *expects* to receive next.

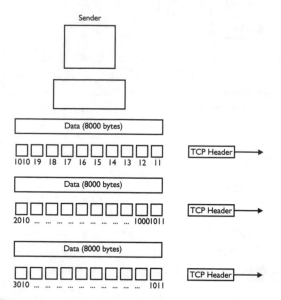

FIGURE 6.4   8000 bytes of data broken down into eight segments

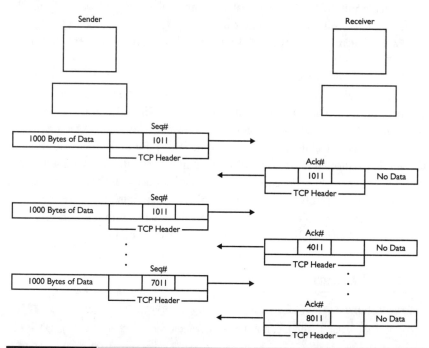

FIGURE 6.5   The relationship between the sequence number and acknowledgment number

Figure 6-6 shows both the sequence number and acknowledgment number for the sender and receiver.

When the receiver is acknowledging the sender, it might not be sending any data, therefore the sequence number the receiver sends to the sender does not increment. However, the sequence number does increment going from the sender to the receiver. This is what is shown in Figure 6-6. This may seem a little strange at first, but it makes perfect sense. In a TCP session, with bidirectional data flow, you have both stations acknowledging data received by each other, ensuring a truly reliable connection.

Port Numbers

When the data is transferred across the network and it reaches the receiver, which application will the data be sent to for processing? This question is answered in the destination port number of the TCP header. It is the destination port number that tells the receiving station to which application thread to forward this data. There are many applications for use with TCP; however, port numbers 1–1024 have been reserved for applications that are widely used. These port numbers are referred to as *well-known port numbers*. For example, Telnet is assigned the port number 23. If a station wants to Telnet to another station, the TCP segment will have a destination port value of 23. The source port number of the segment will have a random number above 1024. This number uniquely identifies this Telnet session and will

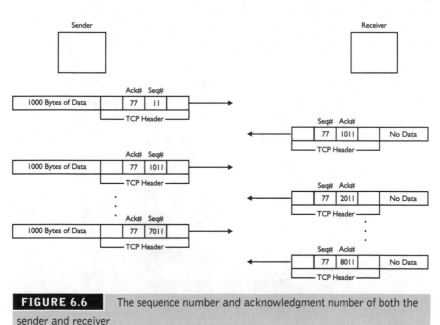

FIGURE 6.6   The sequence number and acknowledgment number of both the sender and receiver

allow the sending station to keep track of multiple Telnet sessions if there are any. Some common TCP applications and their port numbers are listed in Table 6-2.

The Three-Way Handshake

At this point you understand how the sequence and acknowledgment number work together to transfer data, but it has not been discussed how the connection begins. A TCP session is established using a procedure called a *three-way hand-shake*. The three-way handshake synchronizes the sequence numbers and ensures that both stations are capable of TCP communication for the desired application.

A good example of a TCP session is a simple Telnet connection. In Figure 6-7, Station A wants to open a Telnet session to Station B. Station A will first pick its sequence number—in this example, it is 66—and then build the TCP header. Because Telnet has a well-known port number of 23, the destination port number will be 23. It will also choose a random number above 1024 as the source port. In this example, Station A chooses 1745. In Figure 6-7, we have also included the code bits SYN and ACK. These code bits indicate if the field has a valid value.

When Station B receives the SYN request, it responds by acknowledging the sequence number of Station A and generating its own sequence number, which in this example is 303. This acknowledgment by Station B is often referred to as a SYN request as well, because it is allowing Station A to learn of its sequence numbers, or in other words, sync up with Station B's sequence numbers. The final process of the three-way handshake is Station A's acknowledgment of Station B's sequence number. At this point data can now flow as described earlier. This process is often referred to as *SYN SYN ACK*—for instance, when using a debugging tool you might tell an engineer to look for the SYN SYN ACK to find the beginning of a TCP session.

The code bits included in Figure 6-7 indicate whether a field is carrying a valid value. The first segment sent by A to B has the SYN bit set, but not the ACK bit. This

TABLE 6.2	Some Popular TCP Applications
Application	**Port Number**
Telnet	23
FTP	20
FTP-Data	21
SMTP	25
HTTP	80

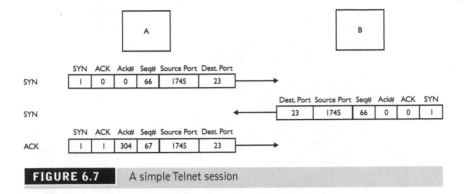

FIGURE 6.7 A simple Telnet session

indicates that only the sequence field is carrying data that is relevant. Notice that Station A simply puts a value of 0 for the acknowledgment field. At this point the acknowledgment field is not in use. When B responds to A, notice that now both bits are set, indicating that both the sequence number and acknowledgment number are valid.

TCP Windowing

As mentioned before, TCP requires an acknowledgment by the receiver to let the sender know that it has received and processed data. If a TCP session were to acknowledge each octet, there would be millions of segments required to acknowledge all the octets of data. Windowing allows the receiver to tell the sender how many unacknowledged octets it can send before it must stop sending and wait for an acknowledgment. This is determined by the receiver's buffer size. The larger this number, the more octets that can be sent without receiving an acknowledgment and the more efficient the network will be.

If the window size is too large, lost packets and the resulting retransmissions that will occur will wreak havoc on the performance of TCP applications. The stations involved will adjust their window sizes based on how successfully they are transferring packets.

To illustrate windowing, we once again turn to the station sending 8000 bytes of data. In Figure 6-8, the receiver has a window size of 4000 bytes. This means

Exam Tip

For simplicity's sake, the windowing process has been reduced to its simplest elements, but there is actually quite a bit happening during the TCP session regarding window size. You will *not* be required to know this for the exam.

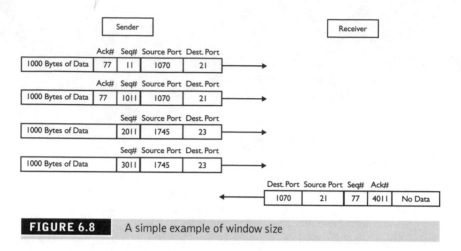

FIGURE 6.8   A simple example of window size

that the receiver will not have to acknowledge each segment as they did in Figures 6-5 and 6-6.

The sender can send up to four segments without receiving an ACK. This will likely save bandwidth on the wire and reduce processing on the stations.

It is also important to note that windowing can be very useful for flow control. By reducing the advertised window size, the receiver can slow down the sender during periods of intense processing or reduced buffer space.

The User Datagram Protocol (UDP)

TCP provides a reliable connection between two hosts, but what about applications that do not require such reliable connections? Or perhaps the reliability is being performed at another layer of the OSI model? For these applications there is the User Datagram Protocol (UDP). UDP is much simpler than TCP since there is no need for sequence numbers or acknowledgment numbers or code bits or on and on and on.

With so few fields (as noted in Figure 6-9 and Table 6-3), there are no services that UDP can perform, such as windowing, flow control, or reliable service. But

Source Port	Destination Port	Length	Checksum
16 Bits	16 Bits	16 Bits	16 Bits

Total of 64 bits or 8 bytes

FIGURE 6.9   The UDP header

TABLE 6.3	Fields of the UDP Header
Field	**Description**
Source Port	The application process where the data is sourced.
Destination Port	The application process the data is being sent.
Length	Length of the UDP header and encapsulated data in octets.
Checksum	Used to verify the integrity of the UDP message.

without all the overhead of a TCP header, UDP's header size is only 8 bytes as compared to TCP's 20 bytes.

Some commonly used UDP applications are listed in Table 6-4. It should be noted that these applications *are* reliable. Just because they use an unreliable Layer 4 service does not mean they are not performing some sort of acknowledgment process at another layer.

Travel Advisory

DNS uses both UDP and TCP as Layer 4 transports. It depends on what DNS function is being performed.

TABLE 6.4	Common UDP Applications
Application	**Port Number**
TFTP	69
SNMP	161
RIP	520
DNS	53

Objective 6.03   # The DARPA Internet Layer

T he DARPA Internet layer is exactly the same as the OSI model's network layer. It is
 responsible for addressing and path determination. A router will use the DARPA
Internet layer address or the OSI model's network layer address to make its forwarding
decision. It is for this reason that we say a router operates at Layer 3 of the OSI model.

> **Exam Tip**
>
> For the CCNA exam you will be required to identify four basic Internet layer
> protocols:
> - Internet Protocol (IP)
> - Internet Control Message Protocol (ICMP)
> - Address Resolution Protocol (ARP)
> - Reverse Address Resolution Protocol (RARP)

The Internet Protocol (IP)

Everyone has heard of IP. This is the protocol that transports the TCP and UDP
segments from all your favorite applications to anywhere on the planet. It seems
like everyone is becoming an expert in IP. The truth of the matter is that IP is a
complex and wonderful protocol. Oh dear, now we sound like the Crocodile
Hunter discussing the latest reptile he terrorizes.

The IP Datagram

The IP protocol keeps all the data in neat, convenient packages so that data can
traverse many networks before reaching its destination. The IP header is illustrated
in Figure 6-10.

Ver	Header Length	TOS	Total Length	Identification	Flags	Fragment offset	TTL	Protocol	Checksum	Surge IP Address	Destination IP Address	Options
bits 4	4	8	16	16	3	13	8	8	16	32	32	0 or 32

= 160 bits
or
20 bytes

FIGURE 6.10   The IP header

In Table 6-5 all the fields of the IP header are listed; however, some fields of note about the IP header are Source IP Address, Destination IP Address, TTL, and Protocol. Other fields, although mentioned briefly here, are beyond the scope of this book.

TABLE 6.5	Description of the IP Header Fields
Field	**Description**
Version	The version of the IP datagram. Currently version 4 is primarily used.
Header Length	The size of the header measured in 32-bit words.
TOS	Often referred to as the service field, it is used to prioritize the encapsulated traffic.
Total Length	This is the size of the entire datagram including the header. The data length can be derived by subtracting the header length from the total length.
Identification	Similar to the sequence number in TCP, but uniquely identifies the entire datagram.
Flags	Used to identify when fragmentation is occurring.
Fragment Offset	Used only when fragmentation occurs and identifies how fragmentation was done.
TTL	The Time To Live (TTL) field identifies the maximum number of routers this packet may traverse. Each router will decrement this field by 1.
Protocol	Identifies the Layer 4 protocol of the encapsulated segment.
Checksum	This checksum verifies the integrity of the header *only*.
Source IP Address	The IP address of the sending station.
Destination IP Address	The IP address of the destination.
Options	This field is optional. If used, the field is 32 bits in length.

One of the main purposes of the Layer 3 header is to identify which station the encapsulated segment is being sent to and where it came from. The destination IP address is used by the routers to make proper forwarding decisions, while the source IP address is used by the receiving station so it knows where the packet came from.

The Time To Live (TTL) field ensures that packets do not roam around an internetwork forever. This is what we call the "Logan's Run Effect." In the movie *Logan's Run*, people were exterminated when they reached age 30. This ensured that the community did not become overpopulated. The TTL field is a way to age a packet, and by killing packets that are too old, the network can keep down traffic. The TTL field will begin at a certain value and then each time it passes through a router the router will decrement the value by 1. If a router ever decrements the TTL to 0, it will *not* forward the frame, but will discard it and send an ICMP message to the sender that it had to kill the packet. This message is called a *TTL expired message* and is discussed in the section "Internet Control Message Protocol (ICMP)."

The Protocol field identifies what type of segment is encapsulated. Is the encapsulated segment a TCP or UDP segment? The Protocol field answers this question.

Exam Tip

A Protocol value of 17 indicates the encapsulated segment is a UDP segment. A value of 6 indicates the encapsulated segment is a TCP segment.

The Address Resolution Protocol (ARP)

The IP address is a Layer 3 address and often referred to as the logical address. This address, although used by the routers, is unreadable by the network interface cards (NICs) of the network nodes. These network nodes use the MAC address to identify traffic that is destined to them. Therefore hosts must use the appropriate MAC address in the Frame header when the IP packet is being encapsulated. To do this, a process called ARP is employed.

When a station encapsulates a packet into a frame, it must determine the correct destination MAC address. Before it encapsulates it will send a broadcast on the wire asking everyone if they are the destination IP address it is looking for. The destination node will see this broadcast and send an ARP reply with its MAC address. The sending station can then properly build the entire frame.

Although we have not yet discussed IP networks in detail, it is important to note that when destination IP addresses are not on the local IP network the station will perform an ARP for the router that is the first hop on its way to the destination IP address. The broadcast would not reach the actual destination IP address because routers do not forward ARP broadcasts.

Stations will keep the IP-to-MAC address mapping in memory in an *ARP cache*. Typically there will be many packets going to the same destination, not just one. The ARP cache prevents stations from continuously doing an ARP for each packet going to the same destination. Only the first packet will trigger the ARP; other packets to the same destination will be encapsulated by doing a lookup in the ARP cache.

Reverse Address Resolution Protocol (RARP)

As its name would imply, the Reverse Address Resolution Protocol (RARP) performs the same function as an ARP, except in reverse. RARP allows a station that knows its MAC address to obtain an IP address. This protocol was commonly used back in the old days (1990) when there were diskless workstations. The network manager was required to statically configure a RARP server with each MAC address and its corresponding IP address. A change in network adapter of a station necessitated a change to the RARP server. Ugh! Because there was nowhere to store parameters such as IP addresses, this was a convenient way for a station to obtain an IP address dynamically. Now, of course, all nodes have memory where this information can be stored. However, the concept proved to be a substantial advantage for administering IP addresses and was updated and replaced by the Dynamic Host Configuration Protocol (DHCP). DHCP allows a station to obtain an IP address dynamically from a DHCP server.

Internet Control Message Protocol (ICMP)

The Internet Control Message Protocol (ICMP) is used for IP nodes to communicate with each other's management information. For example, when the TTL field reaches 0, it is ICMP that relays a "TTL Expired" message to the sender that its packet has been killed.

Another extremely useful command is the Ping application. Ping uses the ICMP protocol. When a station pings another station, it sends out an ICMP message called "echo." The receiving station responds with another ICMP message called "echo reply" (see Figure 6-11).

Although Ping indicates whether a destination is reachable, it is the Traceroute application that will indicate not only whether the destination is reachable, but

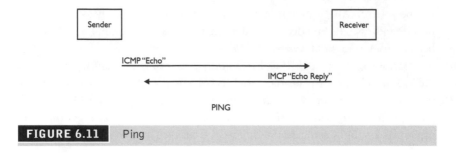

FIGURE 6.11   Ping

also the path packets will take to get there. Using the ICMP messages we already understand easily explains how this is done.

In Figure 6-12, Station A performs a traceroute to Station B. Station B is accessible only through Routers X and Y. Station A will send a UDP segment to Station B with a port value that is most probably not used. This is a random value above 30,000. The UDP segment is then encapsulated into an IP datagram to the destination. However, the TTL value of the first packet is set to 1. When the Router X receives the frame, it decrements the TTL field to 0, kills the packet, and sends an ICMP "TTL Expired" message to Station A. Bingo! Station A now knows the first hop on the way to Station B by examining the Source IP Address field of the ICMP message.

Station A then repeats the process, but instead of using a TTL value of 1, it changes it to 2. When Router X receives the packet, it decrements the TTL from 2

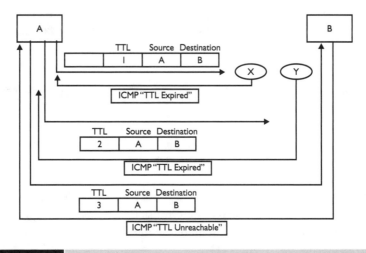

FIGURE 6.12   Traceroute

to 1 and forwards the packet to Router Y. When Router Y receives it, the TTL is decremented to 0 and an ICMP "TTL Expired" message is sent to Station A. Examining the source IP address of the second "TTL Expired" message yields the second hop on the way to Station B.

When Station A sends out the third packet, it traverses both Routers X and Y to reach Station B. When Station B examines the Protocol field of the IP packet, it forwards the encapsulated segment to the UDP process where the UDP process realizes that the port specified in the UDP segment from Station A is not in use. When this occurs, Station B responds back to Station A with an ICMP message "Port Unreachable." When Station A receives the "Port Unreachable" ICMP message, Station A knows that the process is complete.

 **IP Addressing**

In the last section, the Source and Destination IP Address fields were discussed, but there was no mention of exactly how the address is derived or read. In this section, you will learn what an IP address is, how it is classified, and how to subnet. If you are new to IP addressing, you may have to read this section several times—don't worry, that's normal.

The IP Address

The IP address itself is 32 bits in length. To make the address readable to humans (or extremely smart animals), we write the IP address, most of the time, in dotted decimal notation. The address is broken into four 8-bit groups, converting each octet to decimal values, and separating these values by dots as shown here:

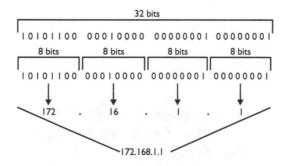

174   MIKE MEYERS' CCNA CERTIFICATION PASSPORT

As you can see, the ability to convert from binary to decimal and back again comes in very handy when working with IP addresses. The good news is that you only need to understand how to convert up to 8 bits at a time. To do this efficiently you must first have an understanding of binary. Binary is simply a Base 2 numbering system. You are already familiar with the Base 10 numbering system; you just need to reapply the same concept.

In Base 10 numbering, each number indicates a power of 10. For example, 1236 is really...

$$1^{10^3} \quad 2^{10^2} \quad 3^{10^1} \quad 6^{10^0}$$

$$(1 \times 10^3) + (2 \times 10^2) + (3 \times 10^1) + (6 \times 10^0)$$

$$(1 \times 1000) + (2 \times 100) + (3 \times 10) + (6 \times 1)$$

$$1000 + 200 + 30 + 6 = 1236$$

The same applies in Base 2 numbering, but the difference is that digits can only be a 1 or 0, which actually makes things much easier. For example, 10110111 is really...

$$1^{2^7} \quad 0^{2^6} \quad 1^{2^5} \quad 1^{2^4} \quad 0^{2^3} \quad 1^{2^2} \quad 1^{2^1} \quad 1^{2^0}$$

$$(1 \times 2^7) + (0 \times 2^6) + (1 \times 2^5) + (1 \times 2^4) (0 \times 2^3) + (1 \times 2^2) + (1 \times 2^1) + (1 \times 2^0)$$

$$(1 \times 128) + (0 \times 64) + (1 \times 32) + (1 \times 16) + (0 \times 8) + (1 \times 4) + (1 \times 2) + (1 \times 1)$$

$$128 + 0 + 32 + 16 + 0 + 4 + 2 + 1 = 1236$$

The trick to binary is to learn the decimal values of each bit for the first 8 bits. This way you can simply start from the left or right and add. The following is the decimal value of each bit value. Simply add the decimal values where there is a 1 present, and you will have the decimal value of the octet.

128	64	32	16	8	4	2	1
1	1	0	0	1	1	0	0
128 +	64 +	0 +	0 +	8 +	4 +	0 +	0

=204

Exam Tip

You must memorize the values 128-64-32-16-8-4-2-1. The easiest way to remember it is to start at 1 and multiply by 2. $1 \times 2 = 2 \times 2 = 4 \times 2 = 8 \times 2 = 16 \times 2 = 32 \times 2 = 64 \times 2 = 128$.

It is often helpful to memorize the decimal value of all 0s and all 1s in an octet, for reasons discussed later. Those values are shown here:

	128	64	32	16	8	4	2	1		
All 0s	0	0	0	0	0	0	0	0	=	0
All 1s	1	1	1	1	1	1	1	1		
	128 +	64 +	32 +	16 +	8 +	4 +	2 +	1	=	255

After practicing this for a little while, you should be ready to try converting from decimal back to binary. To do this, simply start from the left of the 8 bit positions. Ask yourself, is the decimal value greater than or less than 128? If it is larger than 128, place a 1 in the 128 position and subtract 128 from the original decimal value and continue the process until you have checked all 8 bit positions. For example, to convert 214 to binary…

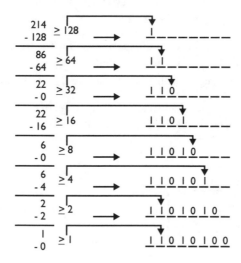

Although the process may seem a little complex now, with practice you will get quicker and quicker.

IP Address Classification

All Layer 3 addresses are broken into two parts, a network portion and a host portion. The network portion identifies the logical segment that a host resides on, and the host portion identifies the host. One useful analogy is the mail system. Your mailing address is very similar to an IP address. You live on Maple Street, and there are many neighbors who also live on Maple Street. To uniquely identify your house, it is assigned a number. This number is analogous to the host number, while the street is analogous to the network number. All hosts on the same network will have the same network number, but individual host numbers will be unique, just like on Maple Street.

The problem you may run into with IP addresses is identifying the network number and host number. Sometimes the network number is the first octet, sometimes it is the first two octets, and sometimes it is half of an octet! IP addresses are broken into classes and this allows you to identify where the network and host numbers reside. There are five classes of IP addresses; A, B, C, D, and E. D and E are reserved for multicasting and research, respectively. A, B, and C are the classes used in the real world for host assignment. The class of address will define what is the network number and what is the host number, as shown in Figure 6-13.

To determine whether an address is a Class A, B, or C address, you need only examine the first several bits of the first octet:

- If the first octet begins with a 0, the address is a Class A address.
- If the first octet begins with a 10, the address is a Class B address.
- If the first octet begins with a 110, the address is a Class C address.

With a little arithmetic, you can identify the range of decimal values that are possible in the first octet for each class, listed in Table 6-6.

Class A
0 0 0 0 0 0 0 0   = 0
⋮
0 1 1 1 1 1 1 1   = 127

Class B
10 0 0 0 0 0 0 0 . 0 0 0 0 0 0 0   = 128.0
⋮
10 1 1 1 1 1 1 1 . 1 1 1 1 1 1 1 1   = 191.255

Class C
110 0 0 0 0 0 0 0 . 0 0 0 0 0 0 0 . 0 0 0 0 0 0 0 0   = 192.0.0
⋮
110 1 1 1 1 1 1 1 . 1 1 1 1 1 1 1 1 . 1 1 1 1 1 1 1 1   = 223.0.0

TABLE 6.6	Possible First Octet Values for Class A, B, and C Addresses
Class Address	**Possible First Octet Values**
Class A	1–127 *
Class B	128–191
Class C	192–223

*0 and 127 are reserved.

Referring to Figure 6-13, you can see that with a Class A address there is a total of 24 bits for the host number, which will yield $2^{24} = 16,777,216$ possible hosts on one network! The possibility of this happening is pretty remote. A Class B address will have a total of 16 host bits, yielding $2^{16} = 65,536$ possible hosts. Only a Class C address has a realistic number of hosts with $2^8 = 256$. You will see in a little bit that you may have to break these larger networks down a bit further.

The Three Fields of IP Addresses

There are several rules to remember when working with IP addresses. They have to do with the three fields of an IP address. Yes, we have only discussed two so far, the Network and Host fields. There is a third that we will discuss shortly.

| FIGURE 6.13 | The network and host portions of Class A, B, and C addresses |

Rule #1: You cannot have all 0s or 1s in the Network field. These addresses are reserved.   The Network field is not exactly as described earlier—the first several bits are not really part of the Network field. They are what might be called the *class identifying bits* (CIBs). These bits are not part of the Network field and therefore don't apply to the rule. Here we see the modification indicating the correct number of Network bits. These bits cannot be all set to 0 or 1.

	7 Bits		24 bits
Class A	0	Network	Host

	14 bits		16 bits
Class B	1 0	Network	Host

		21 bits	8 Bits
Class C	1 1 0	Network	Host

This explains why 0 and 127 are not listed in Table 6-6 as valid first octets of a Class A address, as you can see here:

$$0 \underbrace{0\,0\,0\,0\,0\,0\,0}_{\text{Network Bits}} = 0$$

$$0 \underbrace{1\,1\,1\,1\,1\,1\,1}_{\text{Network Bits}} = 127$$

Rule #2: When the Host field is all 0s, this is a special address called the network address. When the Host field is all 1s, this is a special address called the broadcast address.   Like the Network field, all 0s and all 1s in the Host field are reserved. The all 0s address is called the *network address*, and the all 1s address is called the *broadcast address*. The all 0s address marks the beginning of an IP network, while the broadcast marks the end of that network. For example, 10.0.0.0 is a Class A address. All 0s in the Host field (10.0.0.0) tells you it is the beginning of the network. All 1s in the Host field (10.255.255.255) tells you it's the end of the network. All addresses in between the network and broadcast addresses are *valid* IP addresses.

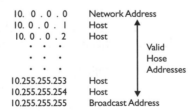

> ### Travel Advisory
>
> The network and broadcast addresses are *not* valid IP host
> addresses. You would never assign these addresses to a host.

These addresses are very important. As mentioned earlier, they identify the range of valid IP addresses for administrators to assign to hosts. Typically the first available or last available is used for the router interface. This is *not* required, but is generally practiced.

If an administrator were going to use the Class C address 192.168.1.0 at a remote site, what would be the valid range of IP addresses that he or she could use?

```
                            ┌─── All 0s in the Host Field
                            ▼
         192.168.1.  0      Network Address
         192.168.1.  1      Router Address
         192.168.1.  2      Valid Host Address
                    .
                    .
                    .
         192.168.1.253      Valid Host Address
         192.168.1.254      Valid Host Address
         192.168.1.255      Broadcast
                    └─── All 1s in the Host Field
```

As can be seen here, the network address and broadcast address tell us what those valid IP addresses are going to be. In the above scenario we used the first available IP address for the router.

The problem you run into while working in the field is when you have networks with 1,000 nodes. These networks are clearly too large for a Class C address (256 – the network and broadcast addresses = 254 possible nodes), but are too small for a Class B address (65,536 – the network and broadcast addresses = 65,534 possible nodes). Why do we keep thinking of Goldilocks and the Three Bears?

To solve this problem, you perform *subnetting*. Subnetting is a procedure whereby you steal bits that rightfully belong to the Host field based on the IP address class and give them to the network number. These bits are referred to as *subnet bits*. This procedure yields the capability to have more networks with a smaller number of valid host addresses. For example, a network with 60,000 nodes would most likely be broken into many networks. Therefore you would need more networks with fewer nodes per network, not just one network that would be yielded by a Class B address! By subnetting, you can divide the Class B network into many subnets, each with a much smaller number of hosts.

This process can be illustrated using an easy example. Let's say Company X has 250 networks with each network requiring 250 hosts. Using a Class B address, 172.16.0.0, you could subnet the Class B address so that of the 16 host bits, 8 bits are stolen from the host bits and given to the network bits. This would give you 8 bits for the Subnet field and 8 bits for the Host field.

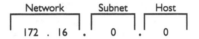

```
    Network          Subnet          Host
 |‾‾‾‾‾‾‾‾‾‾|      |‾‾‾‾‾‾|        |‾‾‾‾‾‾|
   172 . 16   .       0     .        0
```

Local Lingo

Subnet   We often times list the Network and Subnet fields separately, but the Subnet field is actually part of the Network field.

Rule #3: You cannot have all 0s or 1s in the Subnet field.   The bits that have been stolen from the Host field and given to the Network field are often referred to as the Subnet field. Rule #3 will cause two subnetworks to be "burned" or unusable.

$$172.16. \underbrace{0\ 0\ 0\ 0\ 0\ 0\ 0\ 0}_{\text{All 0s}} = 172.16.0.0$$

$$172.16. \underbrace{1\ 1\ 1\ 1\ 1\ 1\ 1\ 1}_{\text{All 1s}} = 172.16.255.0$$

By subnetting the 172.16.0.0 Class B address, you burned the networks 172.16.0.0 and 172.16.255.0.

Local Lingo

Zero subnets   These two networks mentioned are often referred to as the zero subnets, even though the last address is actually the "all 1s subnet." It just doesn't sound cool calling it the "all 1s subnet."

The question still remains: what are the valid subnetwork numbers and host addresses? Keeping in mind that the network and broadcast addresses of each subnet will be all 0s in the Host field and all 1s in the Host field yields the following results:

172.16. 0 . 0	Invalid (Zero Subnet)	
172.16. 1 . 0	Netowrk Address	
172.16. 1 . 2ss	Broadcast Address	
172.16. 2 . 0	Net	
172.16. 2 . 2ss	BC	
172.16. 3 . 0	Net	
172.16. 4 . 2ss	BC	

172.16. 5 . 0	Netowrk Address	
172.16. 5 . 2ss	Broadcast Address	
• • • • •		
• • • • •		
172.16.254. 0	Net	
172.16.254. 2ss	BC	
172.16.255. 0	Invalid (Zero Subnet)	

The first available subnet is the 172.16.1.0 network. This network has a broadcast address of 172.16.1.255 (all 1s in the Subnet field, see Rule #2) and a valid range of host addresses from 172.16.1.1 to 172.16.1.254. The same will go for 172.16.2.0 to 172.16.254.0. Of course, network 172.16.255.0 is burned due to the fact there are all 1s in the Subnet field. This is rudimentary subnetting, and we will discuss more complex implementations shortly.

Exam Tip

Subnetting does *not* yield more IP addresses, as is commonly stated by inexperienced engineers. Subnetting yields more networks, not more hosts. As could be seen previously, subnetting actually reduced the number of host addresses due to the zero subnets and new network and broadcast addresses.

Subnetting

As noted in the previous section, subnetting is performed to allow you to fit the assigned Class A, B, or C address into the topology of the network. Different companies may employ different subnet masks. How do hosts know if subnetting is occurring and exactly what is the host number and what is the network number?

The Subnet Mask

To tell hosts what portion of the address is the network and what portion is the host you use the *subnet mask*. The subnet mask is a sort of adjective—it describes the IP address it immediately follows. Its sole purpose in life is to distinguish what bits refer to the network and what bits refer to the host. The mask looks like an IP address, but it is far from it. It is 32 bits represented in dotted decimal notation, but there are 1s in the bit positions that are part of the network number and 0s in the bit positions that are in the host number. Looking at the subnetting example from the previous section, you can see the mask will be as follows:

Notice that the subnet is part of the network number and therefore will have 1s in the subnet mask. Of course, this is a simple example, because you have subnetted along the octet boundaries. An octet is either 0 or 255 when performing simple subnetting. In complex subnetting, only a portion of an octet is allocated to the network number. However, the network number is always contiguous, therefore there are only several other decimal values that can be used in the subnet mask.

```
0 0 0 0 0 0 0 0 =  0
1 0 0 0 0 0 0 0 = 128
1 1 0 0 0 0 0 0 = 192
1 1 1 0 0 0 0 0 = 224
1 1 1 1 0 0 0 0 = 240
1 1 1 1 1 0 0 0 = 248
1 1 1 1 1 1 0 0 = 252
1 1 1 1 1 1 1 0 = 254
1 1 1 1 1 1 1 1 = 255
```

These are the *only* possible values used with a subnet mask. Noncontiguous subnet masks are not supported.

When there is no subnetting occurring you must still specify a subnet mask on the host. This mask is called the *default subnet mask*. For example, the default subnet mask of the 172.16.0.0 Class B network (or any Class B network, for that matter) will be 255.255.0.0. A Class A address would have a default mask of 255.0.0.0 and a Class C address would have a default mask of 255.255.255.0.

If you were to see the address 10.1.2.34 with a subnet mask of 255.255.255.0 on a host, it could easily be established that the 10.0.0.0 Class A address had been subnetted and that the subnet field was 16 bits as shown here:

Default Mask   255. 0 . 0 . 0
Given Mask   255.255.255. 0

2 octets
beyond default = 16 bits

By comparing the given subnet mask to the default subnet mask the size of the subnet field can be established. It is very important that you be able to read the IP address and subnet mask properly.

Complex Subnet Masking

Up to this point, we have only discussed subnetting along octet boundaries. However, many times the subnet field does not encompass an entire octet. This is sometimes referred to as *complex subnet masking*.

Small companies may only have several locations with a few number of hosts per location. Company Y has three locations, as illustrated in Figure 6-14.

With such a small number of nodes (28 nodes) only a Class C address will be assigned to Company Y. Clearly there is the need for six networks with a maximum of 12 nodes per network. In this case, Company Y needs more networks with fewer nodes per network.

Travel Advisory

The number of nodes listed at each location should include any potential new users, devices such as routers, printers, or servers, and any other device that may require an IP address—not just users!

The only way to get more networks is to perform complex subnetting. If Company Y were assigned the Class C address 192.168.1.0, they would have to create a subnet scheme to allow each network to have an IP address for every node. A Class C address has only 8 host bits. If you were to steal 4 bits from the Host field, that would yield a 4-bit Subnet field and a 4-bit Host field. What is the number of

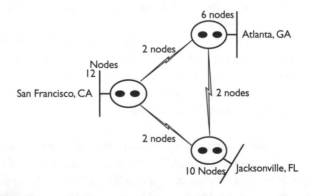

| **FIGURE 6.14** | Company Y's network topology |

networks and the number of valid host addresses per network? The following is a list of all the possible values based on a 4-bit subnet field.

Sub-network Field (4 bits)

```
0 0 0 0 = 0
0 0 0 1 = 1
0 0 1 0 = 2      1 0 0 1 = 9       16 Total Addresses
0 0 1 1 = 3      1 0 1 0 = 10
0 1 0 0 = 4      1 0 1 1 = 11
0 1 0 1 = 5      1 1 0 0 = 12
0 1 1 0 = 6      1 1 0 1 = 13
0 1 1 1 = 7      1 1 1 0 = 14
1 0 0 0 = 8      1 1 1 1 = 15
```

Notice that there are a total of 16 possible values (0–15) but 0 and 15 cannot be used because they would break Rule #3. Thus there will be 14 possible values (1–14). Of course, you have to remember that this is *only* the first half of the octet. These decimal values will never actually show up in the address. The first available network address will be 192.168.1.16, as shown here:

```
            Subnet | Host
192.168.0. 0 0 0 1|0 0 0 0 = 192.168.1.16
                  |  ‾‾‾‾‾
                  |  All 0s for
                  |  a Network Address
```

As stated in Rule #2, the Host field has had all its bits set to 0, while the Subnet field gets the first *valid* subnet number. All 0s is not valid and therefore cannot be used. The next available subnet number is 0010 in binary or 2; however, this is only the first 4 bits of the last octet and the remaining 4 bits must be set to all 0s to yield the actual network number. All possible network addresses and broadcast addresses are listed in Figure 6-15.

In Figure 6-15, all the network addresses have the Host field set to 0, while the broadcast addresses have the Host field set to 1. The all 0s and all 1s subnets are invalid because of Rule #3; this leaves 14 available networks.

Is there a shortcut to listing out all these network numbers? It appears there is a pattern. The first network number was 16, the second 32, the third 48, and so on. Each network is a multiple of 16. Indeed, the simple formula is to obtain this multiplier and build your network and broadcast addresses based on it. The broadcast address is simply one less than the next network number. The formula to determine the multiplier is quite simple: 2^X where X is the number of host bits, in this case 4, therefore $2^4 = 16$.

Now that the network addresses and broadcast addresses have been established, it would be a good idea to figure out the subnet mask. This should be fairly

Subnet | Host

192.168.1	0000 0000 = 16	INVALID		
	0000 1111 = 31			
1st	0001 0000 = 32		11th	1011 0000 = 176
	0001 1111 = 47			1011 1111 = 191
2nd	0010 0000 = 48		12th	1011 0000 = 192
	0010 1111 = 63			1011 1111 = 207
3rd	0011 0000 = 64		13th	1011 0000 = 208
	0011 1111 = 79			1011 1111 = 223
4th	0100 0000 = 80		14th	1011 0000 = 224
	0100 1111 = 95			1011 1111 = 239
5th	0101 0000 = 96		15th	1011 0000 = 240 INVALID
	0101 1111 = 111			1011 1111 = 255
6th	0110 0000 = 112			
	0110 1111 = 123			
7th	0111 0000 = 124			
	0111 1111 = 137			
8th	1000 0000 = 138			
	1000 1111 = 143			
9th	1001 0000 = 144			
	1001 1111 = 159			
10th	1010 0000 = 160			
	1010 1111 = 175			

FIGURE 6.15 All network and broadcast addresses for a Class C address with a 4-bit Subnet field

straightforward. The first 4 bits of the fourth octet have been stolen from the Host field and given to the Network field and therefore the fourth octet will have a mask of 11110000 = 240. Of course, the first three octets will all be 255 because they are all 1s, therefore the subnet mask is 255.255.255.240.

The final step is to assign the ranges of IP addresses to each of the networks shown previously in Figure 6-14. In Figure 6-16, we have assigned the IP addresses as indicated.

Each router interface must be assigned an IP address. The valid range of IP addresses for workstations at each location has been listed.

When performing subnet planning, it is important to follow these steps:

1. Document the topology and maximum number of nodes at each location as we did with Company Y.
2. Calculate the number of networks and the number of hosts per network that you will need. To calculate the number of subnet bits and host bits necessary, remember the two formulas:
   - $2^Y - 2$ = the number of hosts per network, where Y is the number of host bits
   - $2^Z - 2$ = the number of networks, where Z is the number of subnet bits

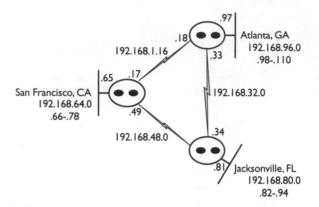

FIGURE 6.16	IP addressing scheme for Company Y

3. Determine the network and broadcast addresses. This can be done using the shortcut mentioned earlier (2^X as the multiplier, where X is the number of host bits).

4. Assign the network addresses to the networks and assign available IP addresses within those networks.

Creating a subnet plan can be easy if you take each step one at a time. Too many times, engineers quickly rush through this process and end up with an unusable addressing scheme.

Recognizing IP Addresses and Subnets

Engineers will often encounter a network that is preexisting. It is important to be able to quickly identify the addressing scheme of this preexisting environment. For example, if you were given an IP address of 172.16.54.74 with a mask of 255.255.255.224, what is the network address and broadcast address of the network where this host resides? This is exactly the opposite of subnet planning. The plan has already been done and now you must figure out the network and broadcast addresses.

The subnet mask is called a mask for good reason. Using a Boolean algebraic logic function called AND, the network number just falls out of the IP addresses because the host bits are *masked* out. An AND is just like a regular "and," but it is done with bits. If someone asks you if you have an apple AND an orange, you will only answer yes if you have both. The same is true with bits—if the first bit is 1 and second bit is 1, and you AND the two together, the result will be 1. However, if either of the bits is 0 or both bits are 0, the result will be 0, as you can see here:

```
         |          |          0          0
    AND  |     AND  0     AND  |     AND  0
         |          0          0          0
```

To calculate the network address, you need only perform a logical AND between the subnet mask and the IP address, as follows:

```
        /172\   .  / 16 \  .  / 54 \  .  / 74 \
        10101000 . 00010000 . 00110110 . 01001010
        11111111 . 11111111 . 11111111 . 11100000  = 255.255.255.225
   AND
        10101000   00010000   00110110   01000000   = 172.16.54.64
        10101000   00010000   00110110   01011111   = 172.16.54.95
```

The mask allows the network bits to fall through while it masks out the host bits. If you logically AND any number with all 1s, you end up with the number you started with, while if you logically AND any number with all 0s, you end up with all 0s. By placing 0s in the host bit positions of the mask, the host bits end up being 0 when logically AND is used, leaving you with the network address.

To determine the broadcast address, simply take the host bits and convert them from 0s to 1s as shown earlier. The address 172.16.54.95 is the broadcast address of the network 172.16.54.64.

Broadcasts

There are two types of broadcasts that a Cisco router will recognize:

- Local broadcast
- Directed broadcast

The Local Broadcast

The local broadcast is always the address 255.255.255.255 and is read by all nodes on an IP network. The router will read but *not* forward these packets, thus keeping them on the local segment—hence the name local broadcast.

The Directed Broadcast

The directed broadcast is what we referred to as the broadcast address in Rule #3. In the real world, this address can also be called the directed broadcast address.

Objective 6.05

Configuring Cisco Devices to Use IP

As mentioned previously, it is very important to assign an IP address to the router interface. This lets the router know which IP network is attached to which interface. In Company Y's scenario in Figure 6-16, each router interface was assigned an IP address—but how would you configure that address on the interface?

Assigning IP Addresses to Router Interfaces

Remembering the configuration modes discussed in Chapter 2, you use the command **ip address** in Interface configuration mode. Referring back to Figure 6-16, to configure the IP addresses on the San Francisco router, the following would be done:

```
SF-Router(config)#interface s0
SF-Router(config-if)#ip address 192.168.1.17 255.255.255.240
SF-Router(config-if)#interface s1
SF-Router(config-if)#ip address 192.168.1.49 255.255.255.240
SF-Router(config-if)#interface e0
SF-Router(config-if)#ip address 192.168.1.65 255.255.255.240
SF-Router(config-if)#
```

All interfaces have been configured on the San Francisco router, but don't forget to use the **no shutdown** command on each interface to bring them up.

To verify the interface has been configured with the correct address, you can use the command **show ip interface** or **show interface**:

```
SF-Router#sh ip interface
Ethernet0 is up, line protocol is up
  Internet address is 192.168.1.65/28
  Broadcast address is 255.255.255.255
  Address determined by setup command
  MTU is 1500 bytes
  Helper address is not set
  Directed broadcast forwarding is enabled
```

```
  Outgoing access list is not set
  Inbound  access list is not set
  Proxy ARP is enabled
  Security level is default
  Split horizon is enabled
  ICMP redirects are always sent
  ICMP unreachables are always sent
  ICMP mask replies are never sent
  IP fast switching is enabled
  IP fast switching on the same interface is disabled
  IP multicast fast switching is enabled
  Router Discovery is disabled
  IP output packet accounting is disabled
  IP access violation accounting is disabled
  TCP/IP header compression is disabled
  RTP/IP header compression is disabled
  Probe proxy name replies are disabled
  Gateway Discovery is disabled
  Policy routing is disabled
  Network address translation is disabled
Serial0 is down, line protocol is down
  Internet address is 192.168.1.17/28
  Broadcast address is 255.255.255.255
  Address determined by setup command
  MTU is 1500 bytes
  Helper address is not set
  Directed broadcast forwarding is enabled
  Outgoing access list is not set
  Inbound  access list is not set
  Proxy ARP is enabled
  Security level is default
  Split horizon is enabled
  ICMP redirects are always sent
  ICMP unreachables are always sent
  ICMP mask replies are never sent
  IP fast switching is enabled
  IP fast switching on the same interface is enabled
```

```
    IP multicast fast switching is disabled
    Router Discovery is disabled
    IP output packet accounting is disabled
    IP access violation accounting is disabled
    TCP/IP header compression is disabled
    RTP/IP header compression is disabled
    Probe proxy name replies are disabled
    Gateway Discovery is disabled
    Policy routing is disabled
    Network address translation is disabled
 Serial1 is administratively down, line protocol is down
    Internet address is 192.168.1.49/28
    Broadcast address is 255.255.255.255
    Address determined by setup command
    MTU is 1500 bytes
    Helper address is not set
    Directed broadcast forwarding is enabled
    Outgoing access list is not set
    Inbound  access list is not set
    Proxy ARP is enabled
    Security level is default
    Split horizon is enabled
    ICMP redirects are always sent
    ICMP unreachables are always sent
    ICMP mask replies are never sent
    IP fast switching is enabled
    IP fast switching on the same interface is enabled
    IP multicast fast switching is enabled
    Router Discovery is disabled
    IP output packet accounting is disabled
    IP access violation accounting is disabled
    TCP/IP header compression is disabled
    RTP/IP header compression is disabled
    Probe proxy name replies are disabled
    Gateway Discovery is disabled
    Policy routing is disabled
    Network address translation is disabled
 SF-Router#
```

The / Notation

In the preceding output, you will notice that the bolded lines have the subnet mask represented as /28. This is an easy way to represent the subnet mask without having to use the long and painstaking 255.255.255.240. It is a little easier to read and much easier to say and write. The number immediately following the / is the number of network bits. Since the subnet mask is a series of contiguous 1s, all you need is the total number of 1s to easily calculate the subnet mask. For example, /28 indicates that there are 28 1s in the subnet mask, therefore it is 11111111.11111111.11111111.11110000— this is 28 1s followed by 4 0s.

If you do not like this notation, it can be changed using the command **term ip netmask-format**. The syntax is as follows:

```
Router#term ip netmask-format [bitcount | decimal | hexadecimal]
```

The **bitcount** option is the default, more commonly called the "slash" notation. **decimal** will represent the mask in standard decimal format. The **hexadecimal** format will display the mask in hexadecimal for truly demented individuals. An example of changing the netmask format is shown here:

```
SF-Router#term ip netmask-format decimal
SF-Router#sh int s0
Serial0 is down, line protocol is down
  Hardware is HD64570
  Internet address is 192.168.1.17 255.255.255.240
  MTU 1500 bytes, BW 1544 Kbit, DLY 20000 usec,
     reliability 255/255, txload 1/255, rxload 1/255
  Encapsulation HDLC, loopback not set, keepalive set (10 sec)
  Last input never, output never, output hang never
  Last clearing of "show interface" counters never
  Queueing strategy: fifo
  Output queue 0/40, 0 drops; input queue 0/75, 0 drops
  5 minute input rate 0 bits/sec, 0 packets/sec
  5 minute output rate 0 bits/sec, 0 packets/sec
     0 packets input, 0 bytes, 0 no buffer
     Received 0 broadcasts, 0 runts, 0 giants, 0 throttles
     0 input errors, 0 CRC, 0 frame, 0 overrun, 0 ignored, 0 abort
     0 packets output, 0 bytes, 0 underruns
     0 output errors, 0 collisions, 31 interface resets
     0 output buffer failures, 0 output buffers swapped out
```

```
    0 carrier transitions
    DCD=down  DSR=down  DTR=up  RTS=up  CTS=up
SF-Router#
```

Notice that we have used the command **show interface** this time to illustrate the second command that can be used to determine the IP address of an interface. Also notice the subnet mask is represented in decimal.

Connecting a Cisco Router to a Catalyst Switch

Back in Chapter 5, we discussed VLANs. Each VLAN is a broadcast domain. A router will typically have each of its interfaces connected to one broadcast domain. However, when using trunking, multiple VLANs can be connected to one router interface. In Figure 6-17, Router A is trunked to a Catalyst switch that has three VLANs configured.

Each of the VLANs is assigned an IP subnet, and to make things easy, the third octet of the IP subnet will match the VLAN number.

Configuring the Router for Inter-VLAN Routing

If a host on one of the VLANs in Figure 6-17 needs connectivity to a host on another VLAN, that traffic must go through the router. However, the router must be configured for inter-VLAN routing. The easiest way to think about this is to examine Figure 6-18, which is a logical representation of the situation shown previously in Figure 6-17.

In Figure 6-18, Router A has three Fast Ethernet interfaces, each assigned the lowest numbered IP address in the available subnet (.1). This is the same as Figure

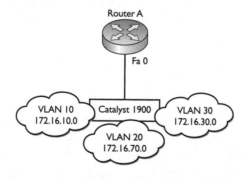

FIGURE 6.17   A router trunked to a Catalyst switch

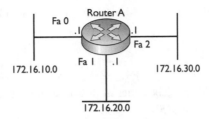

FIGURE 6.18   Logical representation of Figure 6-17

6-17 logically. The only difference is that the interfaces in Figure 6-17 are separate physical interfaces while in Figure 6-18 there is only one interface. The following is the configuration that would be used on Router A if it was configured for Figure 6-18. Nothing is new; we are just simply placing the IP addresses on the interfaces.

```
RouterA(config)#interface FastEthernet 0
RouterA(config-if)#ip address 172.16.10.1 255.255.255.0
RouterA(config-if)#interface FastEthernet 1
RouterA(config-if)#ip address 172.16.20.1 255.255.255.0
RouterA(config-if)#interface FastEthernet 2
RouterA(config-if)#ip address 172.16.30.1 255.255.255.0
```

The configuration for Figure 6-17 is not much different. Instead of specifying the three individual interfaces as above, you specify subinterfaces off the main physical interface. You also need to specify which VLAN each subinterface will be responsible for. Here is the configuration of Router A for Figure 6-17:

```
RouterA(config)#interface FastEthernet 0.10
RouterA(config-subif)#encapsulation isl 10
RouterA(config-subif)#ip address 172.16.10.1 255.255.255.0
RouterA(config-subif)#interface FastEthernet 0.20
RouterA(config-subif)#encapsulation isl 20
RouterA(config-subif)#ip address 172.16.20.1 255.255.255.0
RouterA(config-subif)#interface FastEthernet 0.30
RouterA(config-subif)#encapsulation isl 30
RouterA(config-subif)#ip address 172.16.30.1 255.255.255.0
```

This configuration is very similar, but the interfaces are now subinterfaces. The .# after the physical interface creates a subinterface. A subinterface needs to be created for each VLAN. Before the IP address can be assigned to the subinterface, a VLAN must be assigned. This is done using the **encapsulation** command as shown here:

```
Router(config-subif)#encapsulation [type of trunking] [VLAN#]
```

The **type of trunking** will be either **isl** or **dot1q**. In the preceding scenario, the Catalyst 1900 only supports ISL.

Using Hostnames with a Cisco IOS Device

In today's Internet, every host has an IP address, but it is very difficult to remember a four-octet number written in dotted-decimal notation. It is for this reason that the real world uses hostnames. A hostname is just a name assigned to a particular host to make it easier to identify. It is a lot easier to refer to a web site as CCPrep.com rather than 172.16.1.17.

Configuring Hostnames on a Cisco IOS Device

When working on the CLI of a Cisco IOS device, you'll often use the Ping and Traceroute utilities. These utilities require that you specify an IP address or a hostname. For the hostname to work, you must first create a translation between the hostname and the IP address. You will do this using the command **ip host** in the following format:

```
Router(config)#ip host [name] [tcp port number] [ip address]
```

The **name** field is replaced with the name of the host, while the **ip address** field is the address to which the hostname is being mapped.

Exam Tip

The **tcp port number** is used to change the default port number of 23 when using the Telnet utility from the CLI. From the CLI of a Cisco IOS device, you can Telnet to other devices.

The following is an example of the **ip host** command:

```
Router(config)#ip host ccprep 172.16.1.17
```

This statement tells the router that any time the hostname ccprep is specified it should be translated to the IP address 172.16.1.17. As many entries as you would like can be created.

Travel Advisory

These hostname to IP address mappings are only valid when using the CLI of the device where they are configured. The Cisco IOS device is *not* behaving as a DNS server for other devices, only its own CLI.

Working with DNS Servers

Configuring all those **ip host** commands can be quite annoying if you have many hosts. Instead of configuring each of these individually, you can configure the Cisco IOS device to query a Domain Name System (DNS) server. A DNS server, to put it simply, is a device that contains many hostname to IP address mappings. To configure the Cisco IOS device to query the DNS server, you simply need to configure the IP address of the DNS server on the Cisco IOS device using the following command:

```
Router(config)#ip name-server [ip address1] [ip address2] … [ip address6}
```

You can specify up to six addresses. The Cisco IOS device will try to resolve the name on the first; if unsuccessful, it will try the second and so forth. Only one need be specified, the others are optional.

For example, to configure the DSL-827 router to always look up DNS 172.16.1.10, the following command will work:

```
DSL-827(config)#ip name-server 172.16.1.10
```

The following is output from a Cisco router configured with a DNS. We are trying to ping www.cisco.com:

```
DSL-827#ping www.cisco.com
Translating "www.cisco.com"...domain server [OK]

Type escape sequence to abort.
Sending 5, 100-byte ICMP Echos to 198.133.219.25, timeout is 2 seconds:
!!!!!
Success rate is 100 percent (5/5), round-trip min/avg/max = 104/111/116 ms
DSL-827#
```

The router simply goes to the DNS, resolves the IP address, and pings the resolved IP address.

Whenever it encounters a name, the Cisco IOS device will first look to the local hostnames, if configured, and then to the DNS. If the DNS is not specified, the router will try to find a DNS using the 255.255.255.255 address.

The ip domain-lookup Command

One of the most annoying, yet mostly useful, features of Cisco IOS is its ability to automatically assume that anything typed in either user mode or privileged mode that is unknown must be a Telnet session request. For example, you could Telnet to the host named "dsl" just by typing **dsl** from the CLI as shown here:

```
CCPrep-AS#dsl
Trying dsl (172.16.1.10)... Open


User Access Verification

Username: lrossi
Password:
Password OK

DSL-827#
```

This appears to make things very easy when Telnetting from one Cisco IOS device to another, but watch what happens if you make a small error when trying to type a valid command:

```
CCPrep-AS#shiw
Translating "shiw"...domain server (255.255.255.255)
% Unknown command or computer name, or unable to find computer address
CCPrep-AS#
```

When trying to type the command **show**, you accidentally typed the command **shiw**. The Cisco IOS device tries to resolve the name "shiw" because it does not recognize it as a valid command and just assumes that you're trying to Telnet to a host named "shiw." No big deal, right? Wrong. The Cisco IOS device will sit at the **Translating 'shiw'** command for about a minute. This locks the CLI and causes you to become very annoyed. You will also notice that the router in which you typed the incorrect command did not have a DNS configured because it tried to find the DNS using the 255.255.255.255 address.

To stop this annoying pause, the **no ip domain-lookup** command can be used. By default the configuration file has the command **ip domain-lookup**—this is the command which enables the feature. However, in a lot of cases it is more of an annoyance. The following is the output when typed on the same router, after the command has been removed from the configuration file:

```
CCPrep-AS#conf t
Enter configuration commands, one per line.  End with CNTL/Z.
CCPrep-AS(config)#no ip domain-lookup
CCPrep-AS(config)#
CCPrep-AS#shiw
Translating "shiw"
% Unknown command or computer name, or unable to find computer address
CCPrep-AS#
```

With the **ip domain-lookup** command disabled, there is no pause on the **Translating** line as the router does not have the capability enabled. This will allow those of us who have problems with typing to work on a Cisco IOS device without having to wait after each typo.

Viewing the Hostname to IP Address Translations

You can view the hostname to IP address translations using the **show ip hosts** command. For example, if you were to configure a static translation to ccprep using the **show hosts** command and ping a host such as www.cisco.com, the **show hosts** command would display the following:

```
DSL-827#sh hosts
Default domain is not set
Name/address lookup uses domain service
Name servers are 172.16.1.10
```

```
Host                    Flags       Age Type  Address(es)
ccprep                  (perm, OK)  0   IP    172.16.1.17
www.cisco.com           (temp, OK)  0   IP    198.133.219.25
DSL-827#
```

This output lists both dynamically learned name to address translations as well as static translations from the configuration file. Upon examination you will notice that the Flags section identifies the static entries as **perm** and the dynamically learned entries as **temp**.

The Age heading refers to the number of hours since the entry was last used. Notice that the example shows 0s in both entries indicating that both have been used in the last hour.

CHECKPOINT

✔ **Objective 6.01: Introduction to the Protocol Stack** In this chapter, we discussed the layers of the DARPA model and contrasted it to the OSI model. The DARPA model consists of four layers and the OSI model consists of seven.

✔ **Objective 6.02: The DARPA Transport Layer** We discussed two protocols, TCP and UDP. TCP is a connection-oriented protocol, and UDP is a connectionless protocol. Although TCP has much greater reliability, it also has much more overhead. UDP enjoys the benefit of a much smaller segment header.

✔ **Objective 6.03: The DARPA Internet Layer** The Address Resolution Protocol (ARP) and Reverse Address Resolution Protocol (RARP) allowed hosts to determine the destination MAC address or their own IP address, respectively. The Internet Control Messaging Protocol (ICMP) allows IP hosts to exchange reachability information. The Internet Protocol (IP) is used for path determination and addressing.

✔ **Objective 6.04: IP Addressing** One of the most important aspects of IP is understanding how its addressing scheme works. IP addresses are separated into classes. There are three primary classes in use today, Classes A, B, and C. Each of these classes specifies which bits of the address represent the network and which represent the host. Sometimes it is necessary to steal bits that rightfully belong to the Host field and give them to the Network field. This is called subnetting.

✔ **Objective 6.05: Configuring Cisco Devices to Use IP** The final section of this chapter described the commands necessary to configure a router for IP.

The most important task when configuring a router to route IP traffic is assigning the correct IP addresses to correct interfaces. This can be done using the following command:

```
Router(config-if)#ip address [ip address] [subnet mask]
```

REVIEW QUESTIONS

1. What layer of the OSI model corresponds to the Internet layer of the DARPA model?

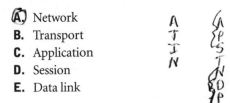

   A. Network
   B. Transport
   C. Application
   D. Session
   E. Data link

2. What Layer 4 field identifies the application to which the encapsulated data belongs?

   A. Reserved
   B. Code Bits
   C. Sequence
   D. Urgent
   E. Port

3. Which of the following accurately depicts the size of the TCP and UDP header?

   A. TCP 20 bytes, UDP 40 bytes
   B. TCP 40 bytes, UDP 40 bytes
   C. TCP 20 bytes, UDP 10 bytes
   D. TCP 20 bytes, UDP 8 bytes
   E. TCP 40 bytes, UDP 8 bytes

4. What is the port number used for Telnet?

   A. 21
   B. 23
   C. 69
   D. 159
   E. Telnet does not use a port number because it uses UDP.

5. Which of the following ICMP message types is used with the popular utility Traceroute?

    A. Destination unreachable

    B. Echo

    C. Echo Reply

    D. TTL Exceeded

    E. All of the above

6. What is the protocol number used by TCP?

    A. 6

    B. 17

    C. 23

    D. 3

    E. 20

7. What is the default subnet mask of the address 10.14.77.89?

    A. 255.255.255.0

    B. 255.255.0.0

    C. 255.0.0.0

    D. 255.255.255.255

    E. Cannot be determined from information given

8. What is the network or subnetwork address that the host 172.16.12.212 255.255.255.224 resides on?

    A. 172.16.0.0

    B. 172.16.12.0

    C. 172.16.10.0.

    D. 172.16.192.0

    E. 172.16.208.0

9. What is the command to disable a router's ability to resolve hostnames to IP addresses using a DNS?

    A. ip domain-lookup

    B. ip name-server

    C. no ip name-server

    D. no ip domain-lookup

    E. no dns-lookup

10. What is the command to configure the router to display subnet masks in dotted-decimal notation?

    A. ip mask-format decimal
    B. ip netmask-format decimal
    C. ip mask-format bitcount
    D. ip netmask-format bitcount
    E. ip subnet-format decimal

REVIEW ANSWERS

1. **A** The Internet layer of the DARPA model corresponds to the network layer of the OSI.

2. **E** The Port field in both TCP and UDP identifies the encapsulated data's application.

3. **D** The UDP header does not contain Sequence, Acknowledgment, Window, Code Bits, or Urgent fields, thus it has the much smaller header size of 8 bytes as compared to TCP's 40-byte header size.

4. **B** Telnet uses port number 23.

5. **A** and **D** Destination Unreachable is message type 3. Echo is type 8. Echo Reply is type 0. Destination Unreachable has seven subvectors called *codes*: 0 = Net Unreachable, 1 = Host Unreachable, 2 = Protocol Unreachable, 3 = Port Unreachable, and so on. Port Unreachable is one of the Destination Unreachable codes. A is a valid answer.

    All the routers along the path to the destination send the TTL Exceeded message when using the Traceroute utility. The destination will respond with a Port Unreachable message.

6. **A** The protocol number used in the IP header to identify the encapsulated segment as TCP is 6.

7. **C** The default mask of a Class A address is 255.0.0.0.

8. **D** The subnet mask tells you that 3 bits of the last octet are being used for subnetting. This yields valid subnetwork addresses of .32, .64, .96, .128, .160,

and .192. The .212 falls into the range of .192 to .223, therefore the network number is 172.16.12.192.

9. **D** The **ip domain-lookup** command enables DNS lookups; however, the question calls for the command to disable it. By placing **no** in front of the command, you disable DNS lookups.

10. **B** The proper command to specify the way the subnet mask is displayed is **ip netmask-format**. The proper option is **decimal**. **bit count** would have displayed the subnet mask in the / notation.

Basic IP Routing Protocols

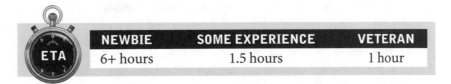

	NEWBIE	SOME EXPERIENCE	VETERAN
ETA	6+ hours	1.5 hours	1 hour

In Chapter 6, we looked at the IP protocol stack and all of its protocols. All IP applications rely on IP to get data to the proper location. As mentioned in the last chapter, a router knows which IP networks it is attached to by the IP addresses assigned to its interfaces. However, what about those networks that are not directly connected to its interfaces?

A router can learn about IP networks in two ways, statically or dynamically. A router will keep a list of these networks in a table, commonly called a routing table. This table is a listing of all the networks that a router has learned about and how to route traffic there, whether the network was learned statically, dynamically, or by the addresses on its interfaces.

Local Lingo

Directly connected networks   Networks that are learned from the IP addresses assigned to a router's interfaces.

This chapter will examine how routes are learned and placed in the routing table.

Objective 7.01   Static Routes

Perhaps the most straightforward way to place routes in the routing table is to statically create routes. To statically create a route, a single command is entered into the router configuration file with all the information necessary.

An entry in a routing table must contain all the information necessary to get packets destined for that network to that network. This includes:

- **Network address**   The router must know the network address itself.
- **Next hop address**   The next hop address is the IP address of the next hop on the way to the destination. This is the IP address of the router that is an intermediate destination on its way to the final destination.

Configuring Static Routes

In Figure 7-1, we have a simple network topology. R1 and R2 are connected together via a serial line.

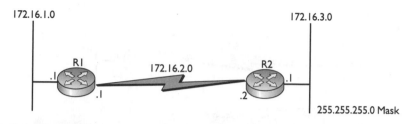

172.16.1.0

172.16.3.0

R1

172.16.2.0

R2

.1

.1

.1

.2

255.255.255.0 Mask

FIGURE 7.1 A simple network topology

A node on the 172.16.1.0 network that wishes to exchange traffic with a node on 172.16.3.0 will have to send traffic through R1. However, R1 only knows its directly connected networks (that it learned via the IP addresses assigned to its interfaces), 172.16.1.0 and 172.16.2.0. When R1 receives traffic destined for 172.16.3.1, R1 drops the packet and sends an ICMP "Destination Unreachable" message to the sender.

Local Lingo

"Destination Unreachable" ICMP message This message is very useful when troubleshooting. It tells the sending station which router does not have the proper routing information.

To solve this problem, R1 must have a route to the destination entered into its routing table. The command to enter a route into the routing table of a Cisco IOS device is **ip route**, used in the following syntax:

```
Router(config)#ip route [Destination Network Address] [Destination
Network's Subnet Mask] [Next Hop Address]
```

There is still a problem, however. When traffic tries to return from the destination node on the 172.16.3.0 network connected to R2, R2 does not know how to return the traffic to the network 172.16.1.0. Therefore you must use the **ip route** command on R2 as well. Figure 7-2 gives the correct syntax for the **ip route** command to allow traffic to flow from 172.16.1.0 to 172.16.3.0 and vice versa.

Travel Advisory

The next hop address *must* be on a known network—in other words, in the routing table.

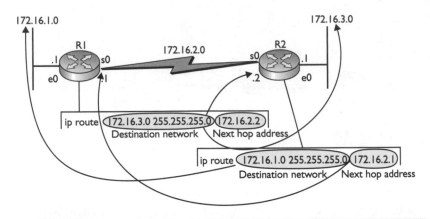

FIGURE 7.2   Routers configured with static routes

The static route may also be directed toward a router interface such as the S0.
Referring back to the scenario in Figure 7-2, Figure 7-3 shows that instead of using
the next hop address, you could use the next hop interface.

Travel Assistance

Any static route pointing to an interface that is down will not be
placed in the routing table. This feature may be overridden using
the **permanent** option at the end of the **ip route** statement.

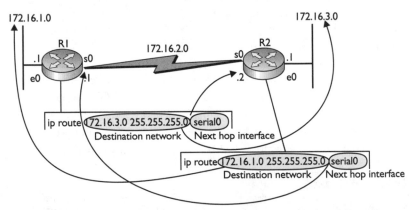

FIGURE 7.3   Routers configured with static routes pointing to directly
connected interfaces

The Default Route

In certain cases like that in Figure 7-4, you will not want to specify all the destination networks individually. In Figure 7-4, there is only one path to all the networks not directly connected to R1.

All traffic from R1 must go through R2 to get to the rest of the corporate networks. It wouldn't make any sense to create a static entry for each and every individual network of the corporate network on R1. This could be quite a few commands all pointing to the same next hop address, which means you have to type a lot.

The solution to this problem is to use a default route, sometimes called the gateway of last resort. The default route is a static route, but with a special destination network. Rather than a specific IP network and subnet mask, the address 0.0.0.0 with a mask of 0.0.0.0 is used. This is, of course, an invalid IP network and mask, but the router knows that this is really the default network. Any traffic destined for a network not explicitly listed in the routing table will be forwarded to the next hop address specified in the default network command.

Referring back to the scenario in Figure 7-4, Figure 7-5 shows the proper command to configure R1 to route traffic to the corporate network.

R1 will route all traffic not destined for the IP network on its e0 to R2. Of course, R2 must know how to get to the IP network on R2's e0 and therefore will probably need a static route pointing to R1.

FIGURE 7.4 A scenario for using the default route

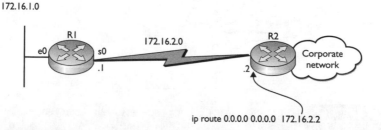

FIGURE 7.5 An example of the default route

Objective 7.02 Dynamic Routes

Static routes are great in small environments that don't change much. But what about those instances when the network is much larger and is constantly having networks added, removed, or changed? Static routes on all the routers would have to be maintained and documented, and this would be become a huge headache. Wouldn't it be nice if the routers could just talk to each other and tell each other about the routes that were being added, removed, and changed, and how to get to all of them? Sure enough, routers can dynamically learn routes via a routing protocol. A routing protocol is a protocol that runs between routers (obviously) to exchange information about networks they know about so they can build a complete routing table.

Routers that learn routes dynamically exchange routing updates with one another so they can learn about all the networks in the topology.

All of the routers in Figure 7-6 will exchange routing information to learn about each other's networks until eventually each router in the topology knows about all the networks in the topology. When all routers in the network topology have all the networks in the topology in their routing tables, the network is said to be *converged*. Convergence is important because it indicates that the

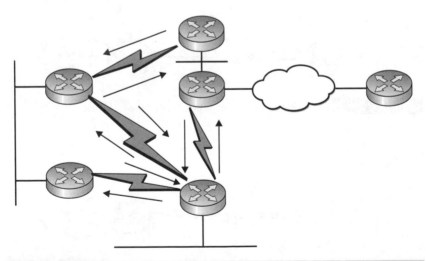

FIGURE 7.6 Routers exchange routing updates to learn about each other's networks.

routers are all in a state of Zen. They know all that is and are at peace with the network. The whole purpose of a routing protocol is get the routers to this Zen state, convergence.

Link State and Distance Vector

Routers go about achieving convergence through the use of a routing protocol. A routing protocol is a way for routers to exchange information about those networks it knows about. There are many different routing protocols, but generally we split them all into two classes, link state or distance vector.

A *distance vector* routing protocol is a routing protocol that exchanges updates on a neighbor-by-neighbor basis. In other words one router tells another router, which tells another router, and so on. This type of routing is sometimes referred to as "routing by rumor" because routing updates only go between neighbors and therefore a router is not learning about a network from the source, unless that router is directly connected to a router that is directly connected to the source network.

In Figure 7-7, Router A learns about Network 1 because it is directly connected. When a distance vector routing protocol is employed, Router A tells Router B via an update that it is directly connected to Network 1. Router B then tells Router C, and Router C tells Router D.

A link state routing protocol is different in that every router receives an update from every other router in the network. This is almost the exact opposite of distance vector's routing by rumor scenario. Every router sends an update to every other router. This update is called a *link state advertisement* (LSA) or *link state update* (LSU), depending on who you talk to.

Both link state and distance vector routing protocols have their advantages and disadvantages. In general, a link state routing protocol is better suited for larger networks, and a distance vector routing protocol is better suited for smaller networks. The CCNA exam requires that candidates have knowledge of what a

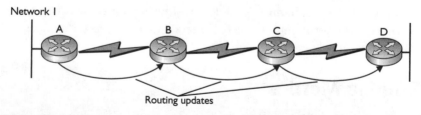

Network 1

Routing updates

FIGURE 7.7 Routing by rumor

link state protocol is, but not the intricacies of any of the link state routing protocols. For this reason, this book will give a brief and general overview of link state routing protocols, but *not* an in-depth look at the different link state routing protocols. However, distance vector routing protocols are required of candidates, and the two routing protocols you will be required to be familiar with are covered in this chapter.

Although everyone is in general agreement that there are two routing protocol classes, Cisco has created a third class called *hybrid routing protocols*. A hybrid routing protocol, of which there is one, is a routing protocol that combines the best attributes of link state and distance vector routing protocols. Think of this as the Six Million Dollar Man of routing protocols. Steve Austin was the combination of Man and Machine, and hybrid routing protocols are the combination of link state and distance vector routing protocols. As mentioned earlier, there is only one of these types of routing protocol and it is Cisco proprietary. The Enhanced Interior Gate Routing Protocol (EIGRP) is an enhancement to Cisco's distance vector routing protocol, the Interior Gateway Routing Protocol (IGRP), as the name implies. The intricacies of EIGRP are not required knowledge for the CCNA exam.

Autonomous System

The autonomous system is a vague concept but an important one. A group of routers that exchange routes or have knowledge of each other's routes *and* are under a common administration are said to be in the same autonomous system (AS). Typically an AS is a group of routers that are all controlled by the same company or department.

Routers inside an AS exchange routes via an Interior Gateway Protocol (IGP). The IGP is either distance vector or link state, but it is controlled and configured by a common administration.

Routers in different ASs exchange routes via an Exterior Gateway Protocol (EGP). The EGP is most likely a distance vector routing protocol, but each router may be configured by a different administration. The Border Gateway Protocol (BGP) is the most common EGP and is used mainly for connectivity to the Internet for sites with a multihomed connection to the Internet. Knowledge of BGP is not required for the CCNA exam.

Routing Metrics

We have already established that routing protocols allow a router to determine the best path from itself to a destination network, but how does it define "best"? We could say that the Florida State University (FSU) Seminoles are the "best" team in the country because they have been ranked in the top five for 14 straight years. However, someone else could argue that the Miami Hurricanes are the best team in the country because they have won the National Championship four times in the last 20 years. Which team is the best? It all depends on what *metric* you use. The metric we used in making the case that FSU is the best was the number of times it was ranked in the top five, while an adversary was using the number of national titles in the last 20 years. Who is right? Neither, unfortunately—the argument could go on forever because the NCAA (the governing body of college football) is too stupid to define a metric such as a playoff system.

On the other hand, there *must* be a metric for the router to use to figure out which route is the best. In Figure 7-8 there is a simple network topology, from Router A to Network Y. What is the best path? Is it through Router B along the serial lines or is it through Router C and the Ethernet links? It all depends on the metric.

Some common metrics are listed in Table 7-1. A routing protocol may use only one or multiple combinations of these metrics.

RIP uses only hop count, while IGRP and EIGRP use a combination of band-width, delay, load, reliability, and MTU. OSPF uses the administrative value cost.

Referring again to Figure 7-8, the best path from Router A to Network Y will depend on the routing protocol. If RIP were being used, both the path through Router B and Router C could be used, while if IGRP were being used Router C would be the best path. As for OSPF it would depend on the cost values assigned to the interfaces, but typically this is based on bandwidth and therefore the path through Router C would be preferred.

It is important to understand these metrics when choosing a routing protocol.

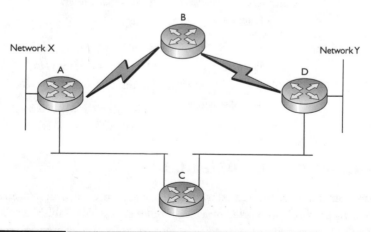

FIGURE 7.8   A simple network topology

TABLE 7.1	Common Routing Metrics
Metric Type	**Description**
Hop count	The number of routers that a packet must pass through to reach the destination.
Bandwidth	The bandwidth of the link; the higher the bandwidth the more preferable the path.
Delay	The amount of time required to reach the destination, usually measured in microseconds.
Load	The amount of bandwidth being used on a link. A link that is overutilized will not necessarily be as good as its bandwidth would indicate.
Reliability	On Cisco routers this indicates the packet error loss on an interface for the last five minutes. An interface with a very low reliability would be less preferable.
Maximum transmission unit (MTU)	The MTU is the largest frame that may be transmitted on a link. The larger the MTU the less overhead there will be for the frame header. A larger MTU would therefore be preferred.
Cost	A value that may be assigned by an administrator as he or she sees fit. The lower cost links will be preferred. Typically cost is assigned based on the bandwidth and is inversely proportional.
Tick	Similar to delay except that time is not measured in microseconds, but rather a unit of time defined by IBM as $1/18^{th}$ of a second.

Administrative Distance

A Cisco router may be configured with more than one routing protocol. Some of the routing protocols supported by a Cisco router are listed in Table 7-2.

IS-IS, OSPF, and EIGRP are advanced routing protocols that are not discussed in this book and are not required knowledge on the CCNA exam.

TABLE 7.2	A Partial List of Supported Routing Protocols on a Cisco Router	
Distance Vector Routing Protocols		**Link State Routing Protocols**
IGRP		OSPF
RIP		IS-IS
EIGRP (sometimes called a hybrid routing protocol)		

With all of these different routing protocols to choose from, there are many instances when multiple routing protocols will be configured on a router. It is also possible that two routing protocols may both know a path to a destination network. The problem arises when the two routing protocols differ as to what is the best path. In Figure 7-9, Router A is configured with both RIP and IGRP.

Since RIP uses hop count as its metric, the best path will be through Router B because there are fewer routers. However, IGRP, which uses a combination of metrics but relies mostly on bandwidth, will choose the path through Routers C and D since the Ethernet bandwidths are substantially greater than the typical serial link. (If you are trying to play the scenario that the serial lines are T3s and the Ethernet links are 10 Mbps and therefore IGRP would agree with RIP, you are overanalyzing.) The router uses a prioritization scheme called *administrative distance* to determine which routing protocol it is going to believe.

Administrative distance is a way for the router to quantify the reliability of a routing protocol. The lower the numeric value of the administrative distance, the more trusted the routing protocol. The administrative distance value assigned to

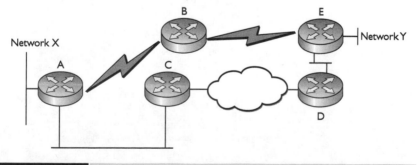

FIGURE 7.9   The best path to Network Y from Router A?

each routing protocol may be changed, but more than likely the default values are going to be used. Table 7-3 is a listing of some of the most commonly used routing protocols and their default administrative distances.

The directly connected network has an administrative distance of 0, indicating that it will always be the best route. This makes perfect sense in that there will be no better path to the destination if you are directly connected to it!

A static route could be configured on a router running a routing protocol. A router that is configured with both static and dynamic routes must be able to prioritize them, and therefore Cisco has assigned a default administrative distance of 1. Clearly, the static route must be more reliable than the dynamic route since someone actually took the time to manually enter it.

BGP is an EGP, as discussed earlier, and will always be believed over the most common IGPs.

Travel Assistance

There is an IGP version of BGP that is commonly referred to as IBGP; its administrative distance is 200, however, so as to not interfere with the common IGPs such as those listed in Table 7-3. To learn more about BGP, visit Cisco's web site at http://www.cisco.com/.

TABLE 7.3 Common Routing Protocols and Their Administrative Distances

Routing Protocol	Default Administrative Distance
Directly connected network	0
Static route	1
BGP	20
EIGRP	90
IGRP	100
OSPF	110
IS-IS	115
RIP	120

IGRP and RIP have values of 100 and 120, respectively. Therefore the scenario in Figure 7-9 would use the IGRP learned route through Routers B and D.

Objective 7.03   Distance Vector and Link State Routing

Up to this point, we have discussed the two types of routing protocols, link state and distance vector, but we have yet to cover exactly how they determine which is the best path to a particular destination.

> **Travel Advisory**
>
> It is important to remember that each routing protocol may use different metrics, but certain metrics do not necessarily mean that a routing protocol is distance vector or link state. There is no correlation between the metric and the type of routing protocol. The route selection process is exactly that, a process.

The Distance Vector Algorithm

An algorithm as defined by Webster's Dictionary is "a set of rules for solving a problem in a finite number of steps." A distance vector routing protocol uses the Distance Vector Algorithm or, as it is sometimes called, the Bellman-Ford Algorithm.

As mentioned earlier, a distance vector router will learn about the networks in its AS by receiving updates from its neighbors. A distance vector router will send out an update every 30 to 90 seconds depending on the routing protocol regardless of whether there have been any changes to the network. This update will contain every route that the router has learned, either from updates or through direct connection. In Figure 7-10 there is a simple network topology. Assuming all routers in Figure 7-10 have just been turned on simultaneously, Router A will come up and automatically populate its routing table with the two directly connected networks W and X. For simplicity, the routers in Figure 7-10 will be running IP RIP, which uses a metric of hop count and sends updates every 30 seconds.

Likewise, Routers B and C populate their routing tables with their directly connected networks, as indicated in Figure 7-10.

Immediately after populating their routing tables with their directly connected networks, each router sends an update out all interfaces to the destination

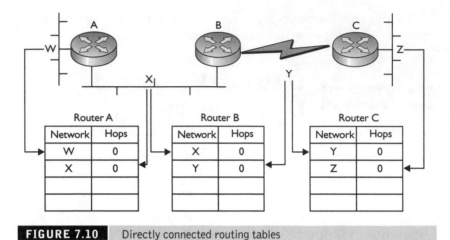

| FIGURE 7.10 | Directly connected routing tables |

address of 255.255.255.255. This address, as you might remember from Chapter 6, will be read by all workstations on the network. This is the first in many problems with older distance vector routing protocols.

When Router A sends its updates to its two directly connected networks, W and X, Router B will receive the update. Router B will look at the routing update and compare it to its own. When it sees that Router A can get to Network W in zero hops, it realizes that if Router A can get there in zero hops, it will be able to reach Network W through Router A and therefore can get there in one hop. Since there is no other route to Network W in Router B's routing table, it places this newfound network in its routing table. The second network in Router A's update to Router B is a different story. Router B realizes that if Router A can get to Network X in zero hops then Router B can get there in one hop. However, when Router B examines its routing table it sees that it already has a route to Network X and that entry has a lower hop count, therefore it ignores the entry in Router A's routing update.

Routers A and C will go through a similar process, yielding the routing tables indicated in Figure 7-11. At this point in time, the network is not converged! Router A does not know of the existence of Network Z, and Router C does not know of the existence of Network W.

At this point, even though the network is not converged, Router B will wait 30 seconds before sending out the update with the new Networks W and Z that it learned about. Once the 30-second update interval is over, the update with the new networks is sent out and the network converges, as indicated in Figure 7-12.

This delay in convergence is yet another problem with distance vector routing protocols. Imagine this scenario with 100 routers instead of 3. The convergence time could become much, much worse. Also imagine the routing updates being

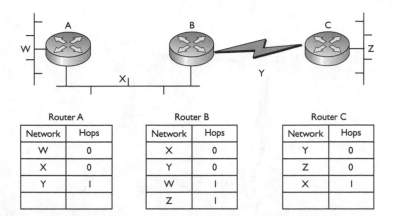

Router A

Network	Hops
W	0
X	0
Y	1

Router B

Network	Hops
X	0
Y	0
W	1
Z	1

Router C

Network	Hops
Y	0
Z	0
X	1

FIGURE 7.11   The first distance vector routing update is sent.

sent out every 30 seconds on all networks! Each update would contain the *entire*
routing table of *every* router. This can be a substantial utilization of network bandwidth and workstation processors. All workstations will receive these updates and
process them because of the destination address of the updates, 255.255.255.255.

Routing Loops

This simple algorithm has several other problems to deal with as well. In large
environments there will undoubtedly be multiple paths to a destination such as in
Figure 7-13.

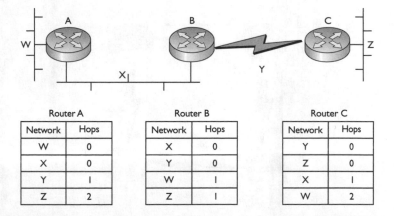

Router A

Network	Hops
W	0
X	0
Y	1
Z	2

Router B

Network	Hops
X	0
Y	0
W	1
Z	1

Router C

Network	Hops
Y	0
Z	0
X	1
W	2

FIGURE 7.12   The network is converged.

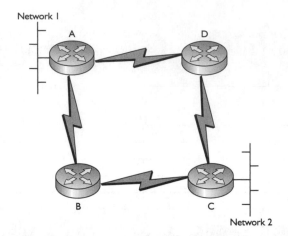

FIGURE 7.13   A redundant network design

The following scenario is to illustrate the necessity of certain features of a routing protocol. The scenario would not actually occur, but could occur if the solutions mentioned in the next section did not exist.

In the event that Network 1 fails, Router A updates its routing table immediately when Network 1 is down. However, Router A has to wait until the current 30-second interval expires before sending updates to Routers B and D, as shown in Figure 7-14.

It is entirely possible that Router D or Router B could send an update to Router A *before* Router A updates Router B or D that Network 1 is down. For example, if

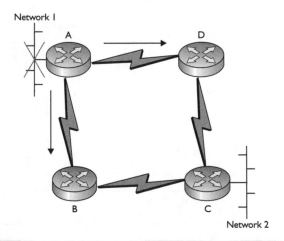

FIGURE 7.14   Network 1 fails.

Router D were to send an update to Router A before Router A has informed Router D that Network 1 is down, Router D will send an update back to Router A indicating that it can get to Network 1 (as shown in Figure 7-15). Router A will then add Network 1 to its routing table thinking that it has a router to Network 1 through Router D in two hops. Of course, Router D is assuming that it can get to Network 1 through Router A, completely unaware that Network 1 is down. If this is starting to sound like a bad episode of *I Love Lucy*, you are getting the hang of it.

Now that Router A has a route to Network 1, it also updates Router B and Router B updates Router C as shown in Figure 7-16.

By the time the update of Network 1 comes back around to Router D, Router D would have figured out that Router A is no longer sending updates with Network 1 being directly connected and would drop Network 1. But now that Router C is updating Router D that it can get to Network 1 in four hops, Router D assumes that it can get to Network 1 in five hops. By this time Router A has stopped receiving the updates from Router D, with Network 1 being one hop away, but it is now five hops away! (See Figure 7-17.)

This process would continue till the end of time or until Network 1 comes back up.

Solutions for Routing Loops

Of course, this problem has been planned for, and there are many different techniques that are used by routing protocols to stop such routing loops. In this section we will explore some of the more commonly used features.

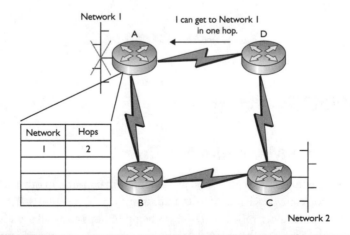

FIGURE 7.15   Router D erroneously updates Router A so it can get to Network 1.

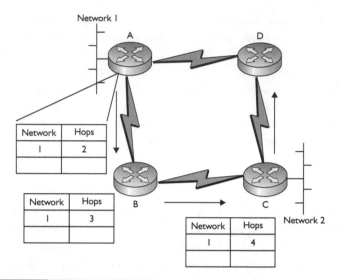

FIGURE 7.16 The route to Network 1 is updated through the loop.

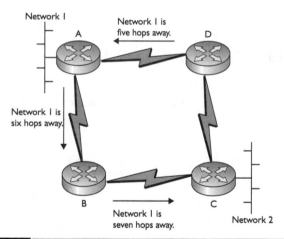

FIGURE 7.17 A routing loop

Defining a Maximum Metric

One of the easiest things to do would be to define a maximum. In other words, do not let the hop count reach infinity—set a maximum. In the case of IP RIP, that maximum is 16. Once a network is advertised as being 16 hops away, all routers receiving the update discard the entry. Referring back to the scenario in Figures 7-13 through 7-17, the maximum metric would prevent the update from circulating forever. Instead, it would end after several trips around the network. Doesn't seem much better, but that's a necessary evil.

Split Horizon

Split horizon is an easy concept that sounds very hard. It simply means that a router cannot send an update back out the interface through which it received that update. Once again referring to the Figure 7-13 problem, you can see that Router D would not be able to send an update to Router A about Network 1, because of split horizon. Since Network 1 was learned on the interface connected to Router A, Router D is unable to send information about Network 1 back out the interface.

I have problems with my split horizon all the time. Sometimes my brother will see a movie before me and tell me that it was great and that I have got to go see it. Several days pass and when I talk with him I mention that I heard this movie is great and that he should go see it. Since he is in the industry, he informs me that my split horizon isn't working because he is the one who told me the movie is great!

Holddown Timers

The holddown timer is a way for routers to not act too quickly when a network goes down. Once again referring to the Figure 7-13 loop, Router D would not immediately change its routing table when learning of a route to Network 1 with a hop count of five as it did in Figure 7-16. The holddown timer allows Router D to keep the entry in the routing table such that it won't accept any updates with a higher metric; however, it will accept an update with a lower metric. (See Figure 7-18.)

The duration that the entry is held in the routing table is configurable, though the default varies by protocol. RIP defaults to 180 seconds; IGRP to 280 seconds.

While the routes are in holddown, they are marked as "Possibly Down" in the routing table. You will see this when viewing the IP routing table with the **show ip route** command discussed later in this chapter.

Exam Tip

There are three ways that a route may come out of holddown: the holddown timer expires, an update with a better metric is received, or the flush timer expires. The *flush timer* is the length of time a router is instructed to wait before completely removing a route from its routing table.

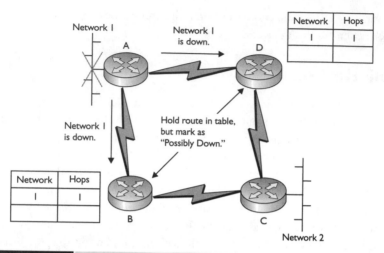

Network	Hops
1	1

Network	Hops
1	1

Network 1

Network 1 is down.

Network 1 is down.

Hold route in table, but mark as "Possibly Down."

Network 2

FIGURE 7.18   Holddown timers

Triggered Updates

One way to speed up the update process and help eliminate erroneous updates like those found in the Figure 7-13 scenario is to use triggered updates. A triggered update does not wait for the update interval to expire. As soon as Network 1 goes down, Router A sends an update to Routers B and D, thus eliminating the possibility that Router A receives an update from one of them first.

The triggered update is not a fix in itself since it still takes time for the triggered update to traverse the network. There is still a chance a router that has not received the update sends an outdated update to a router that has received the triggered update.

Route Poisoning

Route poisoning is a process by which a router can tell other routers that a network has gone down by immediately setting the metric to that network to infinity, hence poisoning the route. Downstream routers see this and know that the network is down. They also send an update back to the source router to let it know that it has received the update. This is called a *poison reverse update*.

Link State Routing Protocols

As mentioned earlier, the CCNA exam will focus on the distance vector routing protocols, RIP and IGRP. However, it is important to understand the basic structure of a link state routing protocol, although not all the details—that is another book!

Link state routing was designed to fix all the problems of distance vector routing. The main differences between link state routing and distance vector routing are as follows:

- Rather than sending the entire routing table, link state routers only send an update with their directly connected networks.
- Link state routers send their periodic updates very infrequently— OSPF every 1800 seconds and NLSP every 7200 seconds, compared to RIP every 30 seconds, IPX-RIP every 60 seconds, and IGRP every 90 seconds.
- Link state routing protocols typically use triggered updates to achieve faster convergence than distance vector protocols. Instead of only sending these updates to directly connected neighbors, these updates are sent to all routers in the network. These updates can be limited by partitioning the autonomous system. OSPF calls these partitions "areas."
- Link state routing protocols typically support features such as variable length subnet masking (VLSM) and router summarization, not discussed in this book or on the CCNA exam.

In a link state network, *all* routers in a partition will know about *all* networks and *all* routers in that partition. In a simple network, there is only one partition, so all routers know all networks and all routers in the autonomous system. This allows the routers to see the entire network, as opposed to distance vector networks where routers see the network through the eyes of their neighbors, so to speak.

A link state router will collect all these updates, commonly referred to as link state packets (LSPs) or link state updates (LSUs) as shown in Figure 7-19, and build a topology table. The link state router will perform these steps:

1. Collect all LSPs into topology database.
2. Build SPF tree.
3. Extrapolate best paths for routing table.

From this topology table the router extrapolates the best routes by using an algorithm called the shortest path first (SPF) algorithm. This algorithm is also sometimes referred to as the Dijkstra Algorithm, after the famous mathematician who designed it.

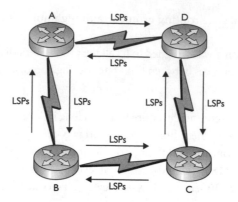

FIGURE 7.19   Link state routing

Routing Information Protocol (RIP)

Objective 7.04

The Routing Information Protocol (RIP) is one of the oldest routing protocols. There are two versions of RIP, RIP Version 1 and RIP Version 2 (not very imaginative names, but effective). RIP Version 1 will be discussed later in this book and on the CCNA exam. RIP Version 2 incorporates several new features such as VLSM and route summarization.

The key features of RIP are as follows:

- RIP is a distance vector routing protocol.
- Routing updates are sent every 30 seconds.
- Hop count is the metric.
- 16 hops indicates a route is unreachable.

Configuring RIP

Configuring a routing protocol on a Cisco router involves two main steps, with many different adjustments and features that can be done as well. The two steps are

1. Define the routing protocol.
2. Define the directly connected networks to run the routing protocol.

Step 1 is performed by using the **router rip** command in global configuration mode. Step 2 is specifying the directly connected networks on which you want the RIP protocol to run. The second step serves two purposes. The first is to define the

---

Exam Tip

When specifying the directly connected networks, you must use the true network number and *not* the subnet number. If by chance you accidentally use the subnet number, the router will automatically correct the mistake. If you don't know that it will change, however, you might think you have made a configuration error or it may lead you to proclaim, "The router is broken."

---

networks that are going to be advertised, and the second is to identify the interfaces to send and receive updates. Networks are specified by the **network** command in the router configuration mode that is entered when using the **router rip** command.

In Figure 7-20, a four-router network is set up using several Class C addresses and several subnets of the Class B address 172.16.0.0. The configuration commands required for each router to run RIP are as follows:

- Router A's configuration:

```
RouterA(config)#router rip
RouterA(config-router)#network 172.16.0.0
RouterA(config-router)#
```

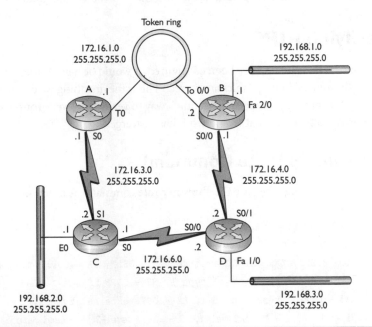

FIGURE 7.20 Sample network environment

- Router B's configuration:

```
RouterB(config)#router rip
RouterB(config-router)#network 192.168.1.0
RouterB(config-router)#network 172.16.0.0
RouterB(config-router)#
```

- Router C's configuration:

```
RouterC(config)#router rip
RouterC(config-router)#network 172.16.0.0
RouterC(config-router)#network 192.168.2.0
RouterC(config-router)#
```

- Router D's configuration:

```
RouterD(config)#router rip
RouterD(config-router)#network 192.168.3.0
RouterD(config-router)#network 172.16.0.0
RouterD(config-router)#
```

Please note that the **router rip** command takes the user into router configuration mode as indicated by the **RouterD(config-router)#** prompt. Each time a modification is made to the RIP configuration you must enter the router configuration mode.

Verifying RIP

Now that all the routers have been configured, it would be a good idea to verify that all the routers' routing tables are correct. This is the first thing we do after configuring the routing protocols. It is a quick way to verify that every router knows about every network or that the network has converged.

The show ip route Command

To verify the routing table, use the **show ip route** command as follows:

```
RouterD#sh ip route
Codes: C - connected, S - static, I - IGRP, R - RIP, M - mobile, B - BGP
       D - EIGRP, EX - EIGRP external, O - OSPF, IA - OSPF inter area
       N1 - OSPF NSSA external type 1, N2 - OSPF NSSA external type 2
       E1 - OSPF external type 1, E2 - OSPF external type 2, E - EGP
       i - IS-IS, L1 - IS-IS level-1, L2 - IS-IS level-2, * - candidate default
       U - per-user static route, o - ODR
```

```
Gateway of last resort is not set

     172.16.0.0/24 is subnetted, 4 subnets
C       172.16.4.0 is directly connected, Serial0/1
C       172.16.6.0 is directly connected, Serial0/0
R       172.16.1.0 [120/1] via 172.16.4.1, 00:00:07, Serial0/1
R       172.16.3.0 [120/1] via 172.16.6.1, 00:00:11, Serial0/0
R     192.168.1.0/24 [120/1] via 172.16.4.1, 00:00:07, Serial0/1
R     192.168.2.0/24 [120/1] via 172.16.6.1, 00:00:11, Serial0/0
C     192.168.3.0/24 is directly connected, FastEthernet1/0
RouterD#
```

This is the routing table of Router D. All networks in your topology are properly showing up in the routing table. In Figure 7-21 each component of the entry for network 172.16.4.0 is explained.

The directly connected network entries are basic in that they only need list the interface to which the network is assigned. The dynamically learned entries such as 192.168.1.0 have more information as shown in Figure 7-22.

The **show ip route** command is the most useful command when troubleshooting routing problems. If an entry does not show up in the table, it indicates that a router is not properly advertising the route. Now it is a matter of figuring out which one.

The show ip protocols Command

Another useful command when troubleshooting routing protocols is the **show ip protocols** command. This command will list all the parameters of all routing protocols configured on a router. The following is a sample output from Router A:

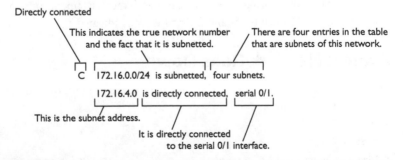

FIGURE 7.21   A show ip route entry examined

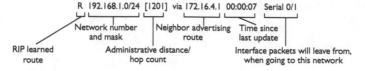

FIGURE 7.22   A RIP entry in the routing table

```
RouterA#sh ip protocols
Routing Protocol is "rip"
  Sending updates every 30 seconds, next due in 11 seconds
  Invalid after 180 seconds, hold down 180, flushed after 240
  Outgoing update filter list for all interfaces is
  Incoming update filter list for all interfaces is
  Redistributing: rip
  Default version control: send version 1, receive any version
    Interface          Send  Recv   Key-chain
    Serial0             1    1 2
    TokenRing0          1    1 2
  Routing for Networks:
    172.16.0.0
  Routing Information Sources:
    Gateway         Distance      Last Update
    172.16.3.2         120        00:00:12
    172.16.1.2         120        00:00:02
  Distance: (default is 120)

RouterA#
```

Some of the more useful information from this output is the administrative distance and the neighboring gateway (router) with their last update time. You will also notice the holddown times and flush times are indicated.

When a Network Goes Down

When a network does go down and the route is placed in holddown, the routing table might look as follows:

```
RouterA#sh ip route
Codes: C - connected, S - static, I - IGRP, R - RIP, M - mobile, B - BGP
       D - EIGRP, EX - EIGRP external, O - OSPF, IA - OSPF inter area
```

```
         N1 - OSPF NSSA external type 1, N2 - OSPF NSSA external type 2
         E1 - OSPF external type 1, E2 - OSPF external type 2, E - EGP
         i - IS-IS, L1 - IS-IS level-1, L2 - IS-IS level-2, * - candidate default
         U - per-user static route, o - ODR

Gateway of last resort is not set

     172.16.0.0/24 is subnetted, 4 subnets
R        172.16.4.0 [120/1] via 172.16.1.2, 00:00:24, TokenRing0
R        172.16.6.0 [120/1] via 172.16.3.2, 00:00:16, Serial0
C        172.16.1.0 is directly connected, TokenRing0
C        172.16.3.0 is directly connected, Serial0
R     192.168.1.0/24 [120/1] via 172.16.1.2, 00:00:24, TokenRing0
R     192.168.2.0/24 [120/1] via 172.16.3.2, 00:00:17, Serial0
R     192.168.3.0/24 is possibly down, routing via 172.16.1.2, TokenRing0
RouterA#
```

The 192.168.3.0 network now indicates that the network is "possibly down." In this case, we have manually disconnected the connection to that network on Router D. In this scenario, we find it useful to use the **clear ip route *** command. This command flushes the entire routing table as though the router were just being booted. Notice the change in the routing table when the command is issued on Router A:

```
RouterA#clear ip route *
RouterA#
RouterA#sh ip route
Codes: C - connected, S - static, I - IGRP, R - RIP, M - mobile, B - BGP
       D - EIGRP, EX - EIGRP external, O - OSPF, IA - OSPF inter area
       N1 - OSPF NSSA external type 1, N2 - OSPF NSSA external type 2
       E1 - OSPF external type 1, E2 - OSPF external type 2, E - EGP
       i - IS-IS, L1 - IS-IS level-1, L2 - IS-IS level-2, * - candidate default
       U - per-user static route, o - ODR

Gateway of last resort is not set

     172.16.0.0/24 is subnetted, 4 subnets
R        172.16.4.0 [120/1] via 172.16.1.2, 00:00:02, TokenRing0
```

```
R      172.16.6.0 [120/1] via 172.16.3.2, 00:00:02, Serial0
C      172.16.1.0 is directly connected, TokenRing0
C      172.16.3.0 is directly connected, Serial0
R    192.168.1.0/24 [120/1] via 172.16.1.2, 00:00:02, TokenRing0
R    192.168.2.0/24 [120/1] via 172.16.3.2, 00:00:02, Serial0
RouterA#
```

Rather than wait for the flush time, the 192.168.3.0 entry is immediately removed.

RIP Load Balancing

By default, RIP will load balance across up to four links with equal distance. With RIP the metric is hop count, which isn't exactly the most accurate measurement. For example, as shown previously in Figure 7-20, Router B has two paths to the network 192.168.2.0. Traffic can flow through Router A or Router D. This is indicated by the two entries in the routing table for the network as shown here:

```
C    192.168.1.0/24 is directly connected, FastEthernet2/0
R    192.168.2.0/24  [120/2] via 172.16.1.1, 00:00:18, TokenRing0/0
                     [120/2] via 172.16.4.2, 00:00:01, Serial0/0
R    192.168.3.0/24  [120/1] via 172.16.4.2, 00:00:02, Serial0/0
```

When two or more paths show up in the routing table, this indicates that load balancing is occurring. With RIP it is a round robin load balancing, with one packet taking the first path and the next packet taking the second. This feature may be adjusted by using the **maximum-paths** command.

In the following example, the maximum paths are set to 1, which indicates there will be no load balancing. Notice what happens to the routing table after the command is applied:

```
RouterB(config)#
RouterB(config)#router rip
RouterB(config-router)#maximum-paths 1
RouterB(config-router)#
RouterB#sh ip route

<output omitted>
     172.16.0.0/24 is subnetted, 4 subnets
C       172.16.4.0 is directly connected, Serial0/0
```

```
R        172.16.6.0 [120/1] via 172.16.4.2, 00:00:02, Serial0/0
C        172.16.1.0 is directly connected, TokenRing0/0
R        172.16.3.0 [120/2] via 172.16.4.2, 00:00:02, Serial0/0
C      192.168.1.0/24 is directly connected, FastEthernet2/0
R      192.168.2.0/24 [120/2] via 172.16.4.2, 00:00:02, Serial0/0
R      192.168.3.0/24 [120/1] via 172.16.4.2, 00:00:02, Serial0/0
RouterB#
```

Now only one entry is listed for the 192.168.2.0 network.

The debug ip rip Command

The **debug ip rip** command can be used to see the updates as they are sent and received. This is an excellent tool when it is necessary to see what networks are being sent by neighboring routers. The following is some sample output from the network shown previously in Figure 7-20:

```
RouterA#debug ip rip
RIP protocol debugging is on
RouterA#
01:16:29: RIP: received v1 update from 172.16.1.2 on TokenRing0
01:16:29:      172.16.4.0 in 1 hops
01:16:29:      172.16.6.0 in 2 hops
01:16:29:      192.168.1.0 in 1 hops
01:16:29:      192.168.3.0 in 2 hops
01:16:31: RIP: sending v1 update to 255.255.255.255 via Serial0 (172.16.3.1)
01:16:31:      subnet  172.16.4.0, metric 2
01:16:31:      subnet  172.16.1.0, metric 1
01:16:31:      network 192.168.1.0, metric 2
01:16:31:      network 192.168.3.0, metric 3
01:16:31: RIP: sending v1 update to 255.255.255.255 via TokenRing0 (172.16.1.1)
01:16:31:      subnet  172.16.6.0, metric 2
01:16:31:      subnet  172.16.3.0, metric 1
01:16:31:      network 192.168.2.0, metric 2
01:16:33: RIP: received v1 update from 172.16.3.2 on Serial0
01:16:33:      172.16.4.0 in 2 hops
01:16:33:      172.16.6.0 in 1 hops
01:16:33:      192.168.2.0 in 1 hops
01:16:33:      192.168.3.0 in 16 hops (inaccessible)
```

```
01:16:57: RIP: sending v1 update to 255.255.255.255 via Serial0 (172.16.3.1)
01:16:57:      subnet  172.16.4.0, metric 2
01:16:57:      subnet  172.16.1.0, metric 1
01:16:57:      network 192.168.1.0, metric 2
01:16:57:      network 192.168.3.0, metric 3
01:16:57: RIP: sending v1 update to 255.255.255.255 via TokenRing0 (172.16.1.1)
01:16:57:      subnet  172.16.6.0, metric 2
01:16:57:      subnet  172.16.3.0, metric 1
01:16:57:      network 192.168.2.0, metric 2
```

This command is very useful because it not only lists the networks that are in each update sent and received, but also the metrics associated with each network. You will notice that Router A is still receiving updates from Router C indicating that network 192.168.2.0 is inaccessible (note the hop count of 16). This is due to the fact that this network has been taken down.

Objective 7.05 Interior Gateway Routing Protocol (IGRP)

The Interior Gateway Routing Protocol (IGRP) is a Cisco proprietary routing protocol designed to improve upon the shortcomings of RIP v1. The main difference between IGRP and RIP is the fact that IGRP has a much higher maximum hop count. IGRP provides for a maximum hop count of 100 while RIP has a maximum of 15. The maximum hop count may be extended to 255 by modifying the configuration. IGRP also uses a much more advanced metric, called a *composite metric*. Unlike RIP, IGRP has an update interval of 90 seconds due to the fact that it uses triggered updates. It is not necessary to have updates every 30 seconds with triggered updates.

The Composite Metric

RIP uses the hop count metric, and this can create environments where the fastest path is not being used. Cisco developed a metric called the composite metric to allow a routing protocol to take into account not just one metric but several.

Some say Troy Aikman is the best quarterback to ever play in the NFL. Dan Marino never won any Super Bowls, but was pretty good too. The NFL, in an effort to more accurately rate a quarterback, developed what is called the "Quarterback Passer Rating." This is a value that in itself is meaningless except when compared to others. The value is actually a formula taking into account many different statistics related to a quarterback's performance, such as touchdowns, pass completion percentage, and so on. The quarterback with the lowest quarterback rating is what the NFL considers to be the "best" quarterback. Essentially IGRP does the same thing but instead of passing completion percentage, you have bandwidth utilization, instead of touchdowns, there is bandwidth, and so on. The composite metric is the same thing except with routing metrics. There are five metrics that make up the composite metric:

- Bandwidth
- Delay
- Reliability
- Load
- MTU

By default, only bandwidth and delay are part of the metric. The metric calculation can be adjusted to not only include the other metrics, but also to weight those that you may feel are more important than others. Typically the default configuration works very well, as you will see when IGRP is used in the same scenario used for RIP earlier.

Configuring IGRP

IGRP is configured exactly the same way as RIP with one small difference. There must be an autonomous system number specified when using the **router igrp** command.

Travel Advisory

All routers *must* have the same AS number to exchange IGRP routing updates.

Once again we refer back to Figure 7-20 to illustrate the network environment.

To configure IGRP on all the routers, they are configured almost exactly the same as in the RIP scenario but with the AS numbers listed. The AS number chosen is 10.

Travel Advisory

The AS number used by IGRP is not to be confused with an IANA-assigned
AS number for Internet access. IGRP is *not* used to advertise or
receive routes from the Internet. That will be done with an
EGP or a static route.

The configuration of all four routers is as follows:

- Router A's configuration:
  ```
  RouterA(config)#router igrp 10
  RouterA(config-router)#network 172.16.0.0
  RouterA(config-router)#
  ```

- Router B's configuration:
  ```
  RouterB(config)#router igrp 10
  RouterB(config-router)#network 192.168.1.0
  RouterB(config-router)#network 172.16.0.0
  RouterB(config-router)#
  ```

- Router C's configuration:
  ```
  RouterC(config)#router igrp 10
  RouterC(config-router)#network 172.16.0.0
  RouterC(config-router)#network 192.168.2.0
  RouterC(config-router)#
  ```

- Router D's configuration:
  ```
  RouterD(config)#router igrp 10
  RouterD(config-router)#network 192.168.3.0
  RouterD(config-router)#network 172.16.0.0
  RouterD(config-router)#
  ```

The configurations still specify the true network number and *not* the subnet
number of those subnets assigned to the interfaces.

Verifying IGRP

To illustrate the fact that two routing protocols may run on a router at the same
time, all routers have not had their RIP configurations removed. The following is
the routing table from Router B:

```
RouterB#sh ip route
Codes: C - connected, S - static, I - IGRP, R - RIP, M - mobile, B - BGP
       D - EIGRP, EX - EIGRP external, O - OSPF, IA - OSPF inter area
       N1 - OSPF NSSA external type 1, N2 - OSPF NSSA external type 2
       E1 - OSPF external type 1, E2 - OSPF external type 2, E - EGP
       i - IS-IS, L1 - IS-IS level-1, L2 - IS-IS level-2, ia - IS-IS inter area
       * - candidate default, U - per-user static route, o - ODR
       P - periodic downloaded static route

Gateway of last resort is not set

     172.16.0.0/24 is subnetted, 4 subnets
C       172.16.4.0 is directly connected, Serial0/0
I       172.16.6.0 [100/8882] via 172.16.4.2, 00:00:23, Serial0/0
C       172.16.1.0 is directly connected, TokenRing0/0
I       172.16.3.0 [100/8539] via 172.16.1.1, 00:00:32, TokenRing0/0
C    192.168.1.0/24 is directly connected, FastEthernet2/0
I    192.168.2.0/24 [100/8639] via 172.16.1.1, 00:00:32, TokenRing0/0
I    192.168.3.0/24 [100/6892] via 172.16.4.2, 00:00:23, Serial0/0
RouterB#
```

The routing table now contains routes with the letter **I** to the left, indicating that these routes were learned via IGRP. The metric is now much larger than the hop counts seen when the entries were learned via RIP. This large value is the composite metric.

It is interesting to note that there is now no load balancing occurring to the network 192.168.2.0. When running RIP, Router B was load balancing between Router A and Router D. Now there is only one route to the network. This makes sense because the Token Ring interface must surely be faster than the serial link between B and D.

If you were curious to see what the metric value was for the 192.168.2.0 update from Router D, you could use the debug command **debug ip igrp transactions**, covered shortly.

At this point, all RIP routes have been replaced in the routing table with IGRP routes. Does this mean that RIP is no longer running on the network? No, and to verify this fact you can use the **show ip protocol** command as follows:

```
RouterD#sh ip protocol
Routing Protocol is "rip"
  Sending updates every 30 seconds, next due in 16 seconds
```

```
Invalid after 180 seconds, hold down 180, flushed after 240
Outgoing update filter list for all interfaces is
Incoming update filter list for all interfaces is
Redistributing: rip
Default version control: send version 1, receive any version
  Interface        Send  Recv  Key-chain
  Serial0/0         1     1 2
  Serial0/1         1     1 2
  FastEthernet1/0  1     1 2
Routing for Networks:
  172.16.0.0
  192.168.3.0
Routing Information Sources:
  Gateway          Distance       Last Update
  172.16.4.1          120         00:03:23
  172.16.6.1          120         00:00:21
Distance: (default is 120)

Routing Protocol is "igrp 10"
  Sending updates every 90 seconds, next due in 20 seconds
  Invalid after 270 seconds, hold down 280, flushed after 630
  Outgoing update filter list for all interfaces is
  Incoming update filter list for all interfaces is
  Default networks flagged in outgoing updates
  Default networks accepted from incoming updates
  IGRP metric weight K1=1, K2=0, K3=1, K4=0, K5=0
  IGRP maximum hopcount 100
  IGRP maximum metric variance 1
  Redistributing: igrp 10
  Routing for Networks:
    172.16.0.0
    192.168.3.0
  Routing Information Sources:
    Gateway          Distance       Last Update
    172.16.4.1          100         00:03:27
    172.16.6.1          100         00:00:13
  Distance: (default is 100)


RouterD#
```

Both routing protocols are listed. The information displayed for IGRP is a little more complex than RIP. This is due to the fact that IGRP is a much more sophisticated protocol. Notice the **K** values, which are in bold. These values can be modified and each one represents one of the five metrics used in the composite metric. Notice that only two have a non-zero integer. As mentioned earlier, only bandwidth and delay are used by default.

Debug IP IGRP Events and Transactions

Unlike RIP, there are two different debug commands to choose from when using IGRP. The **debug ip igrp events** command is not very useful. This command will only show when an update is sent or received, not the contents of that update, as shown here:

```
RouterB#debug ip igrp events
IGRP event debugging is on
RouterB#
00:15:18: IGRP: received update from 172.16.1.1 on TokenRing0/0
00:15:18: IGRP: Update contains 1 interior, 1 system, and 0 exterior routes.
00:15:18: IGRP: Total routes in update: 2
00:15:22: IGRP: received update from 172.16.4.2 on Serial0/0
00:15:22: IGRP: Update contains 4 interior, 3 system, and 0 exterior routes.
00:15:22: IGRP: Total routes in update: 7
00:15:27: IGRP: sending update to 255.255.255.255 via Serial0/0 (172.16.4.1)
00:15:27: IGRP: Update contains 4 interior, 3 system, and 0 exterior routes.
00:15:27: IGRP: Total routes in update: 7
00:15:27: IGRP: sending update to 255.255.255.255 via TokenRing0/0 (172.16.1.2)
00:15:27: IGRP: Update contains 3 interior, 2 system, and 0 exterior routes.
00:15:27: IGRP: Total routes in update: 5
00:15:27: IGRP: sending update to 255.255.255.255 via FastEthernet2/0 (192.168.1.1)
00:15:27: IGRP: Update contains 0 interior, 3 system, and 0 exterior routes.
00:15:27: IGRP: Total routes in update: 3
RouterB#
```

The **debug ip igrp transactions** command is much more useful in that the entire update is shown, as shown here:

```
RouterB#debug ip igrp transactions
IGRP protocol debugging is on
```

```
RouterB#
00:16:38: IGRP: received update from 172.16.4.2 on Serial0/0
00:16:38:      subnet 172.16.4.0, metric 8882 (neighbor 6882)
00:16:38:      subnet 172.16.6.0, metric 8882 (neighbor 6882)
00:16:38:      subnet 172.16.1.0, metric 8945 (neighbor 6945)
00:16:38:      subnet 172.16.3.0, metric 12476 (neighbor 10476)
00:16:38:      network 192.168.1.0, metric 8892 (neighbor 6892)
00:16:38:      network 192.168.2.0, metric 8982 (neighbor 6982)
00:16:38:      network 192.168.3.0, metric 6892 (neighbor 110)
00:16:41: IGRP: received update from 172.16.1.1 on TokenRing0/0
00:16:41:      subnet 172.16.3.0, metric 8539 (neighbor 8476)
00:16:41:      network 192.168.2.0, metric 8639 (neighbor 8576)
00:16:42: IGRP: sending update to 255.255.255.255 via Serial0/0 (172.16.4.1)
00:16:42:      subnet 172.16.4.0, metric=6882
00:16:42:      subnet 172.16.6.0, metric=4294967295
00:16:42:      subnet 172.16.1.0, metric=688
00:16:42:      subnet 172.16.3.0, metric=4294967295
00:16:42:      network 192.168.1.0, metric=110
00:16:42:      network 192.168.2.0, metric=8639
00:16:42:      network 192.168.3.0, metric=4294967295
00:16:42: IGRP: sending update to 255.255.255.255 via TokenRing0/0 (172.16.1.2)
00:16:42:      subnet 172.16.4.0, metric=6882
00:16:42:      subnet 172.16.6.0, metric=4294967295
00:16:42:      subnet 172.16.3.0, metric=4294967295
00:16:42:      network 192.168.1.0, metric=110
00:16:42:      network 192.168.3.0, metric=4294967295
00:16:42: IGRP: sending update to 255.255.255.255 via FastEthernet2/0 (192.168.1.1)
00:16:42:      network 172.16.0.0, metric=688
00:16:42:      network 192.168.2.0, metric=8639
00:16:42:      network 192.168.3.0, metric=4294967295
00:16:42: IGRP: received update from 172.16.1.1 on TokenRing0/0
00:16:42:      subnet 172.16.6.0, metric 4294967295 (inaccessible)
00:16:42:      subnet 172.16.3.0, metric 8539 (neighbor 8476)
00:16:42:      network 192.168.2.0, metric 8639 (neighbor 8576)
00:16:42:      network 192.168.3.0, metric 4294967295 (inaccessible)
```

The two entries that are in bold are the two updates for the 192.168.2.0 network. The update from Router A has a composite metric value of 8639, while the update from Router D has a value of 8982. The route with the lowest metric will be used, which is why only Router A is listed as a route to 192.168.2.0.

The last line of the code indicates that 192.168.3.0 is still unavailable. The metric is clearly higher than anything normal.

Load Balancing with IGRP

In the last scenario, you saw two routes to the network 192.168.2.0 with metrics that were very close; however, IGRP will only load balance across multiple paths with equal metrics by default. IGRP has the ability to load balance across paths with unequal metrics but this must be configured manually. Using the **variance** command, you can specify a range of metrics that are acceptable to load balance over. The actual range is not specified, but rather a degree of tolerance based on the best metric.

For example, the network 192.168.2.0 has a metric of 8639. If you wanted to load balance on a route that had a metric no more than two times that of the best route (that is, a metric value less than 17278), the command **variance 2** would be entered in router configuration mode. Going back to our scenario, the command is issued, and now notice the routing table:

```
RouterB(config)#router igrp 1
RouterB(config-router)#variance 2
RouterB(config-router)#
RouterB#sh ip route
Codes: C - connected, S - static, I - IGRP, R - RIP, M - mobile, B - BGP
       D - EIGRP, EX - EIGRP external, O - OSPF, IA - OSPF inter area
       N1 - OSPF NSSA external type 1, N2 - OSPF NSSA external type 2
       E1 - OSPF external type 1, E2 - OSPF external type 2, E - EGP
       i - IS-IS, L1 - IS-IS level-1, L2 - IS-IS level-2, ia - IS-IS inter area
       * - candidate default, U - per-user static route, o - ODR
       P - periodic downloaded static route

Gateway of last resort is not set

     172.16.0.0/24 is subnetted, 4 subnets
C       172.16.4.0 is directly connected, Serial0/0
I       172.16.6.0 [100/8882] via 172.16.4.2, 00:00:02, Serial0/0
C       172.16.1.0 is directly connected, TokenRing0/0
```

```
I       172.16.3.0  [100/8539] via 172.16.1.1, 00:00:01, TokenRing0/0
C    192.168.1.0/24 is directly connected, FastEthernet2/0
I    192.168.2.0/24 [100/8982] via 172.16.4.2, 00:00:02, Serial0/0
                    [100/8639] via 172.16.1.1, 00:00:01, TokenRing0/0
I    192.168.3.0/24 [100/6892] via 172.16.4.2, 00:00:03, Serial0/0

RouterB#
```

Both routes now appear in the routing table even though the metrics are not the same. Load balancing will not be equal either. IGRP load balances between the two routes proportional to their metrics. In other words, more packets will be sent through the 172.16.1.1 neighbor than the 172.16.4.2 neighbor. This behavior can be modified using the **traffic-share min** command. To return to proportional load balancing, use the **traffic-share balanced** command.

IP Classless

Earlier in this chapter, there was a discussion of the default route. There is sometimes a scenario where the default route does not work exactly as it should. In Figure 7-23, there is a network very similar to the one discussed in the previous section, except now Router B does not have any routing protocols configured on it. Router B will now rely on a default route.

Router B is said to have a *stub network*. There is no reason to run a routing protocol on Router B since it only has one route to the rest of the world—that is, through 172.16.1.1. When the routing table is examined, the default route and the locally connected networks are present:

```
Gateway of last resort is 172.16.1.1 to network 0.0.0.0

     172.16.0.0/24 is subnetted, 1 subnets
C       172.16.1.0 is directly connected, TokenRing0/0
C    192.168.1.0/24 is directly connected, FastEthernet2/0
S*   0.0.0.0/0 [1/0] via 172.16.1.1
```

The default route has also set the "gateway of last resort." The problem occurs when Router B pings the network 172.16.6.1. Even though Router A has a route to the destination network, the ping is unsuccessful:

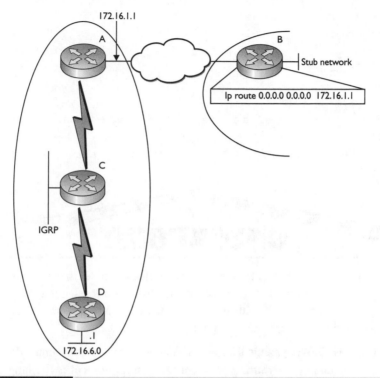

FIGURE 7.23 A stub network

```
RouterB#ping 172.16.6.1

Type escape sequence to abort.
Sending 5, 100-byte ICMP Echos to 172.16.6.1, timeout is 2 seconds:
.....
Success rate is 0 percent (0/5)
RouterB#
```

This is due to the fact that the **ip classless** command is absent from the configuration. Without the **ip classless** command, a router will not forward frames to an unknown subnet of a known true network. In this case, Router B knows about one of the 172.16.0.0 subnets and therefore will not use the default route for any of the 172.16.0.0 subnets, even though only the 172.16.1.0 network is present in the routing table.

To fix this problem, simply use the **ip classless** command, as follows:

```
RouterB(config)#ip classless
RouterB(config)#
RouterB#
RouterB#ping 172.16.6.1

Type escape sequence to abort.
Sending 5, 100-byte ICMP Echos to 172.16.6.1, timeout is 2 seconds:
!!!!!
Success rate is 100 percent (5/5), round-trip min/avg/max = 32/34/36 ms
RouterB#
```

CHECKPOINT

✔ **Objective 7.01: Static Routes**   Static routes are routes that are manually entered into the configuration of a router. In certain cases, it may be necessary to create a default route which is a catch-all for any packets intended for destinations not explicitly listed in the routing table.

✔ **Objective 7.02: Dynamic Routes**   Dynamic routes are routes entered in the routing table via a routing protocol. A routing protocol is the language routers use to exchange information about networks they have learned. There are two types of routing protocols, distance vector and link state.

✔ **Objective 7.03: Distance Vector and Link State Routing**   Distance vector routing protocols exchange routes with their directly connected neighbors, with each neighbor communicating with its neighbor. This "routing by rumor" method is prone to routing loops and therefore there are several features such as holddown timers, poison reverse, split horizon, and triggered updates to help prevent routing loops. Link state routing protocols use much smaller updates and send updates to all other routers, thus eliminating the "routing by rumor" method.

✔ **Objective 7.04: Routing Information Protocol (RIP)**   The Routing Information Protocol (RIP) is a distance vector routing protocol with a 30-second update time. It can easily be configured on a Cisco router using the following commands:

```
Router rip
Network [the directly connected true network]
```

One entry is necessary for each true network that RIP is running.

✔ **Objective 7.05: Interior Gateway Routing Protocol (IGRP)**   The Interior
Gateway Routing Protocol (IGRP) is also a distance vector routing protocol,
which has a 90-second update time. It is much more scalable due to its triggered updates and its very large maximum hop count (100 by default).

REVIEW QUESTIONS

1. Which of the following are ways that a route may be learned by a router?
   (Choose two.)

   A. Static
   B. Fluid
   C. Dynamic
   D. Cisco Express Forwarding (CEF)
   E. Routers cannot be learned by a router

2. Which of the following best describes the administrative distance value?

   A. An assigned priority to a particular route
   B. A rating of trustworthiness of a routing protocol
   C. A value indicating how near or far a route is located
   D. An integer greater than 0 that indicates how reliable a particular route is
   E. An industry standard value used to measure the trustworthiness of a
   routing protocol

3. What will prevent a static route from being removed from the routing table
   when the interface connected with the static route fails?

   A. Static routes will always remain in the routing table.
   B. A static route will always be removed from the routing table in case the
   source interface goes down.
   C. By changing the administrative distance of a static route.
   D. By setting the static route priority level to 0.
   E. By using the **permanent** option at the end of the static route command.

4. What is meant by the term "convergence" when referring to routers?

   A. Convergence is when all the routers get together once a year to discuss
   the pros and cons of being a router.
   B. Convergence is when all the routers in an autonomous system have a
   consistent and complete view of the network topology.

   C. Convergence refers to the priority a routing protocol has over another.

   D. Convergence is a type of routing protocol not supported by Cisco routers, but often used in the industry.

   E. Convergence refers to how close in proximity a router is to the center of a network topology.

5. What statement best describes a link state routing protocol?

   A. A link state routing protocol uses small updates that propagate throughout the network, allowing routers to build a topology table of the entire topology.

   B. A link state routing protocol will send updates out every 30, 60, or 90 seconds depending on the particular protocol.

   C. A link state routing protocol is used mostly in smaller environments that do not require the scalability of distance vector routing protocols.

   D. Link state routing is not supported on Cisco routers.

   E. Link state routing protocols will send updates only to its neighbors, thus creating a "routing by rumor" environment.

6. Which of the following is *not* a characteristic of link state routing protocols?

   A. Updates are only sent when there is a change or at long intervals.

   B. Updates include only directly connected networks.

   C. Link state routing protocols send updates only to neighbors.

   D. Link state routing protocols are much more scalable than distance vector routing protocols.

   E. Link state routing protocols rely on the shortest path first algorithm.

7. When a router does not send an update about a network out the interface in which it learned of that network, the router is using which of the following?

   A. Triggered updates

   B. Poison reverse

   C. Holddown timers

   D. Defining a maximum

   E. Split horizon

8. Which of the following routing protocols is link state?

   A. EIGRP

   B. RIP

   C. IGRP

   D. OSPF

   E. RIP v2

9. Which one of the following is *not* a characteristic of the RIP routing protocol?

    A. RIP is a distance vector routing protocol.

    B. RIP has a maximum hop count of 15, while 16 is inaccessible.

    C. RIP has two versions, 1 and 2.

    D. RIP does not support split horizon.

    E. RIP allows load balancing over paths with equal metrics.

10. What is the command to view the known networks of a Cisco router?

    A. show ip route

    B. show route

    C. show running-config

    D. show ip protocols

    E. show ip interface

REVIEW ANSWERS

1. **A** and **C** Routers can be either manually configured with a route (static), or they may be configured with a routing protocol where they will dynamically learn about routes (dynamic). Cisco Express Forwarding is a concept not discussed in this book, but has to deal with how a Cisco router forwards a frame from one interface to another.

2. **B** The administrative distance is the mechanism that allows a router to prioritize learned routes based on the routing protocol they were learned. The lower the AD, the more trustworthy the routing protocol.

3. **E** The **permanent** option will cause the static route to remain in the routing table regardless of whether the interface pointing to the route is up or down. Changing the AD value of the static route will have no effect on whether it shows up in the routing table based on the interface.

4. **B** Convergence is when the routers all are in agreement as to the whereabouts and routes to all networks in the AS. Convergence has nothing to do with the proximity of a router to the center of the network.

5. **A** Link state routing involves every router sending out a small update of directly connected networks called a link state advertisement or link state update (LSA or LSU). This update is sent to every router in the area or the network depending on the type of link state routing protocol and its configuration.

6. **C** One of the advantages of a link state routing protocol is that each router receives updates from all routers in the network or area. This allows the link state router to see the entire network from the routers directly connected to the networks, rather than through its neighbors.

7. **E** Split horizon is when a router does not forward updates back out the interface in which those updates were learned.

8. **D** The open shortest path first (OSPF) routing protocol is a link state routing protocol.

9. **D** RIP supports split horizon, and therefore answer D is not a characteristic of RIP.

10. **A** The **show ip route** command will display the networks known to the router as well as the next hop on the way to the destination.

IP Access Lists

CHAPTER 8

	NEWBIE	SOME EXPERIENCE	VETERAN
ETA	4+ hours	1.0 hours	.5 hours

Have you ever taken a trip out of the country and had to pass through the Customs inspectors when you returned? Those friendly civil servants went through your luggage and told you what you were allowed to bring in and what had to be thrown away. Their decisions are based on where you came from and what you wanted to bring back into the country. Some of the items are allowed and some are not.

Customs officials typically look at your passport to see what country you have just visited and then proceed to tell you what items you may or may not be allowed to bring into the country. Certain items are disallowed due to agricultural or political concerns. You might be able to bring in some wine or leather goods, but not fruits or vegetables or other perishables. The inspector's decisions are based on the source of the items as well as the items themselves.

When we examine the functionality of access lists, we begin to see that a similar decision process can be applied to router interfaces. Access lists function like the Customs inspector: they compare the packets flowing across the router interface against the rules imposed by the access list you have applied. In the case of a standard access list, you can only check the source of the traffic, while an extended access list can check source address, destination address, port numbers, and traffic type.

This chapter will go in greater detail regarding the design and implementation of both standard and extended access lists. We will also cover named access lists, which allow you to assign a name to the access list for ease of use. Rounding out the chapter will be the **access-class** command and how it can be utilized to restrict access to Telnet sessions.

Objective 8.01   Access List Introduction and Operation

Access lists are used to restrict traffic coming in or out of an interface. It is important to remember when reading this chapter that traffic to be restricted doesn't necessarily come from the outside world, but may in fact come from the inside of your organization.

Rules of the Road

There are some practices that you should follow when creating and applying access lists that will make life much easier if you later have to go back and make changes to what you have already configured.

- **Proper planning prevents poor performance.**   Plan out your access lists on paper before you even touch the router. Try and figure out on paper what an access list is going to do for you. This will give you a better picture of the effect the access list is going to have on your network.
- **Location, location, location.**   This is an old marketing adage that means location is everything. It is also relevant to the application of access lists. You need to apply access lists where they are going to do the most good. You typically want to place an access list as close to the traffic origination point as possible. It would be a waste of bandwidth to send the traffic out onto the network only to have it filtered once it reaches its destination.
- **An ounce of prevention is worth a pound of cure.**   Consider creating your access list in such a way that it gets the most amount of work done in the least number of router CPU cycles. Why have a bunch of access lists that take little bites of traffic when you can create one big one that grabs a whole bunch at one time?
- **Access denied.**   If you remember nothing else after reading this chapter, please remember something called the **implicit deny** statement. The **implicit deny** statement refers to the fact that a router will block any traffic that it hasn't first been told to allow. This nemesis rears its ugly head the moment you apply your first access list to a router interface. The **implicit deny** statement will make you instantly "popular" at work if you forget about it. We cover this particular subject in detail later on the chapter.

Now that we've gotten all the rules and regulations out of the way, let's continue with the fun stuff.

Exam Tip

Where an access list should be placed is very important. You may want to file that piece of information away for a later date since you never know when you might find yourself needing to know this.

Uses for Access Lists

In the previous analogy, we stated that we can create an access control list that inhibits certain types or categories of traffic from entering or exiting a router, but there is more to the story. Access control lists can be utilized to *permit* or *deny* inbound traffic (traffic coming from the Internet or another external network) and/or outbound traffic (traffic leaving a private network that is bound for an external network like the Internet). The placement of the access control list on a router interface is what achieves the desired result. Traffic flows *bidirectionally* through a router interface and you can either allow it, **access-list 100 permit**, or prevent it, **access-list 100 deny**, from flowing by utilizing the correct command line syntax. (See Figure 8-1.)

This all sounds rather complicated on the surface, but the underlying concept is really pretty simple. If you want to permit or deny a certain type of traffic from leaving your network, you create an outbound access list. If you want to permit or deny certain types of traffic from entering your network, you create an inbound access list. Let's put the whole permit/deny thing aside for a moment and look at one more piece of functionality that access lists give you. They also have the power to manage traffic based on the information shown in Table 8-1.

The items in Table 8-1 are just a few examples that we'll cover in this chapter. We wanted you to see that you can do some amazing things with access lists that you may not have known about.

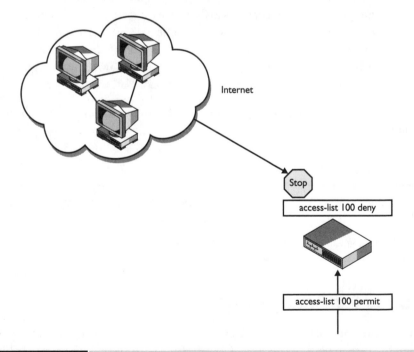

FIGURE 8.1   Filtering inbound and outbound traffic with an access list

TABLE 8.1	Possible Configurations and Their Corresponding Access List Type
Configuration	**Access List Type**
A single host address	Standard access list
A range of host (or subnet) addresses	Standard access list
The destination address of a host on another subnet	Extended access list
The protocol type of the traffic	Extended access list
Port number(s)	Extended access list

The last thing we'll discuss before moving on is that an access list will do nothing until it's been applied to an interface. You can enter access lists commands all day long, but until you issue the command that binds that access list to a specific interface, it is completely useless. An access list must be assigned to an interface for it to be active. Without assigning it to an interface, it is just taking up space in your configuration file.

Access List Structure and Operation

Before we dive too deeply into the subject of access list configuration, we need to take a moment and identify the different types of access lists you have at your disposal. Each type of access lists is represented by a number (generally in blocks of 100 numbers) that identifies the type of traffic that will be affected by whatever access list you are creating. In this chapter, we are going to narrow our focus and concentrate only on IP access lists.

For a complete listing of access list types, you can invoke the command shown here:

```
Router (config)# access-list ?
  <1-99>      IP standard access list
  <100-199>   IP extended access list
  <200-299>    Protocol type-code access list
  <300-399>   DECnet access list
  <400-499>   XNS standard access list
  <500-599>   XNS extended access list
```

```
<600-699>    Appletalk access list
<700-799>    48-bit MAC address access list
<800-899>    IPX standard access list
<900-999>    IPX extended access list
<1000-1099>  IPX SAP access list
<1100-1199>  Extended 48-bit MAC address access list
<1200-1299>  IPX summary address access list
```

Exam Tip

You will be expected to know both IP and IPX access lists for the exam. IPX access lists are covered in Chapter 9.

Since you know that standard access lists are numbered from 1 to 99, you easily identify that a standard access list is being configured if you issue the command **access-list 99**.

As you can see from the output of the **access-list** command, there are a number of access list types that you can use, but again, you are only going to be concerned with IP access list configuration.

- Standard access lists are numbered from 1 to 99.
- Extended access lists are numbered from 100 to 199.

As mentioned previously, a standard access list restricts traffic based on the source address only, while the extended access list restricts traffic based on various other parameters, including the source address.

Access List Processing

Whether you are using an extended access list or standard access list, there are several rules that will apply. When a packet header is checked against an access list, the packet header will be compared to each statement in the access list starting from the first statement entered until it encounters a match. A match occurs when the packet header matches the test condition that has been entered in the access list statement. Once a packet is matched to an access list statement, it is either denied or permitted depending on the access list statement. For example, if the first line in an access list denies traffic coming from the 172.16.1.0 network, all traffic coming from that network will be denied, regardless of any statements after the first statement. This can be very important when entering your test conditions or statements into an access list.

How Access Lists Work

In the previous section, we talked about how an access list looks for a match. What this means is that you tell the router to look for certain conditions to exist and, when they do, to execute the instructions found in an access list that is bound to that particular interface. Read through the description that follows to see how this process works. We will be getting quite a bit more technical in this section, so make sure you understand the logic flow of this operation as indicated in Figure 8-2.

1. A packet comes into your backbone router (the router that connects to the Internet) destined for a host on your Ethernet0 interface.
2. The router knows that is has access list 99 bound to Ethernet0 for traffic exiting Ethernet0.
3. The router looks at the instructions in access list 99 and sees that host 192.168.1.14 is not allowed to send outbound traffic across the Ethernet0 interface.

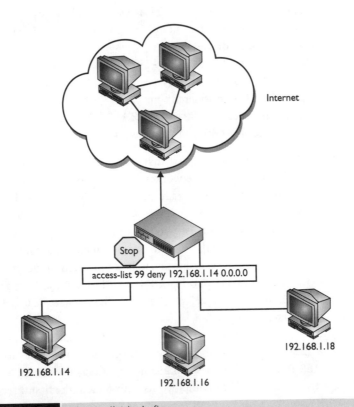

FIGURE 8.2   Access list logic flow

4. The router sees that the source address of the packet trying to exit Ethernet0 is 192.168.1.14.
5. Since the source address of the packet and the source address in access list 99 match, the router blocks the packet and stops processing any other access list 99 statements.

Since you now have a simplified understanding of how access lists work, we need to move on to a more technical discussion. We are going to look at the actual mechanics involved in how a router matches packet information to the conditions that exist in an access list.

Let's start the discussion by using the example standard IP access list that follows:

```
router(config)#access-list 99 deny 192.168.1.84 0.0.0.255
```

The easiest way to understand what affect this command is going to have on the router is to break it down into its base elements, adding them up as we go:

- **router(config)#access-list 99**   This is a standard IP access list.
- **router(config)#access-list 99 deny**   It's going to be denying traffic from a specified source address.
- **router(config)#access-list 99 deny 192.168.1.84**   The router will read the wildcard mask that comes next to determine how much of the source address will be considered a match.
- **router(config)#access-list 99 deny 192.168.1.84 0.0.0.255**   It will deny access to the entire 192.168.1.0 network.

You may be asking why we stated that the access list is going to deny access to the entire 192.168.1.0 network when you told it to look at the 192.168.1.84 IP address. The answer is found in the **0.0.0.255** portion of the command line syntax.

Since this is a standard IP access list, you know that you can only manage traffic based on the source address of the packet, but how much of the source address gets looked at is determined by what appears to be an inverted subnet mask. The **0.0.0.255** statement is the exact opposite of a standard subnet mask. In a regular subnet mask, the **255** tells the router "match this number," while the **0** says "don't care." This is illustrated in Figure 8-3.

When you create an access list, you use the opposite logic. A **0** says "match this" while a **255** says "don't care." So if you apply these new rules to the IP address 192.168.1.84, you see that **0.0.0.255** netmask tells the router "match – match – match – don't care" or in other words, only look at the first three octets of the packet's source address. Pretty cool, huh? Take a minute and see if you

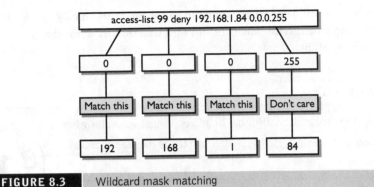

FIGURE 8.3   Wildcard mask matching

can figure out how much of the source address will be considered in the following examples:

```
router(config)#access-list 99 deny 192.168.1.84 0.0.255.255
```

(Only looks at the first two octets.)

```
router(config)#access-list 99 deny 192.168.1.84 0.255.255.255
```

(Only looks at the first octet.)

```
router(config)#access-list 99 deny 192.168.1.84 0.0.0.0
```

(Looks at all four octets.)

Another example can be seen below. What traffic is the following access list statement denying?

```
router(config)#access-list 85 deny 192.168.1.1 0.0.0.255
```

The entire 192.168.2.0 network is going to be prevented from sending traffic right out the router interface.

The entire 192.168.1.0 network will be denied. Yes, it is true that the address specified is 192.168.1.1; however, the wildcard mask tells you that the value of the fourth octet is meaningless.

As you can see from these examples, a network admin can block either a single host address or an entire subnet just by manipulating the netmask that comes at the end of the access list statement.

There are a couple of other command variations you can play around with when creating an access list statement, but we'll wait till later in the chapter before going into any of that.

Exam Tip

Know how wildcard bits affect the IP addresses that you enter when creating an access list. Pay close attention to the number of zeros in the mask.

Objective 8.02 ## Standard IP Access Lists

Configuring a standard IP access list is about as easy as it gets. It has very few parameters to configure and is relatively easy to troubleshoot. Unlike the extended IP access list, standard IP access lists are only concerned with the source address of the packets that cross the router interface. This makes the configuration much easier in terms of determining what traffic you are going to be managing.

If you remember from a previous section, we mentioned that you need to bind or apply an access list to a router interface for it to be able to manage the traffic crossing that interface. This is actually the second part of a two-part process. The first thing you need to do is create the access list, then you can apply it to a router interface.

Before you begin entering the commands needed to create an access list, you need to remember three words: context, context, context. You need to be at the correct router prompt context in order to enter the **access-list** command. You need to be in global configuration mode. This command line context is identified by the word **config** in parentheses followed by the pound sign (#):

```
router(config)#
```

Creating a Standard IP Access List

In this first example, you are going to be blocking or filtering outbound traffic for an entire subnet of IP addresses (as shown in Figure 8-4). Take a look at all the commands needed to correctly configure this type of access list:

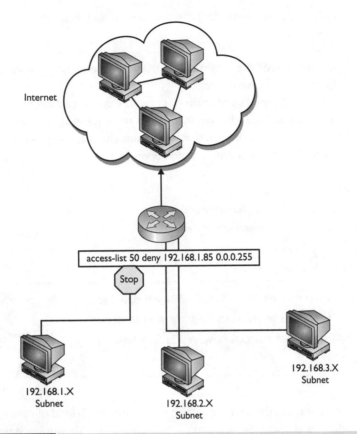

FIGURE 8.4 Blocking an entire subnet

```
router(config)# access-list 50 deny 192.168.1.85 0.0.0.255
router(config)# interface ethernet0
router(config-if)# ip access-group 50 out
```

We will be going over these commands step by step, with a brief discussion at each step of the way. After connecting to your router, issue the command **enable** (press ENTER), then issue the command **config terminal**. This will put you at the correct command prompt.

```
router>
router>enable
Password:
router#config terminal
```

```
Enter configuration commands, one per line.  End with CNTL/Z.
router(config)#
```

If you have entered the commands in the proper sequence, you should see a prompt like the one shown above.

The next thing you'll want to do is try out the contextual help system. This means the router will see what command you are requesting help on and show you what options are available for that command. This is accomplished by typing a question mark after the command and pressing ENTER:

```
router(config)#access-list ?
  <1-99>       IP standard access list
  <100-199>    IP extended access list
```

Travel Advisory

Even CCIEs who have been in the field for a hundred years use the contextual help system. Don't be afraid to use it. No one can memorize all the options that are associated with every command.

Let's move on to the next step, which is deciding which kind of access list you are going to be creating. Since we are in the section titled "Creating a Standard IP Access List," the choice has been made for you. The first step is define the access list number, as shown here:

```
router(config)#access-list 50
```

Why are we using the number "50"? No special reason really—50 just sounds good and it makes no difference as long as it falls in the range from 1–99.

Next, you decide if you are going to permit traffic or deny it:

```
router(config)#access-list 50 ?
  deny     Specify packets to reject
  permit   Specify packets to forward
  remark   Access list entry comment
```

Go ahead and deny traffic from crossing the router interface:

```
router(config)#access-list 50 deny ?
  Hostname or A.B.C.D  Address to match
  any                  Any source host
  host                 A single host address
```

You now need to decide which IP address you are going to deny access to the router interface:

```
router(config)#access-list 50 permit 192.168.1.85 ?
  A.B.C.D  Wildcard bits
  log      Log matches against this entry
  <cr>
```

You have entered an IP address, and you can block either that single source address or the entire subnet that it's on.

```
router(config)#access-list 50 deny 192.168.1.85 0.0.0.255
```

Judging from the wildcard mask that has been entered, it looks like you will be denying access to the entire 192.168.1.0 subnet.

So far, you have entered the commands that create an access list capable of blocking traffic from the entire 192.168.1.0 subnet. Are you done with this access list? Absolutely not! At this point, you must remember the implicit **deny any** at the end of an access list. This access list denies the entire 192.168.1.0 subnet, but it also implicitly denies everything else! When creating an access list to specifically filter traffic, it is important the access list end with a statement permitting all traffic. With the keyword **any** it is quite simple, as used in the following example:

```
router(config)#access-list 50 permit any
```

The second line of the access list now permits all traffic other than the traffic coming from the 192.168.1.0 subnet that will be denied by the first statement.

Applying the Standard IP Access List to a Router Interface

Having created an access list is only half the process. The next step is to apply the access list to a router interface, which is a very simple process. Access lists are created in global configuration mode; however, to apply them to an interface it is necessary to enter the interface configuration mode of the interface you want to apply the access list to.

Once in the interface configuration mode, simply use the command **ip access-group** to apply the access list either in or out. Be sure to apply it in the correct direction. Is this access list restricting traffic going *in* the interface or *out* the interface? The proper syntax is as follows:

```
router(config-if)#ip access-group ?
  <1-199>     IP access list (standard or extended)
  <1300-2699> IP expanded access list (standard or extended)
  WORD        Access-list name
```

Since you want to use access list number 50 on this interface, you are going to enter that information on the command line:

```
router(config-if)#ip access-group 50
```

Now let's look at how to prevent traffic from the 192.168.1.0 subnet from leaving or entering the interface Ethernet0.

```
router(config-if)#ip access-group 50 ?
  in   inbound packets
  out  outbound packets
```

You can choose either **in** for inbound traffic (traffic coming from outside the network) or **out** for outbound traffic (traffic attempting to leave the network). You don't want the 192.168.1.0 subnet to be able to access the Internet, so use the **out** syntax, as follows:

```
router(config-if)#ip access-group 50 out
```

Next, you want to make sure your commands have been entered properly and applied to the correct interface. This can be accomplished by going back to enable mode and issuing the **show running config** command. If you are still at the interface configuration mode prompt, you can type the word **exit** twice to quickly get back to the enable mode prompt:

```
router(config-if)#exit
router(config)#exit
router# show run
```

The **show run** command will display the contents of the router's configuration script. You are concerned with the section that deals with the Ethernet0 interface:

```
interface Ethernet0
 ip address 192.168.1.1 255.255.255.0
 ip access-group 50 out
```

Do you see how the command **ip access-group 50 out** is now associated with the Ethernet0 interface? This tells you that the router is going to process the contents of access list 50 when traffic crosses that interface.

You can apply access list 50 to any interface on the router. All you need to do is go into global configuration mode, enter the interface's name, and apply the access list utilizing the **ip access-group 50 out** command. It's just that simple.

Creating an access list and applying it to an interface is only half the battle. Your next adventure is going to be verifying that the access list is functioning.

Verifying the Operation of a Standard IP Access List

Once you have created and applied an access list to a router's interface, the next logical step would be to perform a test and see if all your efforts have been successful. This is actually the easiest part of the whole operation.

There are two commands that prove useful in testing to see if you have correctly configured the access list:

```
show ip interface <interface name>
show access-lists <access-list #>
```

The command line syntax for the first command, **show ip interface**, is shown here:

```
router#show ip interface ?
  BRI      ISDN Basic Rate Interface
  Ethernet IEEE 802.3
  Null     Null interface
  brief    Brief summary of IP status and configuration
  |        Output modifiers
  <cr>
```

For the purposes of this example, you will issue the command **show ip interface ethernet0** since you applied access list 50 to the Ethernet0 interface on your router:

```
router# show ip interface ethernet0
Ethernet0 is up, line protocol is up
  Internet address is x.x.x.x/24
  Broadcast address is 255.255.255.255
  Address determined by non-volatile memory
  MTU is 1500 bytes
  Helper address is not set
  Directed broadcast forwarding is disabled
  Multicast reserved groups joined: 224.0.0.9
  Outgoing access list is 50
  Inbound  access list is not set
  Proxy ARP is enabled
  Security level is default
  Split horizon is enabled
  ICMP redirects are always sent
  ICMP unreachables are always sent
  ICMP mask replies are never sent
  IP fast switching is enabled
  IP fast switching on the same interface is disabled
  IP Null turbo vector
  IP multicast fast switching is disabled
  IP multicast distributed fast switching is disabled
  Router Discovery is disabled
  IP output packet accounting is disabled
  IP access violation accounting is disabled
  TCP/IP header compression is disabled
  Probe proxy name replies are disabled
  Policy routing is disabled
  Network address translation is disabled
  Web Cache Redirect is disabled
  BGP Policy Mapping is disabled
```

In the previous output notice the line in bold. Since you applied an outbound access list to interface Ethernet0, you should see that fact reflected in the output of the **show ip interface ethernet0** command.

If the screen output had said "Outgoing access list is not set," you would need to go back and see if you had forgotten to apply or bind the access list to the desired interface. Since it displays "Outgoing access list is 50," you know that you have done everything correctly.

Your next verification command is the **show access-lists** command. The command line syntax for this command is as follows:

```
router# show access-lists ?
  <1-2699>  ACL number
  WORD      ACL name
  |         Output modifiers
  <cr>
```

You can use variations of this command to display different information, as follows:

- **show access-lists** Shows all configured access lists
- **show ip access-lists** Shows all configured IP access lists
- **show access-list 50** Shows a specific number access list

You are going to issue the **show access-list 50** command since you only have one access list configured at this point:

```
router# show access-list 50
Standard IP access list 50
    deny   192.168.1.0, wildcard bits 0.0.0.255
    permit any
```

As you can see in the preceding output, you have confirmed that traffic from the entire 192.168.1.0 subnet is going to be subject to the rules you established in access list 50. This is confirmed by the line that reads:

```
deny 192.168.1.0, wildcard bits 0.0.0.255
```

Remember our rules about how the inverse subnet mask or wildcard bits determine how much of the specified IP address is going to be considered by the access list? You entered **192.168.1.85 0.0.0.255**, which tells the router to match all the way up to the third octet, which will cause the router to block the entire 192.168.1.0 subnet.

Let's do another quick example before we move on to extended IP access lists.

Create an Access List to Block Traffic from a Single Host Address

Since you already know how to block an entire subnet's traffic from exiting the Ethernet0 interface on your router, let's quickly take a look at the steps needed to block a single host's IP address's traffic like the scenario in Figure 8-5. It is essentially the same command structure but with one addition. We talked about it in the "Creating a Standard IP Access List" section.

You first need to specify the address that will be explicitly blocked:

```
router(config)#access-list 50 deny 192.168.1.85 0.0.0.0
```

You enter the host's IP address, **192.168.1.85**, followed by **0.0.0.0** which tells the router to match all the octets. This makes the router examine the entire source

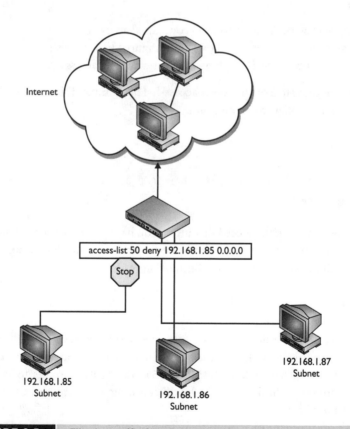

Filtering traffic from a single host

address of the packet, which is exactly what you want it to do. If you only matched the first three octets (as in the previous example), you would block the entire subnet, which is *not* what you want to do in this case.

The next thing you do is enter a command that will allow the rest of the host addresses on that subnet to exit the interface freely. The options available for this command are shown here:

```
router(config)#access-list 50 permit ?
  Hostname or A.B.C.D  Address to match
  any                  Any source host
  host                 A single host address
```

You can either use the **0.0.0.0 255.255.255.255** command syntax or the word **any** which means "any host." Either syntax will work.

```
router(config)#access-list 50 permit 0.0.0.0 255.255.255.255
```

This command overrides the **implicit deny** statement that is always present whenever access lists are called into action. Routers are very literal in their thinking. Once you apply an access list to a router interface, it will do what you tell it to do. But it will also say to itself, "Well, they said to block this one guy, but they didn't tell me to let everyone else through, so I won't." This is the **implicit deny** statement coming back to haunt you.

Let's take a look at all the commands needed to correctly configure an access list that prevents a single host address from exiting the Ethernet0 interface on your router:

```
router(config)# access-list 50 deny 192.168.1.85 0.0.0.0
router(config)# access-list 50 permit 0.0.0.0 255.255.255.255
router(config)# interface ethernet0
router(config-if)# ip access-group 50 out
```

You will notice that this is the same access list used earlier, but instead of using the keyword **any** the source address 0.0.0.0 255.255.255.255 is being used.

You now need to check your work and make sure that the commands you entered have taken effect:

```
router#sh access-lists 50
Standard IP access list 50
    deny   192.168.1.85
    permit any
```

So far, so good. Let's issue one more command just to be sure:

```
router#show ip interface ethernet0
Ethernet0 is up, line protocol is up
  Internet address is 192.168.1.1/24
  Broadcast address is 255.255.255.255
  Address determined by non-volatile memory
  MTU is 1500 bytes
  Helper address is not set
  Directed broadcast forwarding is disabled
  Multicast reserved groups joined: 224.0.0.9
  Outgoing access list is 50
  Inbound  access list is not set
  Proxy ARP is enabled
  Security level is default
  Split horizon is enabled
  ICMP redirects are always sent
  ICMP unreachables are always sent
  ICMP mask replies are never sent
  IP fast switching is enabled
  IP fast switching on the same interface is disabled
  IP Null turbo vector
  IP multicast fast switching is disabled
  IP multicast distributed fast switching is disabled
  Router Discovery is disabled
  IP output packet accounting is disabled
  IP access violation accounting is disabled
  TCP/IP header compression is disabled
  Probe proxy name replies are disabled
  Policy routing is disabled
  Network address translation is disabled
  Web Cache Redirect is disabled
  BGP Policy Mapping is disabled
```

It really is an easy task to accomplish if you take it step by step. Just make sure to remember that if you configure an access list to block traffic from a single host on a subnet, you must enter a corresponding **permit** statement in order to let the other hosts on that subnet have access to the router interface the access list has been applied to.

Objective 8.03   Extended IP Access Lists

If you were to compare access lists to automobiles, the standard access list would be a four-cylinder economy car while the extended access list would be a cross between a high performance racecar and a sport utility vehicle. Both types of access lists are used to block or filter traffic based on a set of rules, but where a standard access list can only block traffic based on source addresses, the extended access list can take the following into account:

- Source address
- Destination address
- Source port
- Destination port
- Protocol type

Despite the fact that there are now quite a few more options available when creating extended IP access lists, the basic operation is essentially the same as you encountered when you were configuring a standard IP access list.

Creating an Extended IP Access List

Even though the basic operation of creating and applying an extended IP access list is superficially the same as that of the standard IP access list, the command line parameters are considerably more plentiful.

Creating an Extended IP Access List that Blocks Web Access from a Specific Subnet

If you are a network administrator and you are constantly battling to conserve bandwidth, you may want to consider blocking access to Internet web sites. This decision will make you hugely unpopular with your coworkers, but it could result in a substantial savings as well as a boost in productivity. An extended IP access list fills this need quite nicely, since they allow you to block traffic based on the protocol and related port numbers. In this case, you are going to be blocking outbound access to port 80, which is the port associated with the HTTP protocol. (See Figure 8-6.)

The command line parameters for creating an extended IP access list are as follows:

```
router(config)# access-list <list number 100-199> < permit | deny >
<protocol> <source address> <source wildcard mask> <destination address>
<destination wildcard mask> <conditional statement and/or port number>
```

To accomplish the task, enter the following commands:

```
router(config)# access-list 100 deny tcp 192.168.1.0 0.0.0.255 any eq www
router(config)# access-list 100 permit ip any any
router(config)# interface ethernet0
router(config-if)# ip access-group 100 out
```

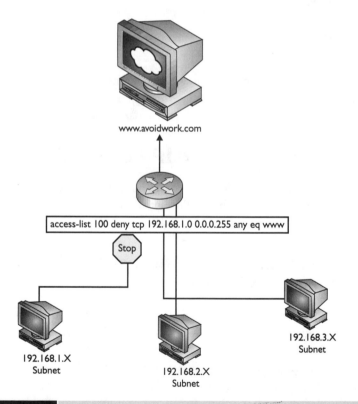

FIGURE 8.6   Filtering Web traffic requests for an entire subnet

Table 8-2 breaks this code down into its components to show exactly what you are telling the router to do when it runs across this access list.

TABLE 8.2	An Analysis of an Extended Access List Command
Command	**Explanation**
router(config)# access-list 100	This tells the router you are going to create an extended access list. Extended access lists have a range between 100–199.
router(config)# access-list 100 deny	You are going to deny traffic coming from somewhere.
router(config)# access-list 100 deny tcp	The TCP protocol is going to be involved. HTTP is part of the TCP protocol.
router(config)# access-list 100 deny tcp 192.168.1.0	The 192.168.1.0 subnet might be involved.
router(config)# access-list 100 deny tcp 192.168.1.0 0.0.0.255	The **0.0.0.255** confirms that you will be filtering the entire 192.168.1.0 subnet.
router(config)# access-list 100 deny tcp 192.168.1.0 0.0.0.255 host	This tells the router the identity of the destination.
router(config)# access-list 100 deny tcp 192.168.1.0 0.0.0.255 any	The **any** tells the router that all destinations are going to be considered. This means that any web site you try to access will be considered.
router(config)# access-list 100 deny tcp 192.168.1.0 0.0.0.255 any eq	The statement **eq** tells the router that you are going to be looking for a port number that equals whatever command comes next.
router(config)# access-list 100 deny tcp 192.168.1.0 0.0.0.255 any eq www	The **www** command says to block access to port 80 traffic. You can enter either **80** or **www** here. The router will understand what you want.

You have now instructed the router that you will blocking web access requests coming from the 192.168.1.0 subnet. You still need to make sure that your newly created access list doesn't catch other subnets behind the router, so you need to enter another command to prevent this:

```
router(config)# access-list 100 permit ip any any
```

This command will tell the router to allow IP traffic originating from any other host address going to any protocol and port number. It's a shorthand version of the 0.0.0.0 255.255.255.255 statement you saw previously. Remember the **implicit deny** statement that always follows you around whenever you implement access lists on a router.

Applying the Extended IP Access List to a Router Interface

The commands needed to apply this access list to the Ethernet0 interface are identical to the commands you used when applying a standard IP access list:

```
router(config)# interface ethernet0
router(config-if)# ip access-group 100 out
```

Verifying the Operation of an Extended IP Access List

You now want to verify that your access list has been applied properly. If you issue the command **show ip interface ethernet0**, you'll see that access list 100 has been applied to the Ethernet0 interface on your router:

```
router# show ip interface ethernet0
Ethernet0 is up, line protocol is up
  Internet address is 192.168.1.1/24
  Broadcast address is 255.255.255.255
  Address determined by non-volatile memory
  MTU is 1500 bytes
  Helper address is not set
  Directed broadcast forwarding is disabled
  Multicast reserved groups joined: 224.0.0.9
  Outgoing access list is 100
```

```
Inbound  access list is not set
Proxy ARP is enabled
Security level is default
Split horizon is enabled
ICMP redirects are always sent
ICMP unreachables are always sent
ICMP mask replies are never sent
IP fast switching is enabled
IP fast switching on the same interface is disabled
IP Null turbo vector
IP multicast fast switching is disabled
IP multicast distributed fast switching is disabled
Router Discovery is disabled
IP output packet accounting is disabled
IP access violation accounting is disabled
TCP/IP header compression is disabled
Probe proxy name replies are disabled
Policy routing is disabled
Network address translation is disabled
Web Cache Redirect is disabled
BGP Policy Mapping is disabled
```

Next, you'll issue the **show access-lists** command. The command line syntax for this command is as follows:

```
router# show access-lists ?
  <1-2699>  ACL number
  WORD      ACL name
  |         Output modifiers

router# show access-list 100
Extended IP access list 100
          deny tcp 192.168.1.0 0.0.0.255 any eq www
permit tcp any any
```

The output of this command shows you once again that you have entered the commands properly, and that the access list has been applied to the Ethernet0 interface on your router.

Creating an Extended IP Access List that Blocks Telnet Access from a Single Host Address

In the previous example, we created an access list that prevented an entire subnet from accessing Internet web sites. While this may cause a momentary rise in your social standing at work, it isn't really considered to be a security measure as such. Suppose for a moment that you work in a company that employs a bunch of network engineers and their support staff. You may decide that you don't want a particularly curious support person to poke around in your firewall router (IP address 192.168.1.2) and cause problems. You can prevent this by denying access to just that one person while allowing everyone else to perform their job functions. This can be accomplished by specifying that person's IP address in your access list command structure as shown here:

```
router(config)# access-list 100 deny tcp 192.168.1.85 0.0.0.0 host
192.168.1.2 eq telnet
router(config)# access-list 100 permit ip any any
router(config)# interface ethernet0
router(config-if)# ip access-group 100 out
```

Table 8-3 breaks this command down into its components to show exactly what you are telling the router to do when it runs across this access list.

Looks a lot like the command structure in the first example, doesn't it? This material really isn't rocket science, it's merely a matter of breaking it down into the base components and knowing how they interact. If you plan out what you want to do before you sit down at the router, things will go a lot more smoothly.

You may have also noticed that the keyword **host** can be used instead of the mask **0.0.0.0**; however, the keyword **host** comes before the address rather than after it like the mask. The **access-list** statement from Table 8-3 could read:

```
router(config)# access-list 100 deny tcp host 192.168.1.85 host
192.168.1.2 eq telnet
```

or

```
router(config)# access-list 100 deny tcp 192.168.1.85 0.0.0.0
192.168.1.2 0.0.0.0 eq telnet
```

Both statements have the same effect.

TABLE 8.3	A Breakdown of an Extended Access List that Is Denying Traffic Between Hosts

Command	Explanation
router(config)# access-list 100	This tells the router you are going to create an extended access list. Extended access lists have a range between 100–199.
router(config)# access-list 100 deny	You are going to deny traffic coming from somewhere.
router(config)# access-list 100 deny tcp	The TCP protocol is going to be involved. Telnet is part of the TCP protocol.
router(config)# access-list 100 deny tcp 192.168.1.85	The 192.168.1.85 subnet might be involved.
router(config)# access-list 100 deny tcp 192.168.1.85 0.0.0.0	The **0.0.0.0** tells the router that only the host address 192.168.1.85 is going to be affected.
router(config)# access-list 100 deny tcp 192.168.1.85 0.0.0.0 host	This tells the router the destination provided will be an individual host's IP address.
router(config)# access-list 100 deny tcp 192.168.1.85 0.0.0.0 host 192.168.1.2	The **192.168.1.2** tells the router that this access list is going to be watching packets that have this destination address.
router(config)# access-list 100 deny tcp 192.168.1.85 0.0.0.0 host 192.168.1.2 eq	The statement **eq** tells the router that you are going to be looking for a port number that equals whatever command comes next.
router(config)# access-list 100 deny tcp 192.168.1.85 0.0.0.0 host 192.168.1.2 eq telnet	Just like in the previous example, you can specify the protocol by name. In this case, you can enter **telnet** and the router understands that you want to restrict access to port 23.

Objective 8.04 Named IP Access Lists

It would be helpful if you could give an access list a name and be able to call it by that name when you needed to use it. With the introduction of Cisco IOS 11.2, you now have the ability to do just that.

Giving an access list a name gives you some administrative flexibility that you did not have previously with the numerically notated variety. In the past, you were limited by the constraints of the number ranges assigned to both the standard (1–99) and extended (100–199) IP access lists. Being able to assign an access list a name breaks that barrier and allows you to create as many access lists as you desire. Along with this new freedom comes a couple of caveats. The most notable restriction is that the name assigned to an access list must be unique. You can't give more than one access list the same name. Other than that, you are pretty much free to do what you want.

Creating a Named IP Access List

The mechanics of creating a named IP access list is very similar to the process you followed for both the standard and extended IP access lists.

Enter the command **ip access-list** to begin the process. This command is a little different than what you're used to, but still looks similar enough to keep your confidence level high.

```
router(config)# ip access-list ?
  extended  Extended Access List
  standard  Standard Access List
```

The next step is to specify whether the named IP access list is going to be standard or extended. You're going to make it a standard access list, as follows:

```
router(config)# ip access-list standard ?
  <1-99>  Standard IP access-list number
  WORD    Access-list name
```

You need to give this access list a name that will help you identify what it does. You want to block your coworker Bob from accessing the Internet through the company firewall, so name your access list **bob**:

```
router(config)# ip access-list standard bob
```

After you press ENTER you will notice that the command prompt context has changed from (config)# to (config-std-nacl). This new command prompt tells you that you are in the configuration mode for a standard named access list. If you had indicated that you were creating an extended IP access list, the prompt would be (config-ext-nacl). From this point on, it's pretty much the conventional access list creation procedure. You are telling the router that you are going to deny access to someone, as follows:

```
router(config-std-nacl)# deny ?
  Hostname or A.B.C.D  Address to match
  any                  Any source host
  host                 A single host address
```

You now give the router Bob's IP address followed by **0.0.0.0** which instructs the router to match all four octets of Bob's IP address:

```
router(config-std-nacl)# deny 192.168.1.85 0.0.0.0
```

The only thing you need to do now is apply the newly created named IP access list to the desired router interface. You do this using the following commands:

```
router(config)# interface ethernet0
router(config-if)# ip access-group bob out
```

Once you submit these commands, Bob is doomed to stay within the confines of the local network. You have successfully prevented him from leaving the network via interface Ethernet0 on your firewall router.

The access-class Command and Router VTY Access

Objective 8.05

In this chapter, we have covered different types of access lists and how they function. We have talked about applying those access lists to router interfaces, which are often referred to as *logical interfaces*, meaning an interface that you can see and touch. Contained within a router are also some *virtual interfaces*. They are more commonly referred to as *VTY interfaces*. VTY means *virtual terminal*, and a VTY interface is the interface that manages Telnet connections for the router. The **access-class** command allows you to apply an established access-list statement to the VTY interfaces on the router.

Access lists block traffic from hosts connected to the router, not the router itself. If you are logged into a router and you initiate a Telnet session to a remote destination router, the access lists on your router are oblivious to what you are doing, because they only watch traffic coming into the router, not traffic originating from it (see Figure 8-7).

Creating and Applying the access-class Command

Applying an access list to a VTY interface is very easy. The commands needed to perform this action are shown here. You need to be in global configuration mode to begin this operation.

First, type in the parameters you want for access list 99. This is the access list that will provide the filtering for VTY lines 0 through 4. This particular access list will be blocking traffic from the entire 192.168.1.0 subnet, as follows:

```
router(config)# access-list 99 deny 192.168.1.85 0.0.0.255
```

The **line vty 0 4** command tells the router you are going to perform some configuration commands on VTY lines 0 through 4:

```
router(config)# line vty 0 4
```

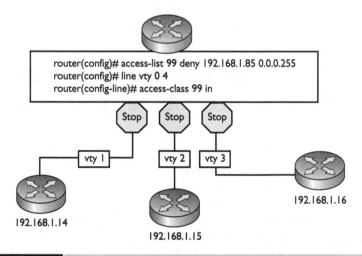

FIGURE 8.7   Limiting Telnet access with the **access-class** command

Notice how the command prompt context changes to reflect that you are in line configuration mode. You now tell the router to apply access list 99 to VTY lines 0 through 4:

```
router(config-line)# access-class 99 in
```

That's all there is to it. You have now protected your router using the **access-class** command.

CHECKPOINT

✔ **Objective 8.01: Access List Introduction and Operation**   An access list can be used to restrict traffic going in or out of a router's interface. Cisco has many different types of access lists. Access lists are a list of test conditions that packets are compared to when entering or exiting a router interface.

✔ **Objective 8.02: Standard IP Access Lists**   A standard IP access list is the simplest of the three access lists discussed in this chapter. A standard IP access list can restrict traffic based on the source address of the packet only. A standard IP access list will be numbered in the range 1–99. Entries will be made using the following command:

```
access-list <1-99> <permit|deny> <source address> <wildcard mask>
```

The wildcard mask indicates the "must match" bits in the preceding address. For example, an address and mask of 192.168.1.0 0.0.0.255 would indicate that any packet that has a source address beginning with 192.168.1 will match the test condition regardless of the value of the last octet.

✔ **Objective 8.03: Extended IP Access Lists**   An extended IP access list uses the range of numbers between 100–199 and allows you to restrict traffic not only based on source address, but also on destination, source port, destination port, and protocol number.

✔ **Objective 8.04: Named IP Access Lists**   Named IP access lists allow you to create access lists that can be modified without having to completely remove the access list. Statements can be removed or added to the last line of the access list, but not inserted. They also make it a little easier to work with due to the fact the access lists are given names rather than numbers.

✔ **Objective 8.05: The access-class Command and Router VTY Access**
The **access-class** command gives you the capability of restricting Telnet
access to and from the router interface. This command can be useful to
restrict traffic going to the router interface without affecting any other type
of traffic.

REVIEW QUESTIONS

1. Which of the following would you use to prevent a single user from accessing Internet web sites?

   A. Special access list
   B. Standard IP access list
   C. Extended IP access list
   D. Web access list
   E. Circular access list

2. What is the recommended location for applying an access list?

   A. As close to the traffic origination point as possible
   B. As close to the traffic destination point as possible
   C. Always place the access list on an Ethernet interface
   D. Always place the access list on a serial interface
   E. Any place is fine

3. What does the command **access-list 99 deny 192.168.1.84 0.0.0.255** do?

   A. It blocks the entire 192.168.2.0 subnet from sending outbound traffic.
   B. It blocks the entire 192.168.2.0 subnet from sending inbound traffic.
   C. It blocks the entire 192.168.1.0 subnet from sending outbound traffic,
   provided the command **ip access-group 99 out** has been entered on the
   desired router interface.
   D. It blocks the entire 192.168.1.0 subnet from sending outbound traffic,
   provided the command **ip access-group 99 in** has been entered on the
   desired router interface.
   E. It does nothing; the syntax is incorrect.

4. The command **access-list 50 permit any** is an example of a(n)
   _____ access list and needs to be entered from a _____
   mode command prompt.

   A. Standard, user

   B. Standard, enable

   C. Extended, global configuration

   D. Extended, user

   E. Standard, global configuration

5. What does the wildcard mask **0.0.0.255** tell the router to do when attempting to match the source address of a packet?

   A. Match – match – match – don't care

   B. Don't care – don't care – don't care – match

   C. Ignore – match – match – ignore

   D. Subtract zero – subtract zero – subtract zero – subtract 255

   E. It has no effect.

6. How many octets of a packet's destination address will the wildcard mask **0.0.255.255** look at when trying to determine a match?

   A. 1

   B. 2

   C. 3

   D. 4

   E. None

7. What operation is being performed if you see the command prompt **router(config-std-nacl)#**?

   A. A standard IP access list is being entered.

   B. A standard named access list is being entered.

   C. An extended IP access list is being entered.

   D. An extended named access list is being entered.

   E. There is no such command prompt.

8. Which of the following commands will override the **implicit deny** statement that is present when deploying access lists on a router interface?

   A. router(config)# access-list 50 disable deny deny

   B. router(config)# access-list 50 deny disabled

   C. router(config)# access-list 50 permit all

   D. router(config)# access-list 50 permit deny all

   E. router(config)# access-list 50 permit any

9. If you wanted to deny traffic based on the packet's destination address, what kind of access list would you use?

   A. Extended access list

   B. Enhanced access list

   C. Standard access list

   D. Circular access list

   E. You cannot deny traffic based on destination addresses.

10. If you wanted to block Telnet traffic originating from a router, what command would you use?

   A. You would use the **access-class** command.

   B. Access lists will work just fine; nothing special is required.

   C. You would use the **VTY Class** command.

   D. You would use the **Access VTY** command

   E. There is no command that will do this.

REVIEW ANSWERS

1. **C** You can only deny port-specific traffic with an extended IP access list. Standard IP access lists can only deny traffic based on source addresses.

2. **A** You want to put an access list as close to the traffic origination point as possible. This keeps unwanted traffic from flying around the network using up valuable bandwidth.

3. **C** The command **access-list 99 deny 192.168.1.84 0.0.0.255** will block traffic that originates from the 192.168.1.0 network because of the wildcard mask **0.0.0.255**, which says "match – match – match – don't care." This tells the router to only look as far as the third octet and then stop when looking for matching source addresses. This command will do nothing until it is applied to a router interface, hence the inclusion of the phrase "provided the command **ip access-group 99 out** has been entered on the desired router interface."

4. **E** The command **access-list 50 permit any** is an example of a standard IP access list. You need to be in global configuration mode to enter this command. Once again, make sure you are at the correct command mode context when entering commands of this nature.

5. **A** The wildcard mask **0.0.0.255** tells the router to only look as far as the first three octets of the packet's source address when attempting to find a match. The phrase "match, match, match, don't care" refers to the bit-matching pattern that is imposed in search of an address match.

6. **B** The wildcard mask **0.0.255.255** tells the router to only look as far as the first two octets of the packet's source address when attempting to find a match. A **0** in the wildcard mask tells the router to try and match this octet, while a **255** tells the router to ignore this octet.

7. **B** The command prompt **router(config-std-nacl)#** indicates that you are about to configure the parameters for a standard named IP access list. Since this command prompt is unlike any other that has been seen in this chapter, it should stand out right away as being something unusual.

8. **E** The command **router(config)# access-list 50 permit any** will override the **implicit deny** statement that is imposed when you apply an access list to a router interface. Once the router processes an access list, it looks around to see what it is supposed to do with traffic that has not been addressed by the access list it just processed. If it sees the **router(config)# access-list 50 permit any** command following the access list it just processed, the router will know to permit any other traffic that it didn't previously know what to do with.

9. **A** Extended IP access lists can permit or deny traffic based on source address, destination address, source port, destination port, protocol type, and port number. Standard IP access lists can only manage traffic based on source address. So if you want to manage traffic based on where the packet is headed, you use an extended access list.

10. **A** The **access-class** command is used to permit or deny traffic to or from a router's VTY interfaces. While an access list is capable of managing traffic originating from outside a router, it has no effect on traffic originating from the router itself. This is where the **access-class** command comes into play. Someone who "router hops" (Telnetting from one router to another) would not be affected by an extended access list that is designed to stop Telnet traffic from a connected host, so you configure an **access-class** command on your router, which directly controls access to the VTY interfaces. Think of it this way: you lock your front door to prevent people outside from coming in your house and using your cable modem to surf the Web. The lock on the front door stops people on the outside of the house, but does not prevent people already inside the house from logging on and Web surfing.

Configuring Cisco IOS Devices for IPX

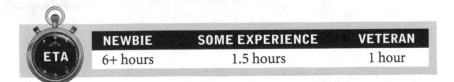

	NEWBIE	SOME EXPERIENCE	VETERAN
ETA	6+ hours	1.5 hours	1 hour

Novell Inc. is one of the oldest companies to produce network operating systems (NOS). Its earliest NOS dates back to 1984 and has evolved to become what is arguably the most stable file and print sharing platform out today. Novell's NOS is a software application called NetWare. NetWare is an operating system that runs on the server and allows workstations to access resources on the server.

In its earliest forms Novell's NetWare uses a protocol called IPX (Internetwork Packet Exchange). NetWare versions 5 and 6, although they still support IPX, run their services using IP. All older versions of NetWare use IPX natively.

In this chapter, we will provide a brief overview of the basics of NetWare and IPX. We will also detail how to configure Cisco devices to operate in an environment containing the IPX protocol.

Novell's Network Operating System

Objective 7.01

As mentioned previously, Novell's claim to fame is its NOS, NetWare. NetWare has gone through many different versions and at the time of this writing NetWare 6 is just being released.

Exam Tip

The CCNA 2.0 exam will expect you to be familiar with Novell's IPX protocol, not the particulars of each version of NOS except as otherwise noted later in this chapter. Although NetWare 5 and 6 rely heavily, if not solely, on IP, the exam will still expect you to have general knowledge of IPX.

Client/Server Operations

Novell's NetWare is a client/server operating system. The server is a PC running Novell's NetWare, while the clients can be almost anything. Currently NetWare supports Microsoft Windows, Apple Macintosh, and almost any Unix-based computers as clients. These clients simply need have installed a piece of software called, appropriately, the NetWare Client.

When the client has the NetWare Client installed on it, it can access any of the resources on Novell servers that the client has connectivity to and to which the

Novell administrator has given access. Cisco routers can be configured to facilitate routing of IPX traffic to support these NetWare devices.

Objective 7.02   Novell's IPX

Clients and servers communicate using the IPX protocol. IPX is a modification of the Xerox Network System (XNS) protocol. If you trace the roots of many of the computer products we use today, you will find that Xerox's Palo Alto Research Center (PARC) has played some part in their development. Ethernet, for instance, was developed by Bob Metcalfe while working at PARC.

The IPX protocol is somewhat different than IP. Unlike many opinions you may have heard, this author considers IPX to be much easier to deal with than IP. The IPX protocol, like IP, is a Layer 3 protocol responsible for packet addressing and routing. Like IP, IPX packets have a source and destination address in their headers, but unlike IP these are IPX addresses.

IPX also doubles as the connectionless Layer 4 protocol used by Novell. IPX can be compared to UDP in that it is used for connectionless delivery, but it is also comparable to IP because of its responsibility for addressing and routing.

The IPX address is 80 bits in length and has two parts, the network number and the host or node number. The network number is 32 bits in length and the node number is 48 bits in length. There is *no* subnet field with IPX. IPX addresses never need to be subnetted. The network portion is assigned to a logical network just as with IP, but the node number is the MAC address of the node rather than an administratively determined value. This provides three advantages over IP:

- IPX node numbers are the MAC address of the station and there is nothing that needs to be configured.
- There are never duplicate IPX addresses since the MAC address is globally unique.
- ARP isn't used to resolve an IPX address to a MAC address.

An administrator need only assign an IPX network number to a logical segment. The stations learn their addresses automatically based on this information, as shown in Figure 9-1.

Notice that with IPX, addressing is written in hexadecimal, not dotted decimal notation as with IP. This will keep the addresses somewhat smaller and more manageable. It should also be noted that Novell applications do not require the use of addresses as do many IP applications.

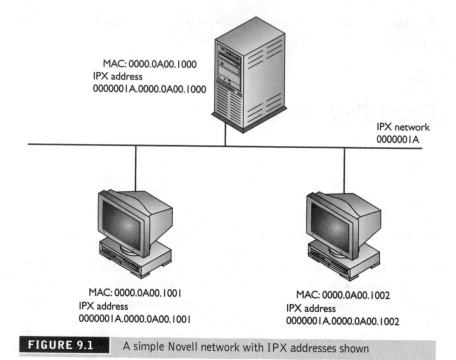

MAC: 0000.0A00.1000
IPX address
0000001A.0000.0A00.1000

IPX network
0000001A

MAC: 0000.0A00.1001
IPX address
0000001A.0000.0A00.1001

MAC: 0000.0A00.1002
IPX address
0000001A.0000.0A00.1002

FIGURE 9.1   A simple Novell network with IPX addresses shown

In Figure 9-1, all nodes receive their addresses automatically via the NetWare server. The workstations need only be configured with the NetWare Client software previously mentioned. If no NetWare server is present on the local LAN, a Cisco router can facilitate the automatic addressing of the client.

Exam Tip

It is not necessary to use leading 0s in the network number. Both Cisco and Novell devices will drop them accordingly. For instance, in Figure 9-1, it is not necessary to type 0000001A; it can be entered as 1A.

Packet Encapsulation

Because IPX is a Layer 3 protocol, it must be encapsulated into a Layer 2 frame. The media will determine the type of frame. For instance, a frame relay link will use a frame relay frame and an Ethernet multicast network will use an Ethernet frame. However, Ethernet has more than one type of frame.

Ethernet Version 2 Frames

IP will always use the Advanced Research Projects Agency (ARPA) frame type. The frame type is called this because it was the frame type used by ARPA when they first started using IP over Ethernet. Cisco will refer to this encapsulation as Ethernet ARPA; however, in the real world, this frame type is more commonly called Ethernet version 2. There was a version 1 of Ethernet that Bob Metcalfe and his team developed, and then they improved on it to create the 10 Mbps version that we know today. The frame itself has only three header fields and an FCS trailer. The destination MAC and source MAC addresses make up the first two fields. The third field is called the Type field (see Figure 9-2). It identifies the type of Layer 3 packet the frame is encapsulating. The field itself is 16 bits in length.

If an IP packet is encapsulated, the Type field will be set to 0800 in hexadecimal (or more commonly written 0x0800 where the "0x" indicates the number is in hexadecimal notation). With IPX, this value is set to 0x8137.

Ethernet RAW or Novell-Ether

When Novell originally created NetWare back in the mid-1980s, their LANs weren't common, and most of the time the LAN would be installed such that *only* NetWare could be used. Back then, "open systems" and "multiprotocol" were not yet household words. In such cases, why would there be a need for a protocol other than IPX? This made the Type field from the Ethernet V2 header and the 802.2 header from the IEEE 802.3 format irrelevant. Novell kept the 802.3 header from the IEEE standard Ethernet frame but dropped the 802.2 (LLC) header. And here's where some confusion sets in. Unfortunately, Novell called this frame type Ethernet_802.3, because it used the 802.3 frame being designed by the 802.3 subcommittee, but without the 802.2 header inside. Only IPX packets can be encapsulated in this frame type (see Figure 9-3). Cisco refers

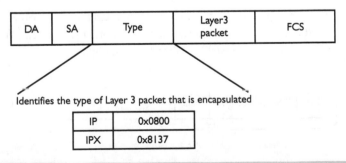

Identifies the type of Layer 3 packet that is encapsulated

IP	0x0800
IPX	0x8137

FIGURE 9.2   An Ethernet Version 2 frame

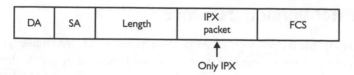

DA	SA	Length	IPX packet	FCS

Only IPX

FIGURE 9.3   Novell-Ether frames

to it as Novell-Ether because only Novell's IPX frames are supported. Sometimes in the real world you will hear it referred to as Ethernet RAW. This was the default encapsulation used by NetWare servers until version 3.12 when it was changed.

The IEEE 802.3/802.2 Header

In an effort to have a standard framing method over Ethernet, the IEEE developed a header by the 802.3 and 802.2 committees. The 802.3 committee defined a header whereby they removed the Type field and replaced it with a Length field. It is the same as Novell's Ethernet frame except that the 802.3 header in itself is not the end of the frame header. The encapsulated packet has not been identified! It was the 802.2 committee's job to come up with a header to identify the encapsulated frame (see Figure 9-4). They called this header the Logical Link Control (LLC).

In the LLC header, the Service Access Point (SAP) fields identify the type of packet that is encapsulated.

Travel Advisory

Do not confuse Service Access Points (SAP) with Novell's Service Advertising Protocol (SAP) discussed later in this chapter.

Cisco refers to this type of frame as SAP. More often than not, you will hear it referred to as the IEEE standard Ethernet encapsulation or IEEE 802.3. This is the default frame type used by Novell NetWare 3.12 and higher.

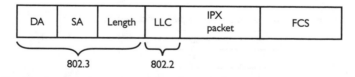

DA	SA	Length	LLC	IPX packet	FCS

802.3   802.2

FIGURE 9.4   The IEEE standard frame header

Travel Advisory

In the real world, the term "802.3 frame type" is tossed around frequently, but depending on who you are talking to it could mean two different frame types. Novell administrators commonly refer to the Novell-Ether frames as 802.3 frames because Novell calls it Ethernet_802.3, while others will refer to the IEEE standard frames as 802.3 frames. It is important for you to make the distinction.

Ethernet SNAP

In an effort to allow vendors more freedom, the IEEE created an extension of the IEEE standard Ethernet frame called Ethernet SNAP. The IEEE added a field after the LLC called the SubNetwork Access Protocol (SNAP) field, as shown in Figure 9-5.

Travel Assistance

The intricacies of Ethernet SNAP are much more detailed than out-lined here. To study these frame encapsulations further, McGraw-Hill's *Catalyst LAN Switching*, by Louis Rossi, has a much more detailed account.

Unlike the other frame types listed, this type is universally called the same name: Ethernet SNAP.

Other Media Types

There are other media types as well as Ethernet. Token Ring, for instance, has two encapsulation types: Token Ring and Token Ring SNAP. Both frame types are used by the IEEE. The SNAP header found in Token Ring SNAP is the same as in Ethernet SNAP.

DA	SA	Length	LLC	SNAP	IPX packet	FCS

FIGURE 9.5   A simplified look at the Ethernet SNAP frame

FDDI interfaces also have different encapsulations, such as FDDI_802.2, FDDI_RAW, and FDDI_SNAP. As you can imagine, they were all derived from the Ethernet frame formats.

Exam Tip

When configuring IPX on serial lines the encapsulation method will always be the encapsulation method used by the serial interface. There can be only one. If the link is **HDLC** or **PPP**, IPX will automatically use the appropriate encapsulation. Only the IPX network number need be configured.

Table 9-1 lists all the LAN frame types and their various names.

When configuring Cisco routers with the proper encapsulation for IPX, it is important to use the terms defined by Cisco and not the others listed.

TABLE 9.1   Frame Type Terminology Summary

Common Name	Novell's Terminology	Cisco's Terminology
IEEE standard Ethernet frame	Ethernet_802.2	SAP
Ethernet RAW	Ethernet_802.3	Novell-Ether
Ethernet version 2	Ethernet_II	ARPA
Ethernet SNAP	Ethernet_SNAP	SNAP
Standard IEEE Token Ring	Token-Ring	SAP
Token Ring SNAP	Token-Ring_SNAP	SNAP
Standard IEEE FDDI	FDDI_802.2	SAP
FDDI RAW	FDDI_Raw	Novell-FDDI
FDDI SNAP	FDDI_SNAP	SNAP

Connecting to the Server

For a Cisco router to facilitate client/server communication may require the router to do a little more than just route IPX traffic. When a Novell Client connects to a NetWare server, it uses a protocol called the Service Advertising Protocol (SAP). More specifically, it uses the Get Nearest Server (GNS) SAP. The GNS is a broadcast by the client to find the nearest server so that it may authenticate into the NetWare network.

The GNS goes out only on the local wire. All Novell servers on the local network respond to the GNS with a Give Nearest Server (GNS) response. The GNS reply contains the IPX address of the server and the IPX address of the local segment. The local station then connects to the nearest server as indicated in Figure 9-6.

What If There Is No Local Server?

In cases where there is no local server, the router must act as a proxy for the remote NetWare server and respond to the GNS request with a GNS reply. How does the router know about other NetWare servers? Novell NetWare servers advertise their services every 60 seconds via SAPs, the Service Advertising Protocol. The router will collect these SAPs and build its own SAP table, sometimes called the SAP Information Table (SIT). The router will then choose the nearest server in the table and then send the GNS reply as in Figure 9-7.

In the past, problems arose when there were local servers and a Cisco router. The Cisco router could potentially respond to the GNS request with a remote server even though there was a local server. In an effort to fix the problem, Cisco created an inherent delay in the GNS reply of .5 seconds to give a local server the opportunity to reply first. It was later realized that the router could determine if there was a local server just by looking at the SIT. If there was a local server, it would be sending SAPs that would be present in the SIT and the router would know if there was a local server. As it stands today, a Cisco router will not respond to a GNS request if there is a local server.

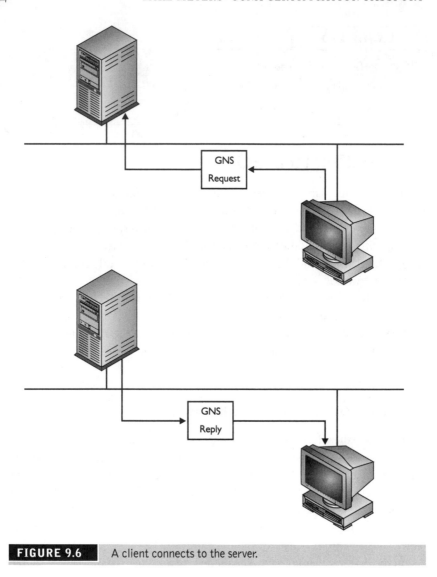

FIGURE 9.6   A client connects to the server.

Connecting to Resources

To access the many services available on NetWare services, Novell has developed a number of upper layer protocols. Although your job as a CCNA will not require you to interact with these protocols on a regular basis (and they will most likely not be covered on your exam), it is good to be aware of them.

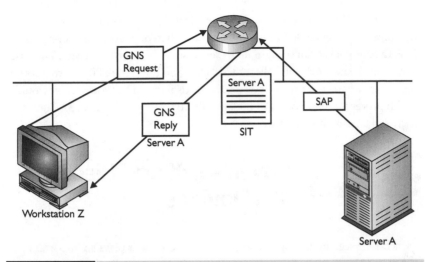

| FIGURE 9.7 | A client connects to a server through a Cisco router. |

Sequenced Packet Exchange

TCP/IP uses TCP for reliable, connection-oriented data delivery at Layer 4. Novell uses the Sequenced Packet Exchange (SPX) protocol for its reliable, connection-oriented data delivery. This protocol will be used with applications requiring guaranteed data delivery at Layer 4. It can be said that IPX is similar to UDP, while SPX is similar to TCP in the way it handles data delivery.

NetWare Core Protocol

The NetWare Core Protocol (NCP) is an upper layer protocol used commonly for file and print services. Clients will retrieve and access these resources via an NCP connection.

Service Advertising Protocol

Unlike the other protocols mentioned in this section, a CCNA does need to be constantly aware of these pesky little packets. As mentioned earlier, a NetWare server will advertise its services via these SAPs every 60 seconds. This can become a nightmare to network administrators and engineers as it can consume copious amounts of the available bandwidth if not carefully managed.

A single NetWare server could have dozens of services running on it, and therefore the server could be sending out more than one SAP packet every 60 seconds (a SAP packet can contain up to seven service advertisements). The Cisco routers in the network will collect these SAPs and build the SIT. The routers will then advertise their entire SIT every 60 seconds just as a NetWare server would.

To prevent unnecessary SAP updates, a SAP filter must be used. SAP filters are discussed later in this chapter.

Objective 7.03 Novell's IPX and Cisco IOS Devices

As can be seen in the last two objectives, a Cisco router plays an important part in the Novell network and it must be configured accordingly. Just like with IP, a routing protocol must be used to learn about the IPX networks available on the internetwork. Currently there are three routing protocols that can be used on Cisco routers to route IPX traffic:

- **Novell's IPX RIP** Very similar to IP RIP. This is the routing protocol discussed in this section.
- **Novell's NetWare Link Services Protocol (NLSP)** A link state routing protocol developed by networking expert Radia Pearlman, who was also responsible for the Spanning Tree Protocol.
- **Cisco's Enhanced Interior Gateway Routing Protocol (EIGRP) for IPX** Cisco's EIGRP works for IP, AppleTalk, and IPX.

IPX RIP

For the CCNA exam, you will be required to understand IPX RIP. NLSP and IPX EIGRP are not required.

IPX RIP is very similar to IP RIP except, of course, for the fact that it carries IPX network information. IPX RIP also has an increased update interval, 60 seconds as opposed to 30 seconds, and a slightly different metric consisting of ticks and hops rather than just hops. Some highlights to remember about IPX RIP:

- It is a distance vector routing protocol.
- The update interval is 60 seconds.
- The metric used is ticks (which are $1/18^{th}$ of a second) and hops.
- It has a maximum packet size of 576 bytes, which will allow for up to 50 networks in a single packet.

Configuring IPX and IPX RIP

Configuring IPX on a Cisco router is much easier than IP. The problem administrators often run into is they are unaware of the proper network numbers and encapsulations used on each network. It is very important that proper documentation is laid out when configuring for IPX. Many times the engineer configuring the router will not be the engineer configuring the NetWare servers. This will require communication between the two and this is often easier said than done.

IPX Documentation

Before configuring the router, it is important to have all the IPX network numbers and their respective encapsulation types.

> **Travel Advisory**
>
> It is possible to have more than one encapsulation type on an interface. This will require that two network numbers be used. It is important to remember that in these cases stations that are on the same wire but different encapsulation types will have traffic traverse the router.

In Figure 9-8, a simple network topology is given with all IPX network numbers and encapsulation types indicated. If you are not the person responsible for the assigning of these numbers, it may be necessary for you to ask the Novell administrator. Don't be afraid, those Novell guys are pretty nice...usually.

It is not necessary to specify the encapsulations on the serial interfaces since there will be only one option on those interfaces. However, there is one problem when looking at the serial interfaces: what address will they use for the node address? There is no MAC address on the serial interfaces, therefore the router has to look elsewhere for an address. In such cases, the MAC address of the lowest numbered local area network interface is used or one may be specified when configuring IPX.

Configuring the Router for IPX Routing

The first step in configuring IPX routing, after putting together your documentation, is to enter the command **ipx routing** in global configuration mode of all routers routing IPX. If you would like to specify the node address to be used on all interfaces

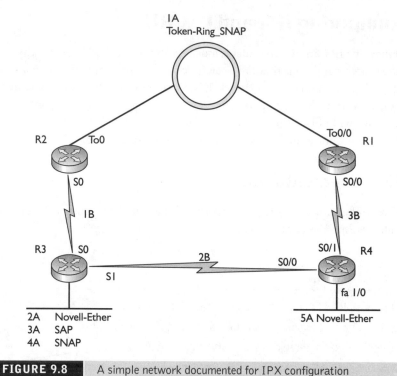

FIGURE 9.8 A simple network documented for IPX configuration

rather than the MAC addresses of the interfaces, you can specify an address at the end of the command. An example of this will follow in the code samples.

This is the only command required, but you may want to enable load sharing across paths with equal costs. By default, there is no load balancing. To configure for load balancing simply use the following command:

```
router(config)#ipx maximum-paths <maximum number of paths>
```

By default the maximum number of paths is 1, hence no load sharing or balancing.

Configuring the Router Interfaces

The final step is to assign the network addresses and encapsulation type to the interfaces. Just like with IP, each interface has to be told what its address is going to be. Unlike IP, however, each interface may have more than one encapsulation type and therefore multiple addresses.

> **Travel Advisory**
>
> It is possible to have multiple IP addresses on a Cisco router
> interface; however, it is not generally considered good design.

To configure an interface to route IPX, use the following command:

```
router(config-if)#ipx network <network number> encapsulation <encapsulation type>
```

If more than one encapsulation is used, a technique called subinterfaces can be used. Rather than configuring just the main interface, multiple subinterfaces are created using the following command:

```
Router(config)#int fa <interface number>.<sub-interface number>
```

For each subinterface a network number and encapsulation can be specified.

Example Configuration

To configure the network outlined in Figure 9-8, the following configs are used. Please note that the configs have had irrelevant information removed.

For R1:

```
Building configuration...
Current configuration : 882 bytes
!
version 12.1
!
hostname R1
ipx routing 0010.7b31.1cc1
!
interface Serial0/0
 encapsulation frame-relay
 ipx network 3B
 !
interface TokenRing0/0
 ipx network 1A encapsulation SNAP
```

```
 ring-speed 16
!
end
```

For R2:

```
Building configuration...

Current configuration:
!
version 12.0
hostname R2
!
!
ipx routing 0007.7816.fe54
frame-relay switching
!
interface Serial0
 ipx network 1B
 clockrate 56000
!
interface TokenRing0
 ipx network 1A encapsulation SNAP
 ring-speed 16
!
end
```

For R3:

```
Building configuration...
 version 11.3
!
hostname R3
!
ipx routing 0000.0000.1138
!
interface Ethernet0.1
 ipx network 2A
```

```
!
interface Ethernet0.2
 ipx network 3A encapsulation SAP
!
interface Ethernet0.3
 ipx network 4A encapsulation SNAP
!
interface Serial0
 ipx network 1B
!
interface Serial1
 ipx network 2B
!
end
```

For R4:

```
Building configuration...
 !
version 12.0
!
hostname R4
!
ipx routing 0010.7b32.9690
!
interface Serial0/0
 ipx network 2B
 clockrate 56000
!
interface Serial0/1
 ipx network 3B
 clockrate 56000
!
!
interface FastEthernet1/0
 ipx network 5A
!
end
```

Although the command **ipx routing** was issued in global configuration mode, each of the routers automatically generated the node address. On R3, a manual address of 0000.0000.1138 was configured.

Verifying IPX Addresses

To verify the addresses of configured interfaces, the command **show ipx interfaces** can be used. Using the network from Figure 9-8, you can verify that the node address 0000.0000.1138 is indeed being used.

```
R3#sh ipx int
Ethernet0.1 is up, line protocol is up
  IPX address is 2A.0000.0c47.6908, NOVELL-ETHER [up]
  Delay of this IPX network, in ticks is 1 throughput 0 link delay 0
  IPXWAN processing not enabled on this interface.
  IPX SAP update interval is 60 seconds
  IPX type 20 propagation packet forwarding is disabled
  Incoming access list is not set
  Outgoing access list is not set
  IPX helper access list is not set
  SAP GNS processing enabled, delay 0 ms, output filter list is not set
  SAP Input filter list is not set
  SAP Output filter list is not set
  SAP Router filter list is not set
  Input filter list is not set
  Output filter list is not set
  Router filter list is not set
  Netbios Input host access list is not set
  Netbios Input bytes access list is not set
  Netbios Output host access list is not set
  Netbios Output bytes access list is not set
  Updates each 60 seconds aging multiples RIP: 3 SAP: 3
  SAP interpacket delay is 55 ms, maximum size is 480 bytes
  RIP interpacket delay is 55 ms, maximum size is 432 bytes
  RIP response delay is not set
  IPX accounting is disabled
  IPX fast switching is configured (enabled)
  RIP packets received 0, RIP packets sent 35
```

```
SAP packets received 0, SAP packets sent 2
Ethernet0.2 is up, line protocol is up
  IPX address is 3A.0000.0c47.6908, SAP [up]
  Delay of this IPX network, in ticks is 1 throughput 0 link delay 0
  Updates each 60 seconds aging multiples RIP: 3 SAP: 3
Ethernet0.3 is up, line protocol is up
  IPX address is 4A.0000.0c47.6908, SNAP [up]
Serial0 is up, line protocol is up
  IPX address is 1B.0000.0000.1138 [up]
Serial1 is up, line protocol is up
  IPX address is 2B.0000.0000.1138 [up]
```

The first interface displays all the information, but each subsequent one has had the material cut for space reasons. Notice that the serial interfaces are both using the node address specified.

Verifying IPX Routing

You may have noticed that IPX RIP was not explicitly configured. This is due to the fact that it is automatically configured by the router. If you are running IPX, the router assumes that you will be running IPX RIP and automatically configures it for you. To verify the routing tables, simply use the **show ipx route** command:

```
R3#sh ipx route
Codes: C - Connected primary network,    c - Connected secondary network
       S - Static, F - Floating static, L - Local (internal), W - IPXWAN
       R - RIP, E - EIGRP, N - NLSP, X - External, A - Aggregate
       s - seconds, u - uses, U - Per-user static

8 Total IPX routes. Up to 1 parallel paths and 16 hops allowed.

No default route known.

C        1B (HDLC),          Se0
C        2A (NOVELL-ETHER), Et0.1
C        2B (HDLC),          Se1
C        3A (SAP),           Et0.2
C        4A (SNAP),          Et0.3
```

```
R         1A [07/01] via       1B.0007.7816.fe54,   46s, Se0
R         3B [07/01] via       2B.0010.7b32.9690,   32s, Se1
R         5A [07/01] via       2B.0010.7b32.9690,   32s, Se1
R3#
```

R3 has three encapsulation types on its E0 interface—notice that the three subinterfaces show up as separate interfaces in the routing table. The other entries were learned via RIP. The values in brackets following the network number are the metrics, ticks/hops. The time interval to the right of these entries indicates how long it has been since the last update.

To view the real-time routing updates, the command **debug ipx routing-activity** can be used:

```
R3#debug ipx routing activity
IPX routing debugging is on
2d05h: IPXRIP: positing full update to 1B.ffff.ffff.ffff via Serial0 (broadcast)
2d05h: IPXRIP: Update len 80 src=1B.0000.0000.1138, dst=1B.ffff.ffff.ffff(453)
2d05h:     network 2B, hops 1,  delay 7
2d05h:     network 5A, hops 2,  delay 13
2d05h:     network 3B, hops 2,  delay 13
2d05h:     network 4A, hops 1,  delay 7
2d05h:     network 3A, hops 1,  delay 7
2d05h:     network 2A, hops 1,  delay 7
2d05h: IPXRIP: update from 1B.0007.7816.fe54
2d05h:     5A in 3 hops, delay 14
2d05h:     3B in 2 hops, delay 8
2d05h:     1A in 1 hops, delay 7
```

The previous output shows the updates as they come in and the advertised metrics of each route.

Another command that may be useful is the **show ipx traffic** command. This command will display statistics of all IPX packets that are received, as shown here:

```
R3#sh ipx traffic
System Traffic for 0.0000.0000.0001 System-Name: R3
Rcvd:    801 total, 20 format errors, 0 checksum errors, 0 bad hop count,
         244 packets pitched, 557 local destination, 0 multicast
```

```
Bcast:   554 received, 277 sent
Sent:    278 generated, 0 forwarded
         0 encapsulation failed, 0 no route
SAP:     1 Total SAP requests, 0 Total SAP replies, 0 servers
         1 SAP general requests, 0 ignored, 0 replies
         0 SAP Get Nearest Server requests, 0 replies
         0 SAP Nearest Name requests, 0 replies
         0 SAP General Name requests, 0 replies
         1 SAP advertisements received, 2 sent
         0 SAP flash updates sent, 0 SAP format errors
RIP:     1 RIP requests, 0 ignored, 1 RIP replies, 8 routes
         93 RIP advertisements received, 241 sent
         16 RIP flash updates sent, 0 RIP format errors
Echo:    Rcvd 0 requests, 0 replies
         Sent 0 requests, 0 replies
         0 unknown: 0 no socket, 0 filtered, 0 no helper
         0 SAPs throttled, freed NDB len 0
Watchdog:
         0 packets received, 0 replies spoofed
Queue lengths:
         IPX input: 0, SAP 0, RIP 0, GNS 0
         SAP throttling length: 0/(no limit), 0 nets pending lost route reply
         Delayed process creation: 0
EIGRP:   Total received 0, sent 0
         Updates received 0, sent 0
         Queries received 0, sent 0
         Replies received 0, sent 0
         SAPs received 0, sent 0
```

The statistics in bold indicate a common problem on IPX networks. The
Ethernet interface of R3 is connected to a network that is being used for another
IPX network by several other devices. In this case, it was done on purpose; however, it is common for network administrators to assign the wrong IPX network
number and end up with these problems, which are very difficult to find. This will
also lead to router configuration errors on the NetWare server and an annoying
beep every 60 seconds.

Testing Connectivity

As with IP, there is a way to ping with IPX. Cisco has developed an IPX echo and echo reply similar to the ICMP ping. It can be executed by using the following command:

```
Router#ping ipx <ipx address>
```

The problem with an IPX ping is that you must specify the IPX address, and these are not commonly known or easily remembered, unlike router interface addresses.

Travel Advisory

The IPX ping used by Cisco on its routers is *not* the same as the IPX ping used on NetWare servers, and therefore they will not ping each other.

 **Objective 7.04** # Restricting IPX Traffic with Access Lists

As with IP traffic, there may be instances when you wish to restrict traffic. Cisco routers have the ability to restrict IPX traffic with three different access lists:

- Standard IPX access lists
- Extended IPX access lists
- SAP filters

Standard IPX Access Lists

Creating and applying access lists on a Cisco router is almost always the same. There are two steps:

1. Create the access list.
2. Apply it to the interface.

IPX standard access lists are no different. They require a number between 800–899 and are applied to the interface using the **ipx access-group** command.

This should be familiar to you considering that with IP access lists the command **ip access-group** was used.

IPX standard access lists can restrict traffic based on source and destination addresses. This is a little different than IP standard access lists—they could only restrict based on the source address. However, it is very rare that IPX traffic need to be restricted in this way; see the "IPX SAP Filters" section later in this chapter.

To configure an IPX standard access list, use the following command to create its entries:

```
Router(config)#access-list <800-899> <permit|deny> <source address>
<destination address>
```

The source and destination addresses are written in hexadecimal with the node addresses optional. For example, to restrict traffic coming from the 1A network going to the 2B network, the following command could be used:

```
R1(config)#access-list 800 deny 1a 2b
```

To apply this access list to an interface, simply use the **ipx access-group** command.

```
R1(config-if)#ipx access-group 800 in
```

This applies the access list to all traffic inbound on the interface.

Extended IPX Access Lists

Extended IPX access lists, much like IP extended access lists, allow you to restrict traffic on a more detailed basis. Instead of just source or destination addresses, you may now specify the protocol or socket (Novell's name for port). You can also use a wildcard mask to restrict specific traffic on a particular IPX network number or multiple IPX network numbers. In reality this is rarely done, but it is a comfort to know that it can be done.

The format of the command is as follows. (The command is much too long to fit on a single line, but it would be entered in one line on the router.)

```
Router(config)#access-list <900-999> <permit|deny> <protocol>
<source> <source socket> <destination> < destination socket>
```

IPX SAP Filters

More often than not, administrators will need to configure a SAP filter to control the numerous SAPs that are being received by the router and then rebroadcast every 60 seconds. To view the SAPs that are currently in the SIT of a Cisco router, the command **show ipx servers** is used, as shown here:

```
R1#show ipx services
Codes: S - Static, P - Periodic, E - EIGRP, N - NLSP, H - Holddown, + = detail
U - Per-user static
7 Total IPX Servers

Table ordering is based on routing and server info

    Type Name                Net     Address      Port    Route Hops Itf
P      4 ARI_FS1             1B.0000.0000.0001:0451   2/01    1  Et0
P      4 ARI_FS2             2A.0000.0000.0001:0451   2/01    1  Et0
P    107 ARI_FS1             1B.0000.0000.0001:8104   2/01    1  Et0
P    107 ARI_FS2             2A.0000.0000.0001:8104   2/01    1  Et0
P    278 ARI_____ 2A.0000.0000.0001:4006   2/01    1  Et0
P    278 ARI_____ 1B.0000.0000.0001:4006   2/01    1  Et0
P    30C 080009A6410800CGHPLJ5 1A.0800.09a6.4108:400C 1/00    1  Et0
```

The types indicate the type of service being offered. A type 4 is a NetWare file server. You may also want to note that the node addresses of all these servers is 0000.0000.0001. All NetWare servers will create an internal network where their services will artificially reside and be identified as node 1 on this internal network. This network will be routed to the external network—that is, the network to which it is connected.

The last SAP is from an HP JetDirect Print Server card, and therefore it does not have the NetWare 0000.0000.0001 address.

A SAP filter is used to reduce the number of entries and the traffic used by these SAPs. In a larger NetWare network, it may not be desirable to have printers in California accessible by users in New York. The advertising of the SAPs from all the printers in California to New York could be a substantial amount of bandwidth on the wide area network connection. A SAP filter could be used to tell the router not to advertise any print services out the wide area interface pointing to New York.

To create a SAP filter, you use the access list range 1000–1099. The format of the command is as follows:

```
Router(config)#access-list <1000-1099> <permit|deny> <source address>
                                         <source mask> <SAP type>
```

The SAP type is the number of the service to be restricted. The mask and the SAP type are optional.

Once the access list has been created, it can be applied to an interface as incoming or outgoing using the following commands.

For incoming filters:

```
Router(config-if)#ipx input-sap-filter <access-list number>
```

Or for outgoing filters:

```
Router(config-if)#ipx output-sap-filter <access-list number>
```

An Example SAP Filter

To deny all type 4 SAPs (file servers) coming into R1, the following can be done:

```
R1(config)#access-list 1000 deny -1 4
R1(config)#access-list 1000 permit -1
R1(config)#int e0
R1(config-if)#ipx input-sap filter
R1(config-if)#
```

The **-1** can be used to indicate any address. This applies to any of the IPX access lists, not just IPX SAP filters. In this case, **access-list 1000** denies all type 4 SAPs and is applied to interface e0 incoming.

The SAP table now becomes:

```
R1#sh ipx server
Codes: S - Static, P - Periodic, E - EIGRP, N - NLSP, H - Holddown, + = detail
U - Per-user static
5 Total IPX Servers

Table ordering is based on routing and server info

   Type Name                   Net     Address    Port   Route Hops Itf
P  107 ARI_FS1                 1B.0000.0000.0001:8104   2/01   1   Et0
P  107 ARI_FS2                 2A.0000.0000.0001:8104   2/01   1   Et0
```

```
P   278 ARI_____        2A.0000.0000.0001:4006    2/01  1  Et0
P   278 ARI_____        1B.0000.0000.0001:4006    2/01  1  Et0
P   30C 080009A6410800CGHPLJ5      1A.0800.09a6.4108:400C    1/00  1  Et0
R1#
```

To view configured IPX access lists, use the command **show ipx access-lists:**

```
R1#show ipx access-lists
IPX sap access list 1000
    deny FFFFFFFF 4
    permit FFFFFFFF
R1#
```

Notice that instead of the **-1** there are now all Fs. This indicates that address is set to all 1s, which indicates any host.

To verify that the SAP filter is correctly applied to the interface, the **show ipx interface** IPX interface command will list the SAP filters that have been applied. The following is a piece of the command issued on R1:

```
CCPrep-AS#sh ipx inte
Ethernet0 is up, line protocol is up
  IPX address is 1A.0000.0c46.e4de, SAP [up]
  Delay of this IPX network, in ticks is 1 throughput 0 link delay 0
  IPXWAN processing not enabled on this interface.
  IPX SAP update interval is 60 seconds
  IPX type 20 propagation packet forwarding is disabled
  Incoming access list is not set
  Outgoing access list is not set
  IPX helper access list is not set
  SAP GNS processing enabled, delay 0 ms, output filter list is not set
  SAP Input filter list is 1000
  SAP Output filter list is not set
  SAP Router filter list is not set
  Input filter list is not set
  Output filter list is not set
  Router filter list is not set
```

CHECKPOINT

✔ **Objective 9.01: Novell's Network Operating System**   Novell's NetWare Network Operating System (NOS) was the first widely used LAN-based NOS. By using simple PCs as their servers and clients, network computing became affordable.

✔ **Objective 9.02: Novell's IPX**   To allow communication between NetWare servers and clients, Novell developed the Internetwork Packet Exchange (IPX) protocol. IPX is a Layer 3 protocol used to transport Novell applications. It can be encapsulated into any of the four Ethernet encapsulation types found today. The IPX address is 80 bits in length, 32 bits for the network number and 48 bits for the node number. The node number is derived from the MAC address of the NIC. If the interface is a serial interface, the lowest numbered local area interface's address is used by all of the serial interfaces.

✔ **Objective 9.03: Novell's IPX and Cisco IOS Devices**   Cisco routers can be configured to route IPX traffic and to assist Novell clients to connect to NetWare servers. Cisco currently supports three IPX routing protocols, but only IPX RIP is required reading for the CCNA exam.

✔ **Objective 9.04: Restricting IPX Traffic with Access Lists**   To restrict IPX traffic, Cisco has three access lists:
- **Standard access lists**   Restrict traffic based on source and destination addresses.
- **Extended access lists**   Restrict traffic based on protocol and socket as well as source and destination addresses.
- **SAP filters**   Restrict pesky SAP updates from eating up bandwidth on connections that are not necessary.

REVIEW QUESTIONS

1. Novell's NetWare servers may be configured on which of the following machines?
   A. Mainframe computers from IBM
   B. Regular PCs
   C. Sun Microsystems stations
   D. High-end Unix-based machines
   E. Any of the above

2. Which of the following protocols most resembles the characteristics of IPX data delivery?

   A. SAP

   B. RIP

   C. UDP

   D. TCP

   E. IPX is unique and there is no other protocol that delivers data like it does.

3. What three IPX routing protocols are supported on a Cisco router and have the capability to route IPX traffic?

   A. IPX RIP, IGRP, NLSP

   B. IPX RIP, EIGRP, IGRP

   C. EIGRP, IGRP, NLSP

   D. IPX RIP, EIGRP, NLSP

   E. IPX RIP, IGRP, IS-IS

4. How is the node number derived when using IPX?

   A. The number is automatically generated randomly.

   B. The node number is based on a combination of the bridge priority and MAC address.

   C. The SPF algorithm calculates it.

   D. The network administrator manually assigns it.

   E. It is the MAC address of the NIC.

5. What encapsulation type is used by default with NetWare 3.11?

   A. Novell-Ether

   B. ARPA

   C. Ethernet_802.2

   D. SAP

   E SNAP

6. What is the maximum number of RIP routes that may be placed in a single RIP packet?

   A. 7

   B. 10

   C. 25

   D. 37

   E 50

7. NetWare servers advertise their services every 60 seconds. Which of the following statements regarding these updates is true?

    A. These updates are called Service Access Points or SAPs.

    B. There can be a maximum of seven services advertised in a single update.

    C. These updates must always be encapsulated in Novell-Ether frames.

    D. NetWare servers only have one service to advertise in these updates.

    E. NetWare servers will send these updates with a source address of the external network.

8. Which command would reset a router to the default load balancing setting?

    A. ipx load balance enable

    B. ipx load balance disable

    C. ipx maximum-paths 2

    D. ipx maximum-paths 3

    E. ipx maximum-paths 1

REVIEW ANSWERS

1. **B** An easy question to get you started. NetWare servers can run on a regular PC—it was one of the reasons why NetWare became so popular.

2. **C** IPX is connectionless, just like UDP. While it's true that IPX is most like IP (Layer 3), when taking the exam, you must choose the best of the offered answers.

3. **D** IGRP and IS-IS do not support IPX routing.

4. **E** IPX node addresses are taken from the MAC address of the NIC. If there is no NIC, there is no way to connect to the network!

5. **A** The older versions of NetWare used the Ethernet RAW version or what Cisco refers to as Novell-Ether.

6. **E** A bit of an obscure question to keep you on your toes. There can be up to 50 routes in a single IPX RIP update.

7. **B** IPX SAPs can have a maximum of seven services contained in a single update. All other statements regarding SAPs are completely false. SAP

does not stand for Service Access Points, but rather Service Advertising Protocol.

8. **E** By default, a Cisco router does not load balance IPX traffic across paths with equal metrics. The **ipx maximum-paths** command can be used to specify the number of paths that may be load balanced over. To configure the router to load balance over only one path, which is no load balancing, simply specify 1.

Serial
Point-to-Point
Connections

	NEWBIE	SOME EXPERIENCE	VETERAN
ETA	5+ hours	2 hours	1 hour

Wide area networks (WANs) are a very important part of internetworking. Local area networks (LANs) are primarily connected by WAN technologies. Knowledge about LANs is far more easily obtained than about WANs simply because of the price of a LAN versus running a WAN. For 20 bucks an Ethernet card can be purchased, and then a few computers, cabling, a cheap router, and switch are all that is required. A small network can be used to create and set up many complex configurations, helping a person to learn about LANs. This only helps with half of the internetwork, though, because the other half is done through WAN connectivity. Basic WAN equipment usually costs more in the lab. In production networks, the WAN connections are extremely expensive when compared to LANs. This is because the technologies involved, the distances that must be covered, and the overhead such as buildings, staff, and many other necessities create huge costs. These costs prevent students from gaining knowledge of these types of networks. Most people can afford a modem to set up a point-to-point connection between two devices, but then to test both ends, simulators may have to be purchased. The terminal equipment required to set up PSTN (modem and ISDN) connections is quite expensive. This is equally true of each WAN technology, so that the WAN seems harder to grasp and many students stay away from learning it. The last portion of this book attempts to help clarify and simplify WAN technologies. While many technologies are referenced, these last three chapters will present a basic overview of WANs and individual discussions of PPP, ISDN, and frame relay.

Objective 10.01   Overview of WAN Connectivity

Both LANs and WANs are networks. They follow many of the same rules and often use the same cabling, but as expected, there are major differences. One major difference is that the WAN uses different equipment that is not used within local area networks. Many WAN connections are run over equipment that is primarily designed to carry voice. The telephone system that runs virtually around the world was not intended to carry user data. It was intended strictly for voice conversations and was all analog, which means that sounds were transmitted by variable physical quantities such as voltages and frequencies.

How WANs Are Different from LANs

When LANs were first created, they were not connected to each other. LANs are all digital networks, which means that voltage and frequency are interpreted by a device as either 0 or 1. However, as the amount of networks increased, it became necessary to connect them. For connecting buildings, LAN wiring with repeaters was installed. Because of cost, this wasn't a viable solution for connecting buildings separated by large distances. The telephone network was already in place, as almost every business was connected by copper telephone wiring installed for their telephones. Modems became a popular way of connecting the LANs over the public telephone network. The modem modulated the signal, changing it from its digital form to analog, so that it could be transmitted across this analog telephone network. When analog signals returned to the modem, they were converted back to digital so the LAN device would understand them.

Today, analog networks are disappearing, but the two-wire copper cabling remains in place. It is connected to almost every house and business in the United States and still provides what it did in the beginning for many LAN networks—an inexpensive way to connect LANs together. The wire that is used for the Public Switched Telephone Network (PSTN) is the same type of wiring that you would find in a CAT5 cable. Instead of two wires, there are eight in the CAT5 cable. The voltage, signaling, frequency, and connectors differentiate technologies for the most part. In many cities, fiber is replacing copper wiring in business buildings; however, most cities have not moved fiber to homes at the time of this writing. As WAN connection demands grew, technologies were developed and new equipment was deployed mostly by telephone companies. WAN protocols are used to format the data in order to traverse the provider's network and return it to a LAN format at a remote site. While in the old days the equipment for the telephone network and LAN network was completely different, today the WAN equipment and LAN equipment is beginning to mesh. Within organizations, the equipment used for data networks is also being used for voice calls.

The WAN is still ruled by the telephone network. Telephone companies provide WAN connections for individuals and businesses that allow technologies such as ISDN, DSL, frame relay, and ATM to be used when connecting LANs. Really, a WAN connection is an interface or translation point used to connect two or more local area networks using a service provider's network. This book does not attempt to explain the switching mechanisms used in the provider's network. Rather, it attempts to describe the behavior and configuration of WAN protocols used to con-

Local Lingo

Link, circuit, channel, line, connection   These terms are often used to refer to a single WAN connection. While there are technical distinctions, the differences are not important for the CCNA.

nect to service providers. WAN technologies such as asynchronous dialup, ISDN, and frame relay are basic protocols used to communicate with a service provider.

Before WAN protocols are explained, we must review some basic terminology and introduce some new definitions.

Earlier in the book, the terms DTE and DCE were explained in terms of clocking and conversion. The DCE is the device that converts the DTE voltage, signals, frequencies, and wiring to the required standards to be sent over the provider's network. Figure 10-1 displays different types of DCE equipment and which WAN technologies typically make use of them.

The three DCE devices depicted in Figure 10-1 are the most common. Modems are used for asynchronous communication and convert digital to analog and back to digital again. The acronym CSU/DSU represents Channel Service Unit/Data Service Unit, often used with WAN encapsulations that run over virtual circuits as assigned by the provider network. For practical purposes, you can think of them as digital modems. The Network Termination 1 (NT1) is used in ISDN BRI for converting the four-wire S/T connection to the two-wire connection to the provider. While there are many differences between these devices, all supply some form of clocking and all are considered DCE.

Other terminology that needs to be defined is CPE, CO, demarc, local loop, toll network, and cloud:

- **CPE**   Customer premise equipment is the telecommunications equipment that resides at the customer's site. The customer doesn't always own CPE equipment. It is terminating equipment such as routers, modems, CSU/DSUs, and NT1s at the customer's site.
- **CO**   Central office equipment is the equipment that resides at the provider's network. This term is the opposite of CPE. If it is not CPE, then it is CO equipment. Often, CO is used to refer to the switching equipment at the provider's location.
- **Demarc**   The demarcation point is where the CPE ends and the CO begins. It usually defines the equipment that the customer is responsible

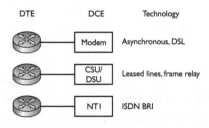

FIGURE 10.1   DCE equipment used for WAN technologies

for providing and maintaining and the equipment that the provider is responsible for maintaining.

- **Local loop**   The local loop is the area between the DCE equipment at the customer site and the switch at the provider; it is also called "the last mile."
- **Toll network**   The toll network is the equipment that makes up the provider's network. The toll network may extend to regional or international locations, which may involve long distance and toll charges for connection. The toll network might include more than one provider, which is often required when customer sites need to be connected.
- **Cloud**   This is a common way of referring to the toll network. It is descriptive of the "hidden" provider network used to connect two or more sites.

These terms are foundational for understanding WAN connections and will be used often throughout the discussions of WAN in this book.

There are three basic types of WAN networks. *Leased lines*, *packet-switched*, and *circuit-switched* are descriptive terms used to classify WAN networks.

- **Leased lines**   These networks are private point-to-point connections used to connect sites with constant demand. Leased lines can come in a variety of speeds from 56 Kbps up to 622 Mbps (OC-12). They offer a privacy factor that the other network types do not. The bandwidth supplied by the service provider will not be shared with anyone else; it is for the customer's private use. The downfall is in cost, as leased lines are very expensive to maintain. Since these networks are not shared, the cost is not shared. If there are long periods of low or no use, this is the wrong choice. This type should be used for connecting two locations requiring consistent bandwidth.
- **Packet-switched**   These networks are used by WAN technologies that forward based on virtual circuit (VC) numbers. Networks that make these types of connections are referred to as non-broadcast multiaccess networks (NBMA). These networks operate like LANs in that multiple devices connect to a single network; however, unlike LANs, they have no broadcast capability. Virtual circuits are a way of defining paths to remote sites. The frame entering a packet-switched network may transverse various service provider switches on the way to a destination. VC numbers point to the destination and are not concerned with which switches pass the frame. VC-based packet-switched networks include frame relay, X.25, and ATM. This type of network is ideal if connecting to locations separated by large geographic areas, and when permanent high-bandwidth connections are required for traffic that is bursty and not constant. The costs are based on usage, a pay-as-you-go provision. Links are shared, and so are costs.

- **Circuit-switched**   These networks are typically used for point-to-point technologies such as asynchronous dialup and ISDN. These technologies make use of the Public Switched Telephone Network (PSTN) to connect sites. Each of the technologies makes use of the two-wire telephone cabling, meaning that these technologies can be deployed almost anywhere throughout the United States. Use this type of network for lower bandwidth applications when periodic connections are required. Use ISDN for telecommuters who need to periodically download large files, and asynchronous dialup for mobile users checking e-mail or downloading small files.

WANs are similar to LANs in that both make use of a data link layer address to communicate with other devices. In a LAN, communication is not achieved by using only an IP or IPX network address. Ethernet, Token Ring, and FDDI all communicate by MAC addresses. These data link technologies do not understand IP. When an upper layer uses the IP address as the destination host, the layer is using logical communication. The destination IP host might not be on the same network as the local host and will have to be passed through a router. Data link layer communication will have to be established between every Layer 3 device in the path to the destination host and is done on a segment-by-segment basis. It is impossible for data link communication to span multiple LAN segments.

Most WAN protocols reside at the data link layer of the OSI. The only addressing these devices communicate by is their respective data link address formats. LANs use MAC addresses, but WAN protocols make use of various addresses depending on the technology. MAC addresses are burned into the device; the WAN data link address is typically not. Table 10-1 displays WAN technologies and their data link layer addressing.

TABLE 10.1	WAN Technology Data Link Layer Addresses	
WAN Protocol	**Data Link Address**	**Meaning**
Frame relay	DLCI	Data link connection identifier
ATM	NSAP	Network service access point
ISDN BRI	TEI	Terminal identifier
X.25	X.121	X.121 address
PPP	Not used	—

With some of these technologies, the data link address is statically configured, while with others it is dynamically configured. Frame relay and ATM may use both methods for obtaining their connection IDs. ISDN BRI will always dynamically be assigned its TEI. For point-to-point connections, it isn't always necessary to have a data link address. Since there can only be two stations connecting, there is no need to have the separate addressing. For PPP it is assumed that there are only two stations connecting, so IP addressing is sufficient.

Objective 10.02   HDLC and Synchronous Serial Connections

The High Data Link Control protocol is the forerunner to PPP. Like PPP, it is used to make connections across point-to-point links. Unlike PPP, there are multiple versions of HDLC, which is a standard defined by the ISO as a bit-oriented connection protocol. In the next section, it will be explained that PPP uses the ISO's HDLC frame format for the basis of the PPP frame. However, the HDLC described here isn't the HDLC used by Cisco routers. Cisco didn't implement the standard HDLC because it didn't support multiple network layer protocols simultaneously using the data link connection. This is because the HDLC frame didn't have a field to indicate the network protocol type. If the frame didn't have a way to distinguish between network layer protocols, it could not distinguish between IP and IPX packets, preventing multiprotocol support. Cisco modified the standard HDLC frame to include a "proprietary" field in the header. This field indicates the network layer protocol encapsulated in the HDLC frame, providing Cisco with a data link layer protocol that can be operated in a multiprotocol environment for point-to-point connections. In fact, Cisco HDLC is the default encapsulation for serial interfaces on Cisco routers.

HDLC is used primarily for synchronous serial lines. Asynchronous or modem communication requires an asynchronous protocol. This is because HDLC has another deficiency in that it doesn't support authentication. It wasn't built as a dialup protocol for asynchronous communication. Synchronous interfaces don't have to dial up and authenticate because these interfaces are always up and connected. SLIP, the forerunner to PPP, was the main option but only supported IP; there was no good choice for dialup connections in a multiprotocol environment. Networking was in need of a protocol that had multinetwork layer support and provided authentication—and the answer was PPP.

Objective 10.03 · Dialup Using Point-to-Point Protocol

Point-to-Point Protocol (PPP) not only fulfilled the multiprotocol and authentication requirements, it also was built with other features that make PPP the most capable asynchronous protocol ever designed, though asynchronous communication isn't the only serial communication supported. PPP can be run on almost any point-to-point serial connection. Specifically, PPP is supported on the following Cisco interfaces:

- Asynchronous serial
- Synchronous serial
- High-speed serial interface (HSSI)
- ISDN

Though ISDN is not a serial connection, it is point-to-point and usually implemented in dialup configurations requiring authentication and multiprotocol support. PPP is the best option for these types of connections. There are three main components to PPP:

- Network Control Protocol (NCP)
- Link Control Protocol (LCP)
- High Data Link Control (HDLC)

HDLC, while listed as a component of PPP, doesn't do anything for PPP. When PPP was created, the designers borrowed the HDLC frame format to use as the basis for the PPP frame. Therefore, the main two components that do all of the work for PPP are NCP and LCP.

Travel Advisory

A common mistake is to confuse Cisco's HDLC frame format with the frame that PPP was built upon. PPP was built on the ISO HDLC frame format.

LCP and NCP

LCP is the main component for making the data link connection. It negotiates the parameters and provides error detection for the link. Specifically, LCP provides the following four services:

- **Authentication** A Cisco router supports two authentication methods: Challenge Handshake Authentication Protocol (CHAP) and Password Authentication Protocol (PAP), offering excellent security and compatibility, respectively. The Cisco device also supports MS-CHAP so that Windows-based workstations and servers are able to authenticate to the router.
- **Compression** Cisco devices support three compression algorithms: stacker, predictor, and Microsoft Point-to-Point Compression (MPPC). Compression can be an important feature used for slower serial connections.
- **Multilink** This is a protocol used to bundle separate connections or channels into a single logical connection. Multilink is primarily used in ISDN BRI so that the two B channels can be bundled together into a single virtual connection. Before multilink, these connections were independent from one another, but now, the two channels can be aggregated together by using PPP.
- **Error detection** This is one of the options negotiated by LCP. It allows not only for error detection, but also for quality report packets to be sent when requested by network layer processes. These reports are quite extensive and comprehensive in describing the quality of the current connection. They can also be requested by SNMP for network management.

Travel Assistance

The error detection provided by LCP can be further studied by looking up RFC 1989 on the Internet. LCP is defined in RFC 2484, multilink in RFC 1990, and authentication in RFC 1334.

LCP provides most of the services that PPP offers. A service not mentioned in the preceding list is multinetwork layer protocol support. As described earlier, multiple network protocol support was lacking in SLIP and HDLC, so the creators of PPP created NCP to provide this service for PPP connections. NCP only

---

Exam Tip

A thorough understanding of LCP and NCP is crucial to understanding PPP. Because of the flexibility and power of PPP, this becomes an important objective for the CCNA program.

does one thing; it supports protocols such as IP and IPX to be sent out the serial interface over the PPP connection. For IP, this is accomplished using Internet Protocol Control Protocol (IPCP). For IPX, it is done through Internet Packet Exchange Control Protocol (IPXCP).

PPP Negotiation

When a PPP connection is initiated, PPP moves through three distinct phases:

- **Link establishment phase**   During this phase, options such as compression and link quality are negotiated. Many of the options are implemented only if both sides are configured for the option.
- **Authentication phase**   While this phase is optional, most of the time it is configured and required. This is when either PAP or CHAP authentication is negotiated. Unless both sides are configured for a common authentication option, authentication will fail. Therefore, if one side is not set for authentication, but the other requires it, the connection will fail. If one side requires CHAP and the other only PAP, the connection will also fail.
- **Network layer phase**   During this phase, NCP configures PPP to pass the network protocols configured on the device as just described.

The first two phases are done by LCP and the last by NCP.

PAP Authentication

PAP or CHAP may be used to authenticate the connection. PAP uses a two-way authentication process in which the username (or router hostname) and password are sent in clear text. The dialup device connects, and during the authentication phase, it sends the username and password. The authenticating router checks its database and either accepts or rejects the connection. The clear text password is a huge security hole because any packet-capturing program can decode the frame and see the password listed for the authentication process. PAP should only be used when compatibility is an issue. Some devices only support PAP, so that in some circumstances, PAP may be the only option, but because of the security limitations, it should be avoided for dialup connections.

CHAP Authentication

CHAP is the preferred authentication mechanism because it supports a three-way handshake in which a seed number is generated on the authenticating device by using the remote host's username and referring to its database for the corresponding username and password. The seed is sent in a packet as a challenge to the host. The host must use the seed number in connection with its username and password to generate a reply that is sent to the authenticating device. When the device receives the reply, it checks for a match. If it does, authentication is successful and options are negotiated. If not, the authentication fails and the connection is dropped.

CHAP increases security by using encryption so that the passwords are not presented in plain text. It also protects against "playback" attacks because a random number is used by the authenticating router for each connection. This prevents a hacker from recording the login packets from the dialup host and repeating them to the authenticating device. Another security measure in CHAP is that the three-step authentication process is initiated by the called system, preventing the caller from trying thousands of consecutive attempts at guessing a password.

Exam Tip

PAP is a poor authentication method and should be avoided. CHAP uses encryption so that passwords are secured. When setting up a dialup connection, CHAP should be used whenever possible.

Configuring Serial Connections Using HDLC and PPP

Objective 10.04

Configuration using HDLC is extremely simple on a Cisco router because it is the default encapsulation for synchronous serial interfaces. Data link protocols or encapsulations are always required for communication on interfaces.

Local Lingo

Protocol, encapsulation These terms are often used interchangeably. Encapsulation specifically refers to data link frames that are used to encapsulate packets. Protocol refers to rules that are used for communication purposes.

The router uses an encapsulation depending on the type of interface used. This can be changed at any time by using the **encapsulation** [*protocol*] command from interface configuration mode. By running the **encapsulation** ? command, the various protocols supported are listed:

```
Rack-02-AS(config-if)#encapsulation ?
  atm-dxi          ATM-DXI encapsulation
  bstun            Block Serial tunneling (BSTUN)
  frame-relay      Frame Relay networks
  hdlc             Serial HDLC synchronous
  lapb             LAPB (X.25 Level 2)
  ppp              Point-to-Point protocol
  sdlc             SDLC
  sdlc-primary     SDLC (primary)
  sdlc-secondary   SDLC (secondary)
  smds             Switched Megabit Data Service (SMDS)
  stun             Serial tunneling (STUN)
  x25              X.25
```

Configuring HDLC

In the following example, the encapsulation is going to be changed to x25 and then changed back to HDLC:

```
Rack-02-AS(config-if)#encap x25
Rack-02-AS(config-if)#
Rack-02-AS(config-if)#encap hdlc
Rack-02-AS(config-if)#
```

The command to view interface encapsulations is **show interface**. This command displays information on how the interface is presently configured and operating. In the output of **show interface serial 0**, the encapsulation is the default HDLC:

```
Serial0 is up, line protocol is up
  Hardware is HD64570
  MTU 1500 bytes, BW 1544 Kbit, DLY 20000 usec,
```

```
      reliability 255/255, txload 1/255, rxload 1/255
   Encapsulation HDLC, loopback not set
   Keepalive set (10 sec)
   Last input never, output never, output hang never
   Last clearing of "show interface" counters 00:03:11
   Input queue: 0/75/0/0 (size/max/drops/flushes); Total output drops: 0
   Queueing strategy: weighted fair
   Output queue: 0/1000/64/0 (size/max total/threshold/drops)
      Conversations  0/0/256 (active/max active/max total)
      Reserved Conversations 0/0 (allocated/max allocated)
   5 minute input rate 0 bits/sec, 0 packets/sec
   5 minute output rate 0 bits/sec, 0 packets/sec
      0 packets input, 0 bytes, 0 no buffer
      Received 0 broadcasts, 0 runts, 0 giants, 0 throttles
      0 input errors, 0 CRC, 0 frame, 0 overrun, 0 ignored, 0 abort
      0 packets output, 0 bytes, 0 underruns
      0 output errors, 0 collisions, 0 interface resets
      0 output buffer failures, 0 output buffers swapped out
      0 carrier transitions
      DCD=down  DSR=down  DTR=down  RTS=down  CTS=down
```

Because HDLC doesn't support many of the options that PPP does, **encapsulation hdlc** is the only command detailed here.

Configuring PPP

PPP is a feature-rich protocol, so the configuration is more complex. Setting the encapsulation on the interface is only the beginning of configuration options that may be used. For the CCNA level, basic configurations using authentication, compression, and multilink are presented next.

Once the command **encapsulation ppp** is entered on the serial or ISDN interface, a group of PPP command options becomes available, as follows:

```
Rack-02-R3(config-it)#ppp ?
  authentication  Set PPP link authentication method
  bap             Set BAP bandwidth allocation parameters
  bridge          Enable PPP bridge translation
```

```
callback        Set PPP link callback option
chap            Set CHAP authentication parameters
ipcp            Set IPCP negotiation options
lcp             PPP LCP configuration
link            Set miscellaneous link parameters
max-bad-auth    Allow multiple authentication failures
multilink       Make interface multilink capable
pap             Set PAP authentication parameters
quality         Set minimum Link Quality before link is down
reliable-link   Use LAPB with PPP to provide a reliable link
timeout         Set PPP timeout parameters
use-tacacs      Use TACACS to verify PPP authentications
```

The first command usually configured after the encapsulation is **ppp authentication**. Use either **ppp authentication chap** or **ppp authentication pap** to set up the authentication method. Below, the PPP interface is configured with CHAP authentication. For the authentication to succeed, the username and password that will be presented by the *remote* device are also entered, as follows:

```
Rack-02-R3(config)#int bri 0
Rack-02-R3(config-if)#encap ppp
Rack-02-R3(config-if)#ppp authentication chap
Rack-02-R3(config-if)#exit
Rack-02-R3(config)#username Rack-02-R6 password ccna
```

The username and password are critical issues when setting up dialup connections. On Windows devices, usernames usually are not case sensitive. On Cisco devices, however, the username as well as the password is case sensitive. In addition, by default when a router uses CHAP to authenticate, the hostname of the remote router is used. This means that when a username is configured for CHAP, it must be the remote hostname of the router authenticating.

Exam Tip

In reality, the username doesn't have to be the remote router's name. For flexibility, there are other PPP commands that can alter this behavior. However, while learning the CCNA material, assume that the username has to be the remote hostname.

When two routers are dialing each other using PPP, the username command will use the other router's hostname and vice versa, as seen in Table 10-2.

This basic configuration requires that the passwords be shared on the devices—and remember that usernames and passwords are case sensitive. In addition, the local router's hostname is never used for a username locally. The username is always the remote name.

Exam Tip

The remote name in the **username** command is case sensitive, as is the password.

Setting up basic multilink is a snap. This is done with the **ppp multilink** command entered on the interface. Compression is also easy to configure—to enable compression, just enter the command **compress [stac | predictor | mppc]**. As shown here, **multilink** and **compression** are added to the interface configuration:

```
Rack-02-R3(config-if)#ppp multilink
Rack-02-R3(config-if)#compress stac
Rack-02-R3(config-if)#
```

The basic commands for setting up PPP are summarized in Table 10-3.

TABLE 10.2   PPP Authentication Between Two Cisco Routers

RouterA Configuration	RouterB Configuration
encapsulation ppp	encapsulation ppp
ppp authentication chap	ppp authentication chap
hostname RouterA	hostname RouterB
username RouterB password IDENtical	username RouterA password IDENtical

TABLE 10.3 PPP Configuration and Troubleshooting Commands

Command	Description
encapsulation ppp	Enables the PPP protocol on the interface.
ppp authentication [chap | pap]	Enables CHAP or PAP authentication on the interface.
ppp multilink	Enables PPP multilink on the interface.
compress [stac | predictor]	Enables stacker or predictor compression on the interface.
hostname	Configures the name of the local router.
username [remote name] password [password]	Configures the username and password presented by the remote device of local authentication. These two devices must share an identical password.
show interface	Used to view the encapsulation and status of the interface.
debug ppp authentication	Displays the PPP authentication process in real time.
debug ppp negotiation	Displays the LCP and NCP negotiation process in real time.

CHECKPOINT

✔ **Objective 10.01: Overview of WAN Connectivity**   There are three types of WAN networks, described as leased lines, packet-switched, and circuit-switched. Leased lines are dedicated point-to-point connections. Packet-switched networks are VC-based multiaccess networks. Circuit-switched networks make use of the existing copper telephone wire to provide asynchronous dialup and ISDN almost everywhere. WAN technologies use data link addresses (as do LANs) to communicate between hosts on the same network segment.

✔ **Objective 10.02: HDLC and Synchronous Serial Connections**   While foundational to other point-to-point protocols, HDLC didn't offer many of the services that were needed for serial connections. Cisco modified the ISO format by adding a proprietary field in the HDLC header so that Cisco HDLC supports multiple network protocols for synchronous serial connections.

✔ **Objective 10.03: Dialup Using Point-to-Point Protocol**   PPP was developed in response to the need to secure serial communications, provide multiprotocol network layer support, and aggregate bandwidth. PPP has two main components, called NCP and LCP. NCP gives multiprotocol support while LCP negotiates authentication, compression, multilink, and error detection for connections.

✔ **Objective 10.04: Configuring Serial Connections Using HDLC and PPP** The **encapsulation** command is used to enable interface encapsulations for LAN and WAN connections. **encapsulation hdlc** and **encapsulation ppp** configure the HDLC and PPP protocols, respectively. PPP has many more options, and these powerful options can be implemented by using commands such as **ppp multilink, compress,** and **ppp authentication.**

REVIEW QUESTIONS

1. Which of the following protocols are used for WAN connections? (Choose three.)

   A. Token Ring

   B. SLIP

   C. HDLC

   D. FDDI

   E. PPP

2. Which of the following protocols are used in connection with VCs? (Choose two.)

   A. Frame relay

   B. ISDN

   C. Asynchronous dialup

   D. ATM

3. A network user wants to work from home and needs a WAN connection. This user needs to download and upload large CAD files periodically throughout the day. Which technology would you recommend?

    A. Asynchronous dialup

    B. ISDN

    C. Frame relay

    D. ATM

    E. Leased line

4. A salesperson needs to access his home network from customer sites to retrieve e-mail and documents. Which technology would you recommend?

    A. Asynchronous dialup

    B. ISDN

    C. Frame relay

    D. ATM

    E. Leased line

5. A business needs to connect to another building across town. The connection needs to be high-bandwidth, and exclusive use of the provider's facility is a requirement. Which technology would you recommend?

    A. Asynchronous dialup

    B. ISDN

    C. Frame relay

    D. ATM

    E. Leased line

6. A business needs to connect its Detroit operations to other sites in Los Angeles and New York. The connection needs to be inexpensive, but must supply high bandwidth. What technology would you recommend?

    A. Asynchronous dialup

    B. ISDN

    C. Frame relay

    D. ATM

    E. Leased line

7. Which of the following WAN technologies list the corresponding name of the data link address correctly?

    A. Frame relay—DLCI

    B. ISDN—SNAP

    C. X.25—NSAP

    D. PPP—TEI

8. Which of the following WAN types have the correct technologies associated with them? (Choose two.)

    A. Leased lines—Asynchronous serial

    B. Circuit-switched—Frame relay

    C. Packet-switched—ISDN

    D. Circuit-switched—Asynchronous

    E. Packet-switched—Frame relay

    F. Circuit-switched—Synchronous serial

    G. Packet-switched—ATM

9. Which definition best describes the toll network?

    A. The area between the DCE equipment at the customer site and the switch at the provider.

    B. A WAN connection to the service provider that is charged based on usage.

    C. The equipment that makes up the provider's network.

    D. The entire network beginning at the customer site, through the provider to other customer sites.

10. What type of connection does PPP support? (Choose two.)

    A. Asynchronous

    B. HSSI

    C. FDDI

    D. SDLC

    E. Etherchannel

REVIEW ANSWERS

1. **B** **C** and **E** Token Ring and FDDI are LAN protocols. By process of elimination, that leaves SLIP, HDLC, and PPP. SLIP and PPP are primarily used for asynchronous communications and HDLC is used for synchronous serial connections.

2. **A** and **D** Frame relay and ATM are both used by packet-switched networks. Packet-switched networks are multiaccess networks, meaning that multiple stations can be connected on a common network segment. ISDN and asynchronous dialup are typically point-to-point connections and categorized as a circuit-switched network.

3. **B** ISDN is clearly the correct answer here. One of the requirements was periodic connection, which is best suited for either asynchronous (modem) or ISDN connections. These technologies are always presented by Cisco as periodic connections. Another requirement was large CAD files, which asynchronous is not suitable for.

4. **A** Everything other than asynchronous dialup is overkill for this solution. Also, the other solutions don't supply the mobility required by a salesperson who is moving between customer sites.

5. **E** This required solution is too big for either ISDN BRI or asynchronous dialup. However, it must have "exclusive use of the provider's facility," which means that leased lines must be used. It is the only technology listed in which the bandwidth is not shared across the provider's network.

6. **C** Frame relay is probably the best choice here. ATM and leased lines are probably too expensive for what this scenario requires. Answers A and B are probably too slow for this.

7. **A** Frame relay uses a Data Link Connection Identifier (DLCI) for communication to other frame relay devices. ISDN uses a TEI, X.25 uses X.121, and PPP has no real data link address. Remember this rule when taking a test: if after studying, you don't recognize an answer from the material, tend not to choose it. This could have been used to quickly eliminate C.

8. **D** and **E** Based on this chapter, these are the best answers. Make sure that you don't reason yourself out of correct answers. Leased lines are presented as dedicated connections, while frame relay and ATM are packet-switched (ATM is cell-switched), leaving asynchronous serial and ISDN as circuit-switched.

9. **C** This is the definition used earlier in the chapter. The toll network is the sum of the "cloud" equipment, which is owned by service providers. Answer A is descriptive of the local loop and D is too broad, including the customer network.

10. **A** and **B** PPP supports most any serial connection, such as synchronous, asynchronous, and high-speed serial interface (HSSI). While PPP has been developed to run on Ethernet and ATM (PPPOE and PPPOA, respectively), this is outside of the CCNA course. CCNA questions should be viewed in light of the Cisco requirements. The CCNA curriculum is intended for foundational understanding, not to explore every technology available.

ISDN BRI Connections

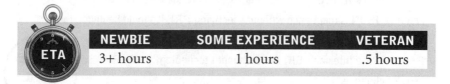

	NEWBIE	SOME EXPERIENCE	VETERAN
ETA	3+ hours	1 hours	.5 hours

333

This chapter's focus is to provide an overview of ISDN BRI technology and basic configuration commands. The first section describes why ISDN is still an important technology in WAN connectivity. The concept of channels, as well as an explanation of terminology and reference points, is an important foundation that has added benefits in that many other technologies make use of the foundation that ISDN has laid. After this, the configuration of ISDN on a router will be explained in two parts that focus on the core commands and on how Cisco presents ISDN as a dial-on-demand routing (DDR) technology. While there are other types of DDR, only Legacy DDR will be looked at for the CCNA.

Objective 11.01   The Importance of ISDN

As far as the CCNA exam is concerned, ISDN is an important objective. In fact, ISDN is an objective that is important throughout the CCNP and CCIE programs. Neither of the higher-level certifications can be passed without learning ISDN. ISDN is a broad topic that includes broadband ISDN, ISDN PRI, and ISDN BRI—the last is the centerpiece of Cisco ISDN discussions and implantations. The other ISDN subjects are not less important, but Cisco emphasizes ISDN BRI because of its availability and capabilities. Through the use of DDR technology, ISDN is implemented throughout the United States, from the smallest sites to the largest corporations. Many students seem to think that because ISDN BRI is much slower than DSL or cable modem technologies that it is not necessary. It is thought that ISDN is going away and that learning it is a waste of time.

Local Lingo

ISDN BRI, ISDN PRI This chapter explains ISDN BRI, not ISDN PRI. Anytime ISDN is mentioned without specifying PRI, it should be understood as ISDN BRI. BRI stands for Basic Rate Interface and PRI stands for Primary Rate Interface. BRI is a 3-channel technology, while PRI uses 24 channels.

ISDN isn't going anywhere for a while! It is a core WAN technology and has a huge installation base. The ISDN technology is used by frame relay and ATM. ISDN technologies such as Q series protocols are found in connection with frame relay. ISDN supports Q.931 and Q.921 for call setup and signaling, respectively.

Frame relay supports Q.931 and Q.921, and originally, frame relay was to be built upon ISDN.

One of the greatest assets of ISDN is that it is offered almost everywhere throughout the United States. DSL is offered only in certain locations, and some forms of DSL are limited for data being uploaded. ISDN BRI is full duplex and all digital. *Full duplex* means that while information is being downloaded at full speed, information can be uploaded at equal speed. *All digital* implies that it is useful for data, voice, and video applications. Because it is available throughout the U.S., ISDN also has value in corporate and branch office sites as a backup to frame relay connections. When a frame relay connection fails, Cisco routers can be programmed to bring up a secondary ISDN connection automatically. The following is a summary of ISDN benefits:

- Uses DDR (dial-on-demand routing) technology, which allows the connection to be made only when needed.
- Faster call setup than a modem, normally under five seconds.
- All digital communication both for inbound and outbound transfers.
- Greater speed than analog dialup. ISDN is 64K per channel with 16K on the D channel for a total bandwidth of 144K.
- Excellent for voice, video, and data requirements.
- Digital end-to-end using existing public switched telephone network using SS7 (signaling system 7).

Objective 11.02 ISDN Channels

ISDN is best described by explaining channels. Channels are common in WAN communications. Because of the long association of voice telecommunications and WAN, it is not surprising to find out that channels in WAN technologies are 64K. This is the lowest bandwidth to allow for voice-grade communications. Often a 64K channel is referred to as a voice channel. ISDN BRI is a three-channel technology made up of two bearer (B) channels and one delta (D) channel. The B channels are used for data and the D channel is used for signaling and call setup. The two data channels are 64K, while the D channel is only 16K. ISDN BRI media has a bit rate of 192K, which includes the bandwidth of the three channels plus some physical framing overhead. But this is different from the bandwidth.

It is often thought that bandwidth is a measurement of how much data is passed across a connection. While this is partially true, what most people miss is that, in some cases, the signaling is included in the bandwidth measurement. For instance, a 28.8 modem has a bandwidth of 28.8K. However, analog communication uses in-band signaling, which means that the signaling is mixed in with the data and uses up some of that precious bandwidth. No one separates the data from the signaling when talking about the bandwidth of the modem connection. This is not the case with ISDN. ISDN supports out-of-band signaling. This means that the signaling isn't mixed in with the data. The signaling is sent apart from the data in a separate channel. The B channels only carry data, and when the two are combined they can carry 128K; the D channel carries 16K of signaling. This makes the combined bandwidth of ISDN 144K, 128K of which can be used strictly for data.

Local Lingo

Bit rate, bandwidth   ISDN bit rate and bandwidth are two different things. The bit rate is the capacity of the physical media. For ISDN BRI the bit rate is 192K. The bandwidth is the combination of the data and signaling only. Two 64K B channels plus 16K of the D channel means that the bandwidth is 144K.

When thinking of channels, imagine a monorail station that has three monorail tracks in it. Each track has its own monorail train for passengers. When the trains leave the station, they follow their track to a location, and maybe two go to the same location. Channelized communication works in a similar fashion. The channels, like tracks, can be used to reach different destinations or aggregated to the same destination. Channelized communication provides flexibility and scalability.

Objective 11.03   # Terminology, Reference Points, and Cabling

ISDN terminology is different from other WAN technologies because ISDN is so intertwined with the telephone network. For ISDN there are two types of equipment, described as *terminal equipment 1* (TE1) and *terminal equipment 2* (TE2). TE1 is terminal equipment that has ISDN capability built in—for instance, routers with ISDN interfaces are TE1. It doesn't matter what type of ISDN interface is built in, just as long as it has an ISDN interface. TE2 is any device that doesn't have ISDN capability natively. This type of equipment must have some type of external device to allow it to communicate using ISDN technology. An easy way to remember the difference between TE1 and TE2 is by the numbers. Let the 1 in TE1 equipment represent the best as far as ISDN is concerned. Here, "best" means native ISDN capability. The 2 in TE2 can then represent second-best equipment, meaning that it doesn't support ISDN natively. Just because the equipment is TE2 doesn't mean it can't be used in conjunction with ISDN. External devices such as an external ISDN modem or a terminal adapter (TA) can be used to add ISDN capability to the device. When adding the TA, the equipment essentially becomes TE1.

Reference Points and Devices Defined

Before continuing this thought, reference points must be explained. A *reference point* is used to describe requirements in equipment, interfaces, cabling, and many other specifications, such as voltage and signaling between equipment. Figure 11-1 presents all of the ISDN reference points necessary for understanding ISDN.

In Figure 11-1, there are two reference points that are combined, the S and the T. They actually are divided by an NT2; however, the two reference points are often combined as they are here. In fact, combining these two makes it easier to understand ISDN, as you will see later when we discuss the two types of ISDN interfaces. The following is a description for each reference point and device:

- Reference points:
  - **R reference point (rate reference point)**   Used for specifications between the TE2 and the TA devices.

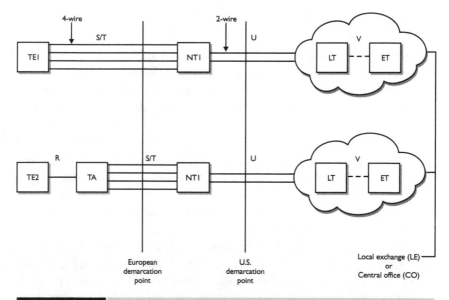

| FIGURE 11.1 | ISDN reference points |

- **S/T reference point (system/terminal reference point)**   Used for specifications between the TE1 and the NT1 devices.
- **U reference point (user reference point)**   Used for specifications between the NT1 and the LT devices.
- **V reference point**   Used for specifications between the LT and the ET.

- Devices and terminology:
  - **CO (central office)**   The ISDN provider's network. It is synonymous with LE (local exchange).
  - **TE1 (terminal equipment 1)**   A device that has ISDN digital capability built in.
  - **TE2 (terminal equipment 2)**   A device without ISDN capability built in. Typically an analog phone, modem, or PC.
  - **TA (terminal adapter)**   Used to make an analog TE2 device ISDN compatible.
  - **NT1 (network termination 1)**   Used to terminate CPE equipment and convert the four-wire S/T interface to the two-wire U interface.
  - **ET (exchange termination)**   Logical connection used to connect customers to the CO.
  - **LT (line termination)**   Functions like NT1, but located at the CO. This is the physical connection from the customer to the CO.

S/T and U Interfaces

Returning to the explanation of Figure 11-1, notice that there are two demarcation points, one in the U reference area and one in the S/T reference area. These are important because the demarcation point is the boundary between the CPE equipment and the CO equipment. In the U.S., the demarcation point is in the U reference area making the NT1 customer premise equipment (CPE). However, in Europe the demarcation is in the S/T reference area, which means the NT1 is CO equipment. This is important when connecting ISDN equipment because, if connecting the equipment in the United States, the customer is responsible for providing the NT1; in Europe, the CO provides it.

When it comes to interfaces, ISDN devices come in two different flavors: S/T and U interfaces. The difference is whether the NT1 is built in or not. With S/T interfaces, the NT1 isn't built into the device. If it is used in the United States, an external NT1 must be provided to make the ISDN connection to the provider. In Europe, an S/T interface is all that is required; the CO will take care of the NT1. Some Cisco devices come with both interfaces built into the device. The two interfaces do not mean that two ISDN cable connections can be made; rather, one of the other may be used. For example, routers like the 766 have both interfaces so they can be sold in Europe or the U.S.

Exam Tip

The location of the NT1 in reference to a given demarcation point is important for CCNA as well as allowing the correct interfaces on a device to be selected for a given router solution.

When connecting ISDN devices, make sure you know what type of ISDN interface is on the device. Many times the interface isn't marked with an S/T or a U. Care should be taken when making connections so that the interface type is determined before the devices are connected. An NT1 should never be plugged into a router with a U interface. Not only is it unnecessary because the U indicates that the NT1 is built in, but the NT1's four-wire S/T interface plugged into the router's two-wire U interface can damage the equipment.

Travel Advisory

Never plug an NT1 into a U interface. Doing so may damage the equipment.

Cabling ISDN

For cabling, CAT5 is typically used for ISDN connections. The S/T interface uses the middle four wires (pins 3, 4, 5, 6) to connect to an external NT1. The U interface also makes use of CAT5 cable, but only two wires are used. See Table 11-1 for a description of these two interfaces. These two wires are the same as any telephone cabling. ISDN technology provides high availability because it uses the same two-wire copper telephone connection to the provider. Unlike ADSL, ISDN cannot share the existing telephone connections; instead, the provider will install another all-digital connection used for the ISDN. Because the ISDN provides two voice channels, the ISDN can replace the normal telephone lines. The benefit is that they are all-digital quality, but the drawback is that if power is lost, so is the telephone service. Each B channel has a phone number associated with it that can be used like any other telephone number.

TABLE 11.1	ISDN Interfaces
S/T Interface	**U Interface**
4-wire interface	2-wire interface
Straight-through cabling	Straight-through cabling
External NT1 required	NT1 built in

Many providers use SPIDs (service provider IDs) which may look something like 72486124310101. In this SPID, the phone number is (724) 861-2431, and the 0101 is appended on the end. The phone number portion can be used just like any other telephone number.

When cabling ISDN, usually CAT5 cables with two RJ45 ends are used. It is sometimes necessary to use an RJ45 connection to the router and an RG11 connector to the wall jack. Today, providers typically install RJ45 wall jacks for ISDN, but because both wall jacks are used, many companies ship ISDN cabling with the router that has an RJ45 connector on one side and RG11 on the other. TE2 equipment will require additional cabling.

A terminal adapter is usually required to connect TE2 equipment to ISDN. It provides full ISDN capability so that with the addition of the TA, the equipment functions as a TE1 device. To put it in mathematical terms, a TE2 plus a TA equals a TE1. However, this is only partially true. TA devices are usually external and provide great flexibility, allowing several other analog devices to be connected via ISDN. The drawback with this is that only two may be in use at any given time. Multiple TAs can be used to connect up to eight devices, but each TA counts as one device. The limitation of no more than two devices transmitting simultaneously greatly limits the number of devices that are used within an office. Often a three-port TA will be used for three devices such as a PC, fax, and telephone. If these devices need continuous use of the ISDN, this solution will not work. Most of the time, the ISDN connection is not continually used. For these situations, the TA can be helpful in providing connectivity to these devices.

ITU ISDN D Channel Protocols

Protocols used in ISDN D channel communication can be categorized as E, I, and Q series protocols. These three series are as follows:

- E series defines telephone network. Specifically, addressing and international phone numbering are defined for ISDN.
- I series deals with concepts, terminology, and interfaces.
- Q series is used for switching and signaling; this would primarily be concerned with the D channel. Link Access Procedure Delta (LAPD) is defined by the Q.921 specification. Also, Q.931 defines call setup and teardown for the ISDN connection.

When considering ISDN, it should be understood as a three-layer technology. Table 11-2 below lists the layers and the corresponding protocols.

The layers help to describe terminology and functions for ISDN.

ISDN B Channel Protocols

While many protocols can be used to configure ISDN B channels, for Cisco, there are primarily two that are discussed: PPP and HDLC. These protocols are discussed in detail in Chapter 10. The main difference between D and B channel protocols is that D channel protocols are used between the CPE and the CO to establish communication with the switch and set up the B channels. B channel protocols are used for the actual router-to-router connections between two sites so that data can be passed. D channel protocols deal with switching functions and data link addressing.

Exam Tip

Two protocols often used for the B channels on Cisco equipment are PPP and HDLC.

TABLE 11.2	The Three Layers of ISDN
Layer	**Protocol/Description**
3	ISDN Q.931
2	LAPD Q.921
1	Framing/bits

Objective 11.04 Core Configuration Commands

Configuring ISDN on Cisco equipment can also be broken into a two-part configuration. The first part can be referred to as the core or basic ISDN configuration. The second part will be covered later and deals with dial-on-demand routing.

Configuring ISDN

The core ISDN setup involves three steps:

1. Configure the switch type.
2. Enter the BRI interface encapsulation.
3. Configure the two SPIDs if required by the provider.

The very first step in configuring ISDN on a Cisco router is to enter the ISDN switch type. The **isdn switch-type** global configuration command is used to select the switch that the provider is using. In Table 11-3, switch types available around the world are listed; the ones used in North America appear first.

When the ISDN is installed, the provider will supply the necessary settings for configuring the ISDN devices. The switch type specified in these settings must be configured first.

TABLE 11.3 ISDN Switch Types

Switch Type	Country/Region
Basic-5ess (AT&T)	United States
Basic-dms (Northern Telecom)	North America
Basic-ni (National ISDN)	North America
Basic-net3	U.K., Europe, Asia, and Australia
ntt	Japan
vn3	France
basic-1tr6	Germany

Before the core configuration commands are entered, the status of the three ISDN layers can be viewed with the **show isdn status** command as follows. Notice that none of the layers listed in the output is functioning, because the ISDN commands have not yet been entered.

```
Rack-02-R3#show isdn status
 **** No Global ISDN Switchtype currently defined ****
ISDN BRI0 interface
        dsl 0, interface ISDN Switchtype = none
    Layer 1 Status:
      DEACTIVATED
    Layer 2 Status:
        TEI = 106, Ces = 1, SAPI = 0, State = TEI_ASSIGNED
        TEI = 107, Ces = 2, SAPI = 0, State = TEI_ASSIGNED
    Layer 3 Status:
        0 Active Layer 3 Call(s)
    Active dsl 0 CCBs = 0
    The Free Channel Mask:  0x80000003
    Total Allocated ISDN CCBs = 0
Rack-02-R3#
```

The switch type may be entered from global configuration or interface configuration mode by using the command **isdn switch-type**. If configuring an ISDN router that connects to only one provider, put the command in at global configuration. However, sometimes an ISDN router might have many BRI interfaces connecting to more than one provider, so that the switch type should be entered on the individual interface.

Exam Tip

The **isdn switch-type** command can be entered at global configuration mode, interface configuration mode, or both.

After entering the switch type, the encapsulation should be changed on the ISDN interface. PPP is usually required for most ISDN installations and is configured using the **encapsulation PPP** command as described in Chapter 10.

Service provider IDs (SPIDs) are required by DMS-100 and National ISDN and are configured on the interface. SPIDs identify the customer's level of service.

The commands **isdn spid1** and **isdn spid2** are used on the interface followed by the SPID numbers supplied by the provider. In the router configuration example that follows, the switch type, encapsulation, and SPIDs are configured:

```
Rack-02-R3(config)#interface bri 0
Rack-02-R3(config-if)#isdn switch-type basic-ni
Rack-02-R3(config-if)#encapsulation ppp
Rack-02-R3(config-if)# isdn spid1 0835866101
Rack-02-R3(config-if)# isdn spid2 0835866301
```

It should be observed that **spid1** and **spid2** don't use a space between the word spid and the number. Also, the numbers begin with 1, not 0. Although the switch type could have been entered at global configuration mode, here it was configured on the BRI interface.

Exam Tip

Service provider identifiers (SPIDs) are required by DMS-100 and National ISDN and are configured on the interface. A SPID identifies the customer's level of service.

These three commands are all that are required for setting up basic ISDN. To verify that things are working correctly to this point, the **show isdn status** command should be entered again, and Layers 1 and 2 should now be functioning as shown here:

```
Rack-02-R3#show isdn status
Global ISDN Switchtype = basic-ni
ISDN BRI0 interface
        dsl 0, interface ISDN Switchtype = basic-ni
    Layer 1 Status:
        ACTIVE
    Layer 2 Status:
        TEI = 108, Ces = 1, SAPI = 0, State = MULTIPLE_FRAME_ESTABLISHED
        TEI = 109, Ces = 2, SAPI = 0, State = MULTIPLE_FRAME_ESTABLISHED
        TEI 108, ces = 1, state = 5(init)
            spid1 configured, no LDN, spid1 sent, spid1 valid
            Endpoint ID Info: epsf = 0, usid = 1, tid = 1
```

```
        TEI 109, ces = 2, state = 5(init)
            spid2 configured, no LDN, spid2 sent, spid2 valid
            Endpoint ID Info: epsf = 0, usid = 3, tid = 1
    Layer 3 Status:
        0 Active Layer 3 Call(s)
    Active dsl 0 CCBs = 0
    The Free Channel Mask:  0x80000003
    Total Allocated ISDN CCBs = 0
Rack-02-R3#
```

At this point, D channel communication is established with the provider's switch, and DDR can then be configured on the device. Unlike the B channels, the D channel should always be connected. This is one of the reasons that ISDN call setup is far quicker than a modem. The D channel stays up, and when a call needs to be made, the router signals the provider's switch across this channel. The typical ISDN call is connected in less than five seconds. If the output of **show isdn status** doesn't look like the one just presented, do not proceed to DDR configuration. If there isn't "MULTIPLE_FRAME_ESTABLISHED" twice with two TEIs and the SPIDs listed as valid, the router isn't communicating with the switch properly. When communication with the switch is established correctly, the next phase of configuration can be implemented.

Objective 11.05   Dial-on-Demand Routing

After basic D channel setup is achieved, the router is ready to be configured to call a remote site. The configuration used for connecting to a remote site is called dial-on-demand routing (DDR). When configuring DDR, it is assumed that the switch type, encapsulation, and SPIDs have all been configured and communication with the provider's switch has been achieved. The setting up of the IP address, authentication, and dialing parameters are all part of DDR setup.

Whenever Cisco describes ISDN, they present it as an "on demand" technology. This means that the connection is not made until a need for the connection arises. On other vendor equipment, ISDN can be a "nailed up" or permanent connection. In the Cisco IOS, there is no such equivalent when using PPP encapsulation. While there are ways to keep the ISDN connection up all the time, all of them are indirect. There is no single command that is designed to specify the connection as permanent. This is for good reason. ISDN BRI was designed so that devices could share the channels. This sharing requires that one device doesn't constantly make use of the channel so that devices make use of the connection as needed. Even when used as a backup to frame relay, the ISDN line is a temporary connection that is used only when the primary fails. While other venders give the capability of permanent connections, Cisco router configuration is designed for periodic connection.

The following steps describe how the DDR connection is made when the BRI interface is idle:

1. A routing table lookup is performed on the destination address in the IP header.
2. A next-hop address and outgoing interface are determined.
3. The packet is sent to the interface and a determination is made using the **dialer-group** and **dialer-list** commands as to whether this traffic is important enough to dial the remote site.
4. If the traffic is determined "interesting," which means it is important enough to dial the remote connection, the router looks for a dialer statement containing a phone number, which it uses to dial.
5. After the connection is authenticated, all traffic intended for this remote connection is sent over the link.
6. If the data being passed over the connection doesn't contain any interesting traffic, the idle timeout will begin. This timer starts at 120 seconds by default, and if it reaches zero, it will disconnect the call even if non-interesting traffic is still flowing. If while the connection is up and the idle timeout has begun to count down, interesting traffic passes the link, it will reset the timer to 120. When there is no interesting traffic, it will begin to count down again.

When setting up DDR, three basic steps should be performed:

1. **Configure a static route.** To have data sent to any interface on a router, there must be a route in the routing table. Static routes are usually used for small sites and will direct the traffic to the BRI interface in order to reach the remote site.
2. **Define interesting traffic.** This is done by using two commands. On the interface, the **dialer-group** [*group number*] command is used to determine what traffic is considered interesting. The group number specified by this command is used to reference the second command, **dialer-list**. The **dialer-list** [*group number*] global configuration command is used to define what is interesting. It can be used in conjunction with an access list to limit what is interesting.
3. **Configure the dialer statement.** The dialer statement is generally specified by the **dialer-map interface** command. There are many options to this command, such as the protocol, next-hop router IP address and name, and phone number.

The configuration that follows illustrates how these steps are implemented:

```
Rack-02-R2#config term
Enter configuration commands, one per line.  End with CNTL/Z.
Rack-02-R2(config)#ip route 140.10.200.0 255.255.255.0 140.10.20.2
Rack-02-R2(config)#dialer-list 1 protocol ip permit
Rack-02-R2(config)#int bri 0
Rack-02-R2(config-if)#ip address 140.10.20.1 255.255.255.0
Rack-02-R2(config-if)#dialer-group 1
Rack-02-R2(config-if)#dialer map ip 140.10.20.2 broadcast name
            rack02 8358662
```

All three elements of DDR are present. The static route is defined from global configuration mode. The IP at the end of the static route statement is the IP address of the router on the remote site, which is the next-hop address for traffic being sent out the interface. The order of the commands entered isn't important for these basic ones, so the dialer list is entered while still at global configuration mode. This dialer list means that everything IP-based is interesting and will trigger the call when passed to the interface; however, IPX and other traffic will not trigger the call. Group number 1 is assigned to the dialer list. After this is done, the interface commands are configured. The IP address is entered, as is the **dialer-group** command. The dialer group has to match the dialer list group number, which it does. Finally, the dialer map is used to say that any traffic destined for the IP gateway address of 140.10.20.2, with the router name rack02, should dial 8358662. The broadcast parameter is optional and allows broadcast traffic to be sent across the link.

Care should be taken when configuring DDR because there are many "gotchas" that can make a configuration fail to work. Hostnames and passwords are always case sensitive—one mistake in one letter can mean the difference between a working and non-working configuration (Chapter 10 explains this further). Another common mistake is often made when configuring the static route. If the router must dial out to a remote site, the static route must have an IP gateway address, not just an interface configured. For instance, the following output is legal to use on point-to-point ISDN connections; however, because the IP-gateway "bri 0" doesn't match the dialer map IP gateway "140.10.20.2", the router will not dial out:

```
Rack-02-R2(config-if)#dialer map ip 140.10.20.2 name rack02 broadcast 8358662
Rack-02-R2(config-if)#exit
Rack-02-R2(config)#ip route 140.10.200.0 255.255.255.0 bri 0
```

If this router only needed to receive calls, this configuration would work, although the telephone number 8358662 would be unnecessary for this and ignored.

While these three steps are used to configure DDR, they are not the only commands that may be required. DDR configuration is often complex, requiring many commands to configure items such as authentication and multilink. A complete solution might look something like what is presented here:

```
username Rack02 password 7 00071A150754
isdn switch-type basic-ni1
interface BRI0
     ip address 140.10.20.1 255.255.255.0
     encapsulation ppp
     isdn spid1 0835866201
     isdn spid2 0835866401
     dialer map ip 140.10.20.2 name rack02 broadcast 8358662
     dialer-group 1
     ppp authentication chap
     ppp multilink
ip route 140.10.200.0 255.255.255.0 140.10.20.2
dialer-list 1 protocol ip permit
```

This configuration has all the elements of core ISDN configuration, including the switch type, encapsulation, and SPIDs. All the other commands are part of configuring DDR. Added to the configuration were the **username, ppp authentication chap**, and **ppp multilink** commands, which are commonly used with ISDN solutions.

Below is an output of **show dialer** which shows BRI channel information such as if the connection is idle or dialed in, what triggered the call, and how long until it will be disconnected:

```
Rack-02-R2#show dialer
BRI0 - dialer type = ISDN
Dial String      Successes   Failures    Last called   Last status
8358661              12          0         00:00:07      successful
0 incoming call(s) have been screened.
BRI0:1 - dialer type = ISDN
Idle timer (120 secs), Fast idle timer (20 secs)
Wait for carrier (30 secs), Re-enable (15 secs)
Dialer state is data link layer up
```

```
Dial reason: ip (s=140.10.20.1, d=140.10.20.2)
Time until disconnect 114 secs
Connected to 8358661 (Rack02)

BRI0:2 - dialer type = ISDN
Idle timer (120 secs), Fast idle timer (20 secs)
Wait for carrier (30 secs), Re-enable (15 secs)
Dialer state is idle
```

From the output, it can be seen that the call was successfully connected and was triggered by interesting traffic, which originated from the IP address 140.10.20.1 and was destined for 140.10.20.2. The "time until disconnect 114 secs" means that it has been six seconds since interesting traffic passed the link; 120 is the default. If 114 seconds pass without receiving interesting traffic, the connection will be terminated. Also, it can be seen that BRI0:2 (the second B channel) is not presently dialed in, but BRI0:1 is.

CHECKPOINT

✔ **Objective 11.01: The Importance of ISDN**   While other technologies now available are faster than ISDN, they don't have the broad availability of ISDN. The standards used are important and can help in understanding other WAN technologies such as frame relay. ISDN standards are well established and by making use of the Public Switched Telephone Network (PSTN), ISDN will be available and in use for many years to come.

✔ **Objective 11.02: ISDN Channels**   Channels are often used in WAN communications. They provide flexibility for bandwidth requirements, scalability, and excellent voice capabilities. ISDN is optimized for voice, video, and data applications. The ability to handle these established ISDN as a core WAN technology.

✔ **Objective 11.03: Terminology, Reference Points, and Cabling**   To understand ISDN, key terms like CPE, CO, TE, NT, and demarcation must be understood. Knowing these terms isn't enough, though; ISDN uses reference points when defining standards the terminology describes. Two of the most important reference points are the S/T and the U that describe the standards among the TE, the NT, and the LT.

✔ **Objective 11.04: Core Configuration Commands** There are two parts to setting up an ISDN connection: core commands and DDR commands. The core commands are used to establish D channel communication with the provider's switch. The commands that are used for this are **isdn switch-type**, **encapsulation PPP**, **isdn spid1**, and **isdn spid2**.

✔ **Objective 11.05: Dial-on-Demand Routing** DDR is best used with ISDN because the technology is suited for small sites that need periodic WAN access. Even though it can be very complex depending on the needs, basic setup can be performed with three steps: defining the route, specifying interesting traffic, and configuring the dialer information.

REVIEW QUESTIONS

1. ISDN supports applications such as...? (Choose three.)

 A. Video

 B. Voice

 C. PVC

 D. SVC

 E. Data

2. Which of the following statements are descriptive of ISDN? (Choose three.)

 A. ISDN is used for small office permanent connections.

 B. ISDN provides digital communication for download and analog for uploads.

 C. ISDN uses SS7 signaling.

 D. ISDN has faster connection setup than a modem.

 E. ISDN uses out-of-band signaling.

 F. ISDN uses in-band signaling.

3. ISDN makes use of which of the following channels?

 A. One B and one C

 B. Two B and two C

 C. Three B and one D

 D. Two B and one D

 E. Two B and two A

4. What is the bit rate of ISDN BRI?

  A. 128
  B. 64
  C. 144
  D. 56
  E. 192

5. In the United States, which of the following equipment is CPE? (Choose three.)

  A. LE
  B. TE2
  C. TA
  D. LT
  E. NT1

6. What type of interface would you purchase on a router if you wanted to just plug it in and work in the United States?

  A. U
  B. S/T
  C. R
  D. V
  E. RJ45
  F. RG11

7. When cabling a U interface, an NT1 should be plugged in before connecting to a wall-jack.

  A. True
  B. False

8. In what way does a TE2 device differ from a TE1?

  A. A TE2 device is directly connected to an NT1 when using the S/T bus for device sharing.
  B. A TE1 is directly connected to an NT1 when using the V bus for device sharing.
  C. A TA is directly connected to a TE2 when using the S/T bus for device sharing.
  D. An NT2 is directly connected to an ET when using the S/T bus for device sharing.

REVIEW ANSWERS

1. **A** **B** and **E** ISDN supports video, voice, and data applications and is all-digital, which means higher quality connections. PVCs and SVCs are reserved for packet-switching networks. ISDN is circuit-switched.

2. **C** **D** and **E** ISDN has the following benefits as listed earlier in the chapter:
   - Uses DDR (dial-on-demand routing) technology, which allows the connection to be made only when needed.
   - Faster call setup than a modem.
   - All-digital communication from end to end.
   - Greater speed than dialup. ISDN is 64K per channel and can be aggregated to a bandwidth of 144K.
   - Excellent for voice, video, and data requirements.
   - Digital end-to-end using existing public switched telephone network using SS7 (signaling system 7).

3. **D** ISDN BRI makes use of two 64K voice quality channels known as bearer (B) channels. It uses one 16K signaling channel known as the delta (D) channel.

4. **E** The bit rate is 192K. This consists of 48-bit frames sent 4000/second. The 48 bits consist of 16 bits for each of the two B channels, 4 bits for the D channel, and 12 bits for managing physical layer framing.

5. **B** **C** and **E** Because the demarcation point is in the U reference area, the customer premise equipment (CPE) is listed here:
   - TE1
   - TE2
   - TA
   - NT1
   - NT2

   If the location had been Europe, NT1 would be omitted from the list.

6. **A** Because the demarcation point is in the U reference area and the U interface means that an NT1 is built in, A is the best answer. However, in Europe, the CPE would provide an S/T interface router.

7. **B** This is not only false, but could also destroy the equipment. Never plug an NT1 into a U interface on a router. The U interface supports two wires for transmit and receive; the S/T has four wires for this.

8. **C** The S/T bus is between the TA and the NT1. A TE2 device must be plugged into a TA to work with ISDN. Eight devices can share the S/T bus for ISDN communication. There is no V bus between the TE1 and NT1; this is the S/T reference point. The V reference point is between the LT and ET. Remember that you cannot connect TE2 equipment directly into an NT1.

Frame Relay Connections

CHAPTER 12

ETA	NEWBIE	SOME EXPERIENCE	VETERAN
	3+ hours	1 hours	.5 hours

355

Frame relay is an ANSI and ITU-T standard used to pass data over a public data network (PDN). In Chapter 11, ISDN was described as a WAN technology that makes use of the PSTN (Public Switched Telephone Network). Frame relay doesn't make use of phone connections; rather, it requires a data-switching network called a public data network (PDN). This network passes data based on virtual connection numbers, which are associated with a given location. These virtual connections are like logical tunnels that identify a destination. There are two types of these virtual circuits, called switched virtual circuits (SVC) and permanent virtual circuits (PVC). The former are rarely used with frame relay, because most providers implement their frame relay using permanent virtual circuits.

Objective 12.01 Introduction and Frame Relay Terminology

To explain frame relay, some of the most common terminology is defined in this section. We suggest that after reading through the entire chapter, you should return and review this terminology again for reinforcement.

- **Committed information rate (CIR)**   The total amount of bits per second that the provider guarantees to transmit. This differs from ISDN; with CIR, when the customer orders frame relay, there is no set bandwidth. The amount paid for the frame relay will be based on bandwidth needed. The CIR is not the total bandwidth the customer may use, it is the guaranteed bandwidth that the customer will receive. For instance, the customer might order a circuit with a 768 Kbps CIR using a T1 speed connection. The customer might be able to attain throughput approaching 1.5 Mbps, but the provider only guarantees that the customer will receive 768 Kbps.
- **Local access rate**   The speed of the connection between the frame relay router and provider switch (the local loop). This is the clock rate configured for the connection.
- **Permanent virtual circuit (PVC)**   This is discussed in Chapter 10, but is repeated here, because this is the primary way that frame relay passes information from one site to another. The PVC is simply a virtual connection that is set up across the provider's network to move information from one location to another. Even though the actual path across the provider's network will vary, it is best to think of the PVC as a tunnel connecting one site to another.
- **Data link connection identifier (DLCI)**   Roughly the equivalent of a MAC address in a LAN environment, the DLCI is frame relay's data link

addressing. Think of the DLCI as the number of the PVC that is used to reach a remote destination. DLCIs are locally significant, which means that a given DLCI is used locally to reach the remote site, but the remote site needs a DLCI assigned to the tunnel. Often the DLCIs are the same number on both ends. More often they aren't. Think of the tunnel as the one that connects England and France. On the England side, the tunnel is labeled "France" because that identifies where it leads from England. The other side uses the "England" label.

- **Encapsulation type**   Frame relay encapsulation, which is used between two routers. Unlike LMI, encapsulation must agree from end to end. If two routers located at different sites are connected by a frame relay network, the encapsulations must be configured the same on both ends. On a Cisco router there are two choices: IETF, which must be used to connect to non-Cisco routers, and Cisco, which is proprietary and requires other Cisco routers to work.

- **Local management interface (LMI)**   Data link layer signaling between the local router and the provider's switch. As the name suggests, it is responsible for management of this connection. It reports to the router information originating from the provider's network. The LMI signaling reports the status of the PVCs in the provider's network giving information on congestion, DLCI assignment, and statistics. The LMI uses a reserved DLCI (which should not be confused with other DLCI numbers assigned for data) for PVC messages. For Cisco LMI type, the reserved DLCI is 1023. The following is an output of **show interface serial 0** showing the LMI type of Cisco and its reserved DLCI 1023. In versions 11.2 and later of the Cisco IOS, the LMI is auto-sensed.

```
Serial0 is up, line protocol is up
  Hardware is HD64570 with 5-in-1 module
  Internet address is 140.10.18.3/28
  (Output Omitted)
  LMI enq sent  9502, LMI stat recvd 9502, LMI upd recvd 0, DTE LMI up
  LMI enq recvd 0, LMI stat sent  0, LMI upd sent  0
  LMI DLCI 1023  LMI type is CISCO  frame relay DTE
```

For frame relay there are three types of LMI:

- **Cisco**   An LMI developed through a joint adventure between Cisco and other companies.
- **ANSI**   Annex D, as described in the ANSI standard T1.617.
- **Q933a**   Referred to as ITU-T Q.933 Annex A referenced in FRF.1.1.

Exam Tip

Be aware that there are two encapsulations (IETF and Cisco) and three LMI (Cisco, ANSI, and ITU-T Q.933a). When learning the LMI types, learn the last one mentioned as ITU-T Q.933a, not just Q.933a.

Congestion Avoidance

The following three terms are fields located in the frame relay frame header. These are three 1-bit fields that can contain the value of 1 or 0 (meaning on or off, respectively). The first two of these terms are used to indicate congestion in the provider's network. Frame relay will always do what is necessary to avoid congestion. If the congestion continues after the following mechanisms are used, frame relay will drop all frames necessary to reduce the congestion.

- **Discard Eligible (DE)**   Any frames sent to the provider's network above the agreed CIR have the DE bit set to 1. If there is ample bandwidth across the provider's network, data in excess of the CIR may be passed to the remote location. If congestion occurs within the provider's network, the frames with the DE bit turned on will be discarded first to free up bandwidth.
- **Backward Explicit Congestion Notification (BECN)**   It is usually best to stop congestion by notifying the sender that congestion has occurred and that it should reduce its rate of output. BECNs accomplish this; the frame relay switch experiencing congestion will wait for a frame sourced from the destination network. It will set the BECN bit to 1 as it forwards this frame to the source router, so that it will reduce its output rate.
- **Forward Explicit Congestion Notification (FECN)**   It is generally not effective to tell the destination that congestion is occurring; rather, it is the source that needs to know so it can reduce its rate of output. When the switch senses congestion, it sets the FECN bit in a frame moving to the destination, notifying the destination that congestion has occurred.

Multiaccess

Frame relay terminology is often tricky and hard to understand. Because frame relay is a multiaccess technology, one site may be connected to many other sites. These sites may not need high throughput, and a single router interface will be used to connect to many remote sites. There are various options available for setting up these connections that can make things complex. The following is an example of a frame relay installation connecting to several sites using only two serial interfaces:

```
Rack-03-RA
interface serial0
 no ip address
 encapsulation frame-relay
 frame-relay lmi-type ansi
!
interface serial0.20 point-to-point
 ip address 10.128.30.17 255.255.255.248
 frame-relay interface-dlci 102
!
interface serial0.30 point-to-point
 ip address 10.128.30.5 255.255.255.248
 ip ospf cost 200
 frame-relay interface-dlci 103
!
interface serial 1
 no ip address
 encapsulation frame-relay
 !
interface serial1.2 multipoint
 ip address 100.120.20.13 255.255.255.248
 frame-relay map ip 100.120.20.6 180 ietf broadcast
frame-relay map ip 100.120.20.7 189 cisco broadcast
ip ospf network non-broadcast
!
interface serial1.3 point-to-point
 ip address 100.120.10.13 255.255.255.248
 frame-relay interface-dlci 101
```

While it is not an objective to learn all of the above commands for Cisco's CCNA program, it serves as a good example of how multiple sites might be connected together. Figure 12-1 shows a diagram of the sites used for this configuration. The figure only shows the interfaces, DLCIs, and IP addresses of the hub router A. Subinterfaces allow the two physical interfaces to be divided so that all five sites can be connected.

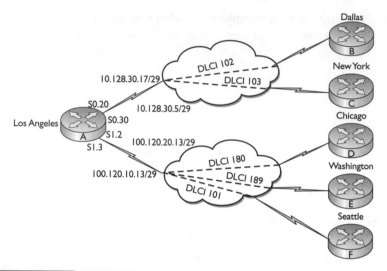

FIGURE 12.1   Elements of frame relay

Objective 12.02   Frame Relay Address Mapping

Frame relay is defined as a packet-switched network, which is far different than ISDN's circuit-switched description. While there are many differences between ISDN and frame relay, many of the standards used with frame relay are borrowed from ISDN. How these networks are implemented is very different. Frame relay uses data link connection identifiers (DLCIs) to pass data from one location to another. ISDN uses TEI addresses to communicate with the provider's switch. Because frame relay uses a packet-switched network, multiple routers are able to participate on one network. ISDN supports multiple stations on the same network, but the implementation is far different. Frame relay resembles a LAN network but without the normal broadcast capability, which stations on a LAN possess. This concept will be explained more in the section "Non-Broadcast Multiaccess Networks."

Exam Tip

The DLCI is the Layer 2 addressing used by frame relay. When learning frame relay, it is important to distinguish characteristics of the DLCI versus characteristics of LMI.

Data Link Addressing

Frame relay, like many WAN technologies, corresponds to the data link layer of the OSI. When connected to a provider, data is passed across a switching network. This entire infrastructure resides at the data link layer of the OSI. The cloud network between sites is not specified in the frame relay specifications. The provider could be using routers or ATM switches (most likely today) that carry the data across the cloud. There is no network layer addressing in the frame relay network. Figure 12-2 displays a full-mesh network, meaning that every site has a connection to all other sites. This shows how all three routers are on the 192.16.1.0/24 network.

When looking at Figure 12-2, don't make the common mistake of thinking the PVC connections are direct from site to site. The equipment and physical paths that the data passes over in the cloud are not significant to the customer, only the concept that a virtual circuit leads to a remote site. Each site in this figure has an interface connecting to the frame relay cloud and is on the same 192.16.1.0/24 network. Notice that router A is 192.16.1.1/24, router B is 192.16.1.2/24, and router C

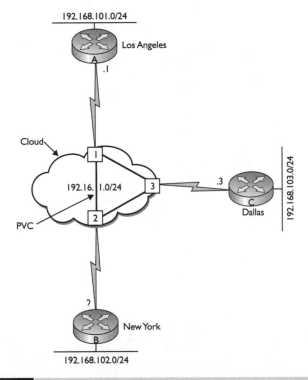

FIGURE 12.2   Single full-mesh frame relay network

is 192.16.1.3/24. Recall that on a LAN, stations had to have some way of resolving a network address to a data link address because directly connected stations do not talk by IP, they talk by data link address. For frame relay, the data link address is called a DLCI (data link connection identifier). This address must be used in order for the routers separated by the cloud to communicate. The PVC connections in Figure 12-2 are described as virtual tunnels connecting routers. The number assigned to these connections is the DLCI, which is supplied by the provider.

In Figure 12-3, the Figure 12-2 drawing is used again, but now there are DLCI numbers added. These DLCI numbers are used to distinguish which PVC is used to communicate between the routers located at the different sites. For router A to communicate with B, it must use the PVC with the DLCI number of 209 to get to the IP 192.16.1.2 address. For TCP/IP in a LAN environment, the process to resolve an IP to data link address is known as ARP. In the frame relay environment, resolving the IP address to a DLCI uses a procedure called *inverse ARP* (INARP). Similar to the MAC address in a LAN environment, the DLCI only has local significance. Local significance means that the DLCI number used to access the remote site doesn't have to be the number used by the remote router to reply.

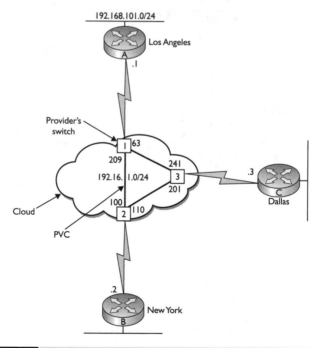

FIGURE 12.3   LAN ARP vs. frame relay inverse ARP

Many things in our society have only local significance. For example, an airline flight has a number associated with it, such as flight 55. This number is used to associate the plane with a destination, such as Los Angeles. This number, however, doesn't indicate what flight is used to return, only the destination. This is what local significance means. In frame relay, a DLCI number indicates the PVC that is used for a single destination. Therefore, in Figure 12-3, each site has a DLCI that is used to reach a destination. To get to Dallas from New York, DLCI 110 must be taken, but to return from Dallas to New York, DLCI 201 must be used.

> ### Exam Tip
>
> Understanding that a DLCI is locally significant is a must for being able to design and implement frame relay.

The data link address allows two devices to communicate on a local network, but network addresses are used for device location and upper layer communication purposes. As stated, INARP is used to automatically associate the network layer address to the data link address, similar to LAN ARP. In Figure 12-4, an example of a LAN ARP is presented.

Here, stations 1 and 2 residing on the 192.168.102.0/24 LAN must ARP for their default-gateway 192.168.102.1, which is the router interface to get to host 3 or 4. Once the information arrives at router A, it must ARP for 192.16.1.3, its next hop router, to get the information to host 3 or 4. Finally, once router B receives the information, it must ARP for the actual host 3 or 4 as needed. The ARP in each case resolves the MAC address for the router interface or end

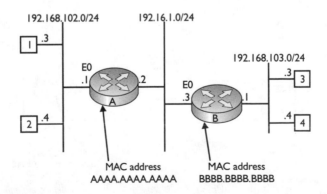

FIGURE 12.4   LAN ARP example

host and associates it with the IP address of the gateway or ultimate destination. So that, in the first communication between host 1 or 2 and router A, the address 192.168.102.1 was mapped to the MAC address AAAA.AAAA.AAAA. When router A performed an ARP for 192.16.1.3, the gateway to the destination hosts, it mapped or associated 192.16.1.3 with the MAC address BBBB.BBBB.BBBB. Finally, router B performed an ARP and associated the destination address of 192.168.103.3 or 192.168.103.4 to the respective MAC addresses of 3333.3333.3333 or 4444.4444.4444. With each ARP, the gateway IP address must be mapped to the gateway MAC address. You could think of a gateway as a departure gate at an airport. For example, a man wants to get on flight 387 to reach New York. For the person to get on the right flight, the flight number and the gate must be associated. This flight leaves at gate 13. Because of the association of the gate with the flight as printed on the boarding pass, he knows that gate 13 can be used to get on flight 387. Using this information, he can reach New York. The mapping process that is crucial to a LAN is important to a WAN also.

Now let's contrast this process with frame relay's inverse ARP process as shown in Figure 12-5. Inverse ARP uses a mapping process to associate the IP address, not to a MAC, but to a DLCI address. In Figure 12-4, hosts 1 and 2 couldn't reach hosts 3 and 4 without the ARP process. In Figure 12-5, the same is true; they will perform an ARP just like in Figure 12-4 for the gateway 192.168.102.1. However, unlike LAN ARP, the router will perform inverse ARP automatically when the link comes up, and it will refresh it every 60 seconds. Router A learns that the gateway is 192.16.1.3. With this mapping to DLCI 110, the router now knows that it must use the PVC 110 to get to that gateway. Once the information reaches router B, the normal LAN ARP as shown in Figure 12-4 will be performed and host 3 or 4 will receive the intended information.

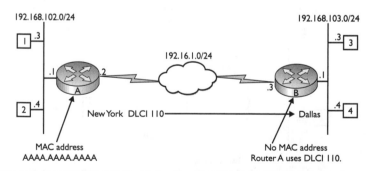

FIGURE 12.5   Inverse ARP example

Manual Mapping vs. Dynamic

Having shown the similarities, the differences must be pointed out. In a normal LAN ARP, the ARP request is done whenever the MAC address isn't listed in the ARP cache. This is done initially when data link communication is required. After this is done, the ARP remains in the cache so subsequent requests can be answered without having to perform an ARP request again. This cache, like most caches, has a timeout period. On Cisco routers, the ARP cache is timed out every four hours by default. For frame relay, the initial mapping is done when the interface is brought up and refreshed every 60 seconds. In LAN ARP, manual ARP entries may be added to the ARP cache that is never timed out. In frame relay, manual map statements may be added to the interface, but when they are, inverse ARP is disabled for any protocol using manual mapping statements on that interface. If a manual map statement for IP is placed on an interface for a remote site, upon reboot, inverse ARP will not perform IP mappings.

Travel Advisory

A manual mapping statement placed on the interface for IP will disable inverse ARP on that interface for IP resolutions. Once a manual statement is used for a protocol, a mapping statement will be required for that protocol on the interface for every remote site.

Another key difference is that ARP uses a broadcast to every station on the local network segment. Frame relay inverse ARP doesn't have normal broadcast capability. The automatic mapping works only because the provider's switch announces DLCI information locally to the router. Because of this, a full-mesh topology, where every router on a network has a direct connection to every other remote router, is required when using inverse ARP. In a hub and spoke topology as shown in Figure 12-6, the mapping must be done manually. Hub and spoke is used when a single router connects to two or more remote routers. Because only one router is the hub, the spokes cannot communicate with each other directly—all communication between spokes must pass through the hub router.

Table 12-1 shows the mapping statements required to make the Figure 12-6 hub and spoke solution work. The IP gateway address must be mapped to the indicated DLCI number on the corresponding router. For example, router A must have a mapping of IP address 192.16.1.2 to DLCI 100 and IP address 192.16.1.3 to

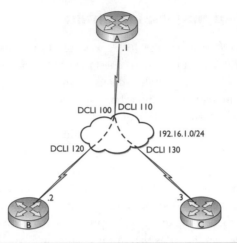

FIGURE 12.6   Hub and spoke requires manual mapping statements.

DLCI 110. What the mapping means here is this: "To get to the IP 192.16.1.2, the router must take PVC (DLCI) 100" and "To get to 192.16.1.3, the router must take PVC (DLCI) 110."

Frame Relay States

When configuring mappings, it is helpful to pay attention to the three frame relay states as reported by the **show frame-relay map** command. They are as follows:

TABLE 12.1   Routers A, B, and C IP to Mapping Requirements

| Router | Mapping | |
	IP Gateway Address	Destination DLCI
A	192.16.1.2	100
	192.16.1.3	110
B	192.16.1.1	120
	192.16.1.3	120
C	192.16.1.1	130
	192.16.1.2	130

- **Active state**   The connections between sites are operational.
- **Inactive state**   The local connection to the frame relay switch is working, but the remote router's connection to the provider's switch isn't.
- **Deleted state**   The local router isn't communicating with the provider's switch.

Here is an output of **show frame-relay map** showing that both mappings are active:

```
Serial0/0 (up): ip 140.10.18.3 dlci 110(0x6E,0x18E0), static,
        broadcast, CISCO, status defined, active
Serial0/0 (up): ip 140.10.18.6 dlci 110(0x6E,0x18E0), static,
        broadcast, CISCO, status defined, active
```

Objective 12.03

Non-Broadcast Multiaccess Networks

In a LAN environment, networks can be described as broadcast multiaccess. *Multiaccess* means that multiple stations attach to the same segment. *Broadcast* means that a station on a segment can send one frame to all the other stations, using a special address known as the *broadcast address*. All the stations recognize this address and interpret the frame as intended for them. In WAN technologies such as frame relay, a single interface on a router can be used to connect to multiple sites using a single segment. As with the LAN, this ability is called multiaccess. The thought of multiple connections on a single segment is still true with frame relay, but without broadcast ability. Multiple frame relay routers located at different sites use interfaces to connect to the segment, which spans the frame relay cloud. It is important to realize that non-broadcast does not mean that broadcast can never be sent on a frame relay link. It means there is no native broadcast ability. Broadcasts can be sent over frame relay links, but each one has to be replicated to each remote router attached to the frame relay segment. To accomplish this, mapping statements are usually required with the **broadcast** parameter configured. If broadcasts need to be sent over the frame relay links, the **broadcast** option is added to the end of each mapping statement as shown here:

```
RouterB(config)#int s0/0
RouterB(config-if)#frame map ip 140.10.18.6 110 broadcast
RouterB(config-if)#frame map ip 140.10.18.3 110 broadcast
```

```
RouterB(config-if)#^Z
RouterB#show frame-relay map
Serial0/0 (up): ip 140.10.18.3 dlci 110(0x6E,0x18E0), static,
            broadcast, CISCO, status defined, active
Serial0/0 (up): ip 140.10.18.6 dlci 110(0x6E,0x18E0), static,
            broadcast, CISCO, status defined, active
```

The two frame map statements define mappings to two IP addresses for DLCI 110. The **broadcast** keyword at the end of the map statements allows broadcast to be sent for two different sites; otherwise, no broadcast could be sent on PVC 110 to the other sites.

Objective 12.04   Configuring Frame Relay

Setting up frame relay between two sites is very easy. But there are some things that must be considered, such as the sites being connected and which interfaces will be used. In a simple installation using point-to-point connections between two sites, the setup is extremely easy. On the main serial interface, enter the encapsulation and the IP address. If the routers are able to run inverse ARP and auto-sense the LMI, the work is pretty much done from a command standpoint. In the following output, the encapsulation and the IP address are all that is configured on the interface:

```
Rack-02-R6#config t
Rack-02-R6(config)#interface Serial0
Rack-02-R6(config-if)# ip address 140.10.18.6 255.255.255.240
Rack-02-R6(config-if)# encapsulation frame-relay
Rack-02-R6(config-if)#^Z
Rack-02-R6#
```

Here is the configuration from the router on the remote site:

```
Rack-02-R3#config t
Rack-02-R3(config)#interface Serial0
Rack-02-R3(config-if)# ip address 140.10.18.3 255.255.255.240
Rack-02-R3(config-if)#^Z
Rack-02-R3#
```

With this minimal configuration, the two routers are communicating using frame relay. The LMI on both sides is auto-detected, and the DLCI is automatically mapped by inverse ARP. The following is an output from **show interface s0** and **show frame-relay map** from Rack-02-R6:

```
Rack-02-R6#sh interface s0
Serial0 is up, line protocol is up
  Hardware is HD64570
  Internet address is 140.10.18.6/28
  MTU 1500 bytes, BW 1544 Kbit, DLY 20000 usec, rely 255/255, load 1/255
  Encapsulation FRAME-RELAY, loopback not set, keepalive set (10 sec)

(output omitted)
  LMI DLCI 1023  LMI type is CISCO  frame relay DTE
  FR SVC disabled, LAPF state down
  Broadcast queue 0/64, broadcasts sent/dropped 0/0, interface broadcasts 0
  Last input 00:00:06, output 00:00:06, output hang never
  (Output Omitted)
Rack-02-R6#sh frame-relay map
Serial0 (up): ip 140.10.18.3 dlci 110(0x6E,0x18E0), dynamic,
              broadcast,, status defined, active
```

From the output above, the IP address 140.10.18.3 is mapped to the dlci 110, and broadcasts are allowed on the frame relay connection. Notice the last word *active* in the configuration means the connection is operational.

Dealing with Split Horizon

While the preceding example might appear to be simple, rarely is it so easy in large frame relay installations. For larger configurations, subinterfaces will probably be necessary and can provide many benefits for frame relay. We looked at distance vector protocols earlier in the book, and saw that split horizon is used to help prevent loops in a network. Split horizon accomplishes this by not allowing a device to advertise information in the direction it was learned from. When connecting to multiple sites through a single serial interface, split horizon will prevent updates from being sent properly. Consider Figure 12-7, which shows a hub router interface connected to two other sites.

When router C broadcasts its RIP updates every 30 seconds, router A will receive them. However, the split horizon rule states that a update must not be sent to the network that it learned the update from. This means that router A will omit

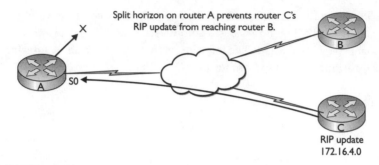

FIGURE 12.7   Frame relay split horizon example

any information learned from router C when it sends its RIP update out serial 0. Therefore, any new information reported from router C will not be received by router B. When the update is to be sent out serial 0, any entry in the route table with a destination route associated with serial 0 will be left out of the update. So with the routing table that follows, the router will omit this route:

```
R       172.16.4.0 [120/1] via 140.10.18.6, 00:00:21, Serial0
```

when sending the RIP update out serial 0. Here is the routing table that this route comes from:

```
RouterA#sir
(Output Omitted)
Gateway of last resort is not set
     140.10.0.0/16 is variably subnetted, 5 subnets, 2 masks
C        140.10.6.0/24 is directly connected, Loopback0
C        140.10.18.0/28 is directly connected, Serial0
R        172.16.4.0 [120/1] via 140.10.18.6, 00:00:21, Serial0
C        140.10.36.0/24 is directly connected, Loopback10
C        140.10.44.0/24 is directly connected, Loopback11
C        140.10.50.0/24 is directly connected, Loopback12
     192.86.2.0/32 is subnetted, 1 subnets
C        192.86.2.2 is directly connected, Loopback20
```

Notice the one route that has an R in the left column. This was learned through the serial 0 interface, and because of this, it will be omitted when this router sends its RIP update out serial 0. This means that router B will never receive information about the 172.16.4.0 network.

Point-to-Point Subinterfaces Prevent Split Horizon

A solution to this problem is to disable split horizon on the serial interface, but this could open the possibility of loops within the network. If routers B and C are stub networks (networks having only one way in and out), this isn't such a big deal. If they are not stub networks, loops may form, and it might be more advantageous to try another solution incorporating subinterfaces. As far as routing is concerned, a subinterface has the same properties as any other interface. In Figure 12-8, a hub router is connecting to two remote sites. Router A now has two subinterfaces to divide the remote sites into two separate networks. Two different interfaces are now listed in the route table as shown below, which means that split horizon is no longer an issue.

A route table will always associate a destination network with an outgoing interface. The route table of router A is displayed here:

```
RouterA#sir
(output omitted)
     140.10.0.0/16 is variably subnetted, 3 subnets, 3 masks
C       140.10.3.0/24 is directly connected, Loopback0
C       140.10.20.0/30 is directly connected, BRI0
C       140.10.21.0/24 is directly connected, Serial0.1
C       140.10.18.0/28 is directly connected, Serial0.2
R       172.16.4.0 [120/1] via 140.10.18.6, 00:00:21, Serial0.2
     192.83.2.0/32 is subnetted, 1 subnets
C       192.83.2.2 is directly connected, Loopback20
```

This route table displays the subinterfaces (in bold italics) as if they were totally separate interfaces. Notice there are two different networks, and as far as

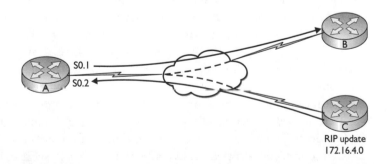

FIGURE 12.8   Subinterface connecting two spoke routers

the routing table is concerned, there are two separate interfaces used to access these networks.

What all this means is that there are no problems with split horizon on interface serial 0. When it passes updates to the sites connected, the router will view each site as accessible through a different interface. RIP updates can arrive on interface serial 0.2 and be sent out interface serial 0.1, and the split horizon rule will not prevent it. The drawback is that each site must be on a different network, one for each subinterface. This may be a problem if network addresses are in short supply. If all your frame relay networks can be accessed via different networks using point-to-point subinterfaces, split horizon will not be an issue with the frame relay connections.

Configuring Point-to-Point Subinterfaces

To configure subinterfaces for point-to-point frame relay connections, perform the following four steps:

1. Remove all network addressing from the main interface, which will be used to make subinterfaces. Then enter the **encapsulation frame-relay** command so that frame relay point-to-point interfaces can be created.
2. Create the point-to-point subinterface using the **interface serial** command. Adding a period followed by the subinterface number and keywords **point-to-point** creates the subinterface. So if it is the first subinterface on serial 0/0, the command is **interface serial 0/0.1 point-to-point**. The prompt will change to subinterface configuration mode, which is denoted by the (config-subif)# prompt.
3. Add network addressing on the subinterface. Each subinterface will have to belong to a unique network different from the other subinterface networks. For IP this is done by using the normal **ip address** command.
4. Configure the DLCI on the subinterface. When using point-to-point subinterfaces with frame relay, the **frame-relay map** command cannot be used. Since there can only be two routers on a point-to-point link, there is no need to specify a gateway IP address to DLCI mapping. All that is needed is to enter a DLCI for the interface. The router will use this DLCI every time it needs to send out the subinterface, which makes sense, knowing that it can only be sent to one station. To do this, use the **(config-subif)#frame-relay interface-dlci [DLCI]** command. This command has no **broadcast** parameter option and is unnecessary on point-to-point links. Of course, point-to-point links don't ever need broadcast capability because there are only two stations on the network.

Here is an example of creating a point-to-point subinterface:

```
Rack-02-R4#config t
Enter configuration commands, one per line.  End with CNTL/Z.
Rack-02-R4(config)#int s0/0
Rack-02-R4(config-if)#no
Rack-02-R4(config-if)#no ip address
Rack-02-R4(config-if)#encapsulation frame-relay
4d02h: %LINEPROTO-5-UPDOWN: Line protocol on Interface Serial0/0, changed
state to up
Rack-02-R4(config-if)#int s0/0.1 point-to-point
Rack-02-R4(config-subif)#ip address 140.10.18.4 255.255.255.240
Rack-02-R4(config-subif)#frame-relay interface
Rack-02-R4(config-subif)#frame-relay interface-dlci 110
```

Remember to put the **encapsulation frame-relay** command and remove the IP address on the main serial interface before creating the point-to-point subinterface or the router will react as shown here:

```
Rack-02-R4(config)#int s0/0.2 point-to-point
                            ^

% Invalid input detected at '^' marker.
Rack-02-R4(config)#
```

Exam Tip

The order of steps in creating a point-to-point subinterface is very important. If steps are performed out of order, the subinterface may not be able to be created.

Multiaccess Networks

Many times it is not possible to have separate networks for each of the frame relay connections. While there are many different configurations possible, we will look at a multipoint situation. *Multipoint* means there are multiple sites connected off a single router interface. There are two ways to set this up on a Cisco router. One way is to use a physical serial interface, which is helpful in full-mesh configurations that rely on inverse ARP for mappings. Another way is to use a multipoint subinterface, which roughly achieves the same effect as the main serial interface. There are pros and cons to using multipoint subinterfaces just like using the physical serial interface for the multipoint connection. The main disadvantage is that inverse ARP doesn't work for any type of frame relay subinterface. This means that even if the multipoint subinterface connects to a full-mesh frame relay network, manual mapping statements will still be required on the multipoint subinterface. Most frame relay connections are hub and spoke or partial-mesh configurations, so mapping statements or interface DLCI statements are required. The main advantage is that other point-to-point connections can be made off the same serial interface at the same time a multipoint connection is being used, as shown here:

```
interface Serial0.1 point-to-point
 ip address 140.10.19.6 255.255.255.240
 frame-relay interface-dlci 140
!
interface Serial0.2 multipoint
 ip address 140.10.18.6 255.255.255.240
 frame-relay map ip 140.10.18.3 110 broadcast
 frame-relay map ip 140.10.18.4 100 broadcast
```

Notice how one subinterface is set up for point-to-point and the other is multipoint. Also, as mentioned earlier, point-to-point subinterfaces must use the **frame-relay interface-dlci** command to configure the DLCI. Multipoint interfaces use **frame-relay map** statements to associate the correct IP with the proper DLCI. Here, the IP address 140.10.18.3 is associated with DLCI 110 and broadcasts are allowed to be passed across this PVC. The other map statement associates 140.10.18.4 with DLCI 100, and it too allows broadcasts to be sent across on the PVC.

Configuring Multipoint Frame Relay Connections

To set up a multipoint subinterface, the procedure is similar to point-to-point subinterfaces, as follows:

1. Remove all network addressing from the main interface, which will be used to make subinterfaces. Then enter the **encapsulation frame-relay** command so that frame relay point-to-point interfaces can be created.
2. Create the multipoint subinterface using the **interface serial** command followed by a period, a subinterface number, and the keyword **multipoint**.

For example, to create a multipoint subinterface on a serial interface, it might look like this: **interface s0.1 multipoint**. The prompt will change to subinterface configuration mode, denoted by the (config-subif)# prompt.

3. Add network addressing on the subinterface. Each subinterface will have to belong to a unique network different from the other subinterface networks. For IP this is done by using the normal **ip address** command.

4. Configure mapping statements for protocols running on the multipoint interface, one per protocol per destination IP address. This is done using the **frame-relay map** command as seen many times throughout this chapter and repeated here:

```
Rack-02-R4(config-subif)# frame-relay map ip 140.10.18.6 110 broadcast
```

After configuring the mapping statements, return to privilege exec and perform a **show frame-relay map** command to make sure the IP and DLCI are mapped and that they are listed as active as shown here:

```
Rack-02-R4(config-subif)#^Z
Rack-02-R4#show frame-relay map
Serial0/0 (up): ip 140.10.18.6 dlci 110(0x6E,0x18E0), static,
          broadcast, CISCO, status defined, active
```

Objective 12.05

Verifying Frame Relay Connections

There are four basic **show** commands for verifying that frame relay is working. Many of these commands have been displayed throughout this chapter. Debug commands should rarely be used for production networks, and so only **show** commands are presented here.

The show interface serial Command

After basic configuration of frame relay has been performed, **show interface serial** is a good command to run. This command will display:

- Layer 1 and Layer 2 information concerning the link
- LMI type used on the link
- Network address

- Various statistics to help determine the stability of the connection to the provider's network
- Encapsulation type (IETF or Cisco)

The following is a sample output of this command:

```
Serial0/0 is up, line protocol is up
  Hardware is PowerQUICC Serial
  Internet address is 140.10.18.4/28
  MTU 1500 bytes, BW 1544 Kbit, DLY 20000 usec,
     reliability 255/255, txload 1/255, rxload 1/255
  Encapsulation FRAME-RELAY, loopback not set
  Keepalive set (10 sec)
  LMI enq sent  78, LMI stat recvd 79, LMI upd recvd 0, DTE LMI up
  LMI enq recvd 0, LMI stat sent  0, LMI upd sent  0
  LMI DLCI 1023  LMI type is CISCO  frame relay DTE
  FR SVC disabled, LAPF state down
  Broadcast queue 0/64, broadcasts sent/dropped 86/0, interface broadcasts 86
  Last input 00:00:07, output 00:00:06, output hang never
  Last clearing of "show interface" counters 00:13:07
  Input queue: 0/75/0/0 (size/max/drops/flushes); Total output drops: 0
  Queueing strategy: weighted fair
  Output queue: 0/1000/64/0 (size/max total/threshold/drops)
     Conversations  0/1/256 (active/max active/max total)
     Reserved Conversations 0/0 (allocated/max allocated)
  5 minute input rate 0 bits/sec, 0 packets/sec
  5 minute output rate 0 bits/sec, 0 packets/sec
     80 packets input, 1177 bytes, 0 no buffer
     Received 0 broadcasts, 0 runts, 0 giants, 0 throttles
     0 input errors, 0 CRC, 0 frame, 0 overrun, 0 ignored, 0 abort
     168 packets output, 5476 bytes, 0 underruns
     0 output errors, 0 collisions, 0 interface resets
     0 output buffer failures, 0 output buffers swapped out
     2 carrier transitions
     DCD=up  DSR=up  DTR=up  RTS=up  CTS=up
Rack-02-R4#
```

The first line "Serial0/0 is up, line protocol is up" means that Layers 1 and 2 are at least partially functional—they are both listed as up. "Encapsulation FRAME-RELAY" is how Cisco encapsulation is displayed. If IETF were being used, it would have read "Encapsulation FRAME-RELAY IETF." The output also lets the user know that Cisco LMI was being used. At the bottom of the output, the "interface resets" and "carrier transitions" provide clues to the stability of the connection into the provider's network.

The show frame-relay map Command

The **show frame-relay map** command is useful for verifying the mapping between the network layer address and the DLCI, as well as the state of the connection. As presented earlier in the chapter, the following is an example of this command:

```
Rack-02-R4#show frame-relay map
Serial0/0 (up): ip 140.10.18.6 dlci 110(0x6E,0x18E0), static,
               broadcast, CISCO, status defined, active
```

Notice that the IP address 140.10.18.6 is mapped successfully to DLCI 110 and that this was done with a static mapping statement. If the mapping had been performed by inverse ARP, it would have stated "dynamic" as shown here:

```
Rack-02-R6#sh frame-relay map
Serial0 (up): ip 140.10.19.2 dlci 140(0x8C,0x20C0), dynamic,
              broadcast,, status defined, active
Serial0 (up): ip 140.10.18.4 dlci 100(0x64,0x1840), dynamic,
              broadcast,, status defined, active
```

The show frame-relay pvc Command

The **show frame-relay pvc** command is used to view each DLCI configured and information about the corresponding PVC in the cloud. This is a statistical command used to display bandwidth and congestion of the individual PVCs as shown here:

```
Rack-02-R6#sh frame-relay pvc
PVC Statistics for interface Serial0 (Frame Relay DTE)
DLCI = 100, DLCI USAGE = LOCAL, PVC STATUS = ACTIVE, INTERFACE = Serial0
  input pkts 515         output pkts 1          in bytes 26532
  out bytes 30           dropped pkts 0         in FECN pkts 0
```

```
   in BECN pkts 0          out FECN pkts 0          out BECN pkts 0
   in DE pkts 0            out DE pkts 0
   out bcast pkts 1          out bcast bytes 30
   pvc create time 01:46:25, last time pvc status changed 01:16:25

DLCI = 110, DLCI USAGE = UNUSED, PVC STATUS = ACTIVE, INTERFACE = Serial0
   input pkts 0            output pkts 343          in bytes 0
   out bytes 10290         dropped pkts 0           in FECN pkts 0
   in BECN pkts 0          out FECN pkts 0          out BECN pkts 0
   in DE pkts 0            out DE pkts 0
   out bcast pkts 343        out bcast bytes 10290
   pvc create time 05:09:26, last time pvc status changed 05:09:26
   Num Pkts Switched 0

DLCI = 140, DLCI USAGE = LOCAL, PVC STATUS = ACTIVE, INTERFACE = Serial0
   input pkts 1            output pkts 1            in bytes 30
   out bytes 30            dropped pkts 0           in FECN pkts 0
   in BECN pkts 0          out FECN pkts 0          out BECN pkts 0
   in DE pkts 0            out DE pkts 0
   out bcast pkts 1          out bcast bytes 30
   pvc create time 05:06:27, last time pvc status changed 05:06:27
```

By looking at the FECN and BECN counters, it can be seen that these PVCs are not experiencing any congestion.

The show frame-relay lmi Command

The **show frame-relay lmi** command displays the LMI type and LMI statistics for each frame relay interface configured. The following is an example of this command:

```
Rack-02-R6# sh frame-relay lmi
LMI Statistics for interface Serial0 (frame Relay DTE) LMI TYPE = CISCO
   Invalid Unnumbered info 0          Invalid Prot Disc 0
   Invalid dummy Call Ref 0           Invalid Msg Type 0
   Invalid Status Message 0           Invalid Lock Shift 0
   Invalid Information ID 0           Invalid Report IE Len 0
   Invalid Report Request 0           Invalid Keep IE Len 0
   Num Status Enq. Sent 36568         Num Status msgs Rcvd 36568
   Num Update Status Rcvd 0           Num Status Timeouts 0
```

The **show interface serial** command also displays the LMI type. It doesn't, however, give the LMI statistical information that this command gives.

Travel Advisory

For more information on frame relay, refer to the Frame Relay Forum web site at http://www.frforum.com/.

CHECKPOINT

✔ **Objective 12.01: Introduction and Frame Relay Terminology**   Because of the speed and multiaccess ability of frame relay, it is the most widely deployed PDN in the United States for high-speed WAN connectivity. Key terminology such as CIR, PVC, local access rate, DLCI, and LMI was described in this section.

✔ **Objective 12.02: Frame Relay Address Mapping**   Frame relay mapping is very confusing to set up. Whether the interface is point-to-point or multipoint will determine if frame relay map statements are used or if the **frame-relay interface-dlci** statement is used. When running multipoint scenarios, it is important to watch out for split horizon problems, which prevent routing updates learned from an interface to be sent out the same interface.

✔ **Objective 12.03: Non-Broadcast Multiaccess Networks**   This terminology describes WANs such as X.25, frame relay, and ATM. These types of networks have no broadcast ability, but retain the multiaccess capability of a LAN network.

✔ **Objective 12.04: Configuring Frame Relay**   While configuring frame relay, there are many issues to pay attention to, and subinterfaces are one of the first that should be determined. Subinterfaces can help with split horizon if used in point-to-point mode. In multipoint mode, they give flexibility so that point-to-point subinterfaces and multipoint can be used simultaneously.

✔ **Objective 12.05: Verifying Frame Relay Connections**   When verifying a frame relay installation, there are four commands that are very useful. Use **show interface serial** when checking line conditions, encapsulation, LMI DLCI, and stability problems. The command **show frame-relay map** displays the network address to DLCI mappings and their present states. The

show frame-relay pvc command is helpful for seeing the DLCIs running on the router and statistics of the PVCs in the provider's network. These statistics will help determine if the network is congested or not. Finally, the **show frame-relay lmi** command is used to see LMI statistics.

REVIEW QUESTIONS

1. What type of network best describes frame relay?

   A. Broadcast multiaccess
   B. Non-broadcast multiaccess
   C. Multiaccess
   D. Point-to-point
   E. Broadband

2. What type of WAN network is frame relay best characterized as?

   A. PSTN
   B. Multipoint
   C. Telephony
   D. PDN
   E. BSTN

3. Which of the following terms best describes the locally significant number that is used in conjunction with the cloud network?

   A. LMI
   B. PVC
   C. CIR
   D. DLCI
   E. TEI

4. Which of the following terms best describes the messages exchanged between a local router and the switch in the provider's network?

   A. LMI
   B. PVC
   C. SVC
   D. Keep-alives
   E. DLCI
   F. DE

5. Which of the following terms best describes an agreement between the customer and provider to transmit an amount of data during a measurement interval?

   A. LMI

   B. PVC

   C. CIR

   D. DLCI

   E. TEI

   F. DE

6. Which of the following commands and associated prompts is correct for enabling Cisco frame relay on an interface?

   A. (config-if)# encapsulation frame

   B. (config-subif)# encapsulation frame-relay

   C. (config-if) # encapsulation frame-relay

   D. (config-subif)# encapsulation frame-relay cisco

7. What command would you use to view the DLCI number 1023 for Cisco LMI?

   A. show frame-relay lmi

   B. show frame-relay map

   C. show frame-relay pvc

   D. show interface serial

8. What command would you use to view the association between frame relay's data link address and a network layer address?

   A. show frame-relay pvc

   B. show frame-relay map

   C. show frame-relay lmi

   D. show frame-relay inarp

   E. show interface serial

REVIEW ANSWERS

1. **B**   Non-broadcast multiaccess best describes frame relay networks. They have no broadcast capability, yet are multiaccess. While frame relay can be used with point-to-point networks, NBMA is the best description.

2. **D** Frame relay is run across a public data network, which is far different from other WAN technologies such as ISDN, which uses the PSTN.

3. **D** The DLCI is best described locally significant because it only provides the number of the PVC to the remote site. This number is meaningless to the other site.

4. **A** The LMI (local management interface) sends messages from the provider's network to the local router. The LMI reports conditions within the provider's network.

5. **C** CIR (committed information rate) is negotiated by the customer and provider. This doesn't mean that only that amount of data may be sent, but rather, it means how much is guaranteed.

6. **A** The (**config-if**)# **encapsulation frame-relay** command is the correct command to enable Cisco encapsulation on a serial interface. None of the other commands will work. One thing that can help memorize Cisco frame relay commands is to understand that there is a hyphen between **frame** and **relay** in almost every Cisco command.

7. **D** **show interface serial** is the only listed command that will display the DLCI number that is being used by the LMI type. The command **show frame-relay lmi** will not display this information, as it is mainly a statistical command. In addition to statistics, it will show the type of LMI being used.

9. **B** The command **show frame-relay map** is used to map or associate an IP address with a DLCI.

About the CD-ROM

Mike Meyers' Certification Passport CD-ROM Instructions

To install the *Passport* Practice Exam software, perform these steps:

1. Insert the CD-ROM into your CD-ROM drive. An auto-run program will initiate, and a dialog box will appear indicating that you are installing the Passport setup program. If the auto-run program does not launch on your system, select Run from the Start menu and type **d:\setup.exe** (where **d** is the "name" of your CD-ROM drive).
2. Follow the installation wizard's instructions to complete the installation of the software.
3. You can start the program by going to your desktop and double-clicking the Passport Exam Review icon or by going to Start | Program Files | ExamWeb | CCNA.

System Requirements

- Operating systems supported: Windows 98, Windows NT 4.0, Windows 2000, and Windows Me
- CPU: 400 MHz or faster recommended
- Memory: 64MB of RAM
- CD-ROM: 4X or greater
- Internet connection: Required for optional exam upgrade

Technical Support

For basic *Passport* CD-ROM technical support, contact Hudson Technical Support:

- Phone: 800-217-0059
- E-mail: mcgraw-hill@hudsonsoft.com

For content/subject matter questions concerning the book or the CD-ROM, contact MH Customer Service:

- Phone: 800-722-4726
- E-mail: customer.service@mcgraw-hill.com

For inquiries about the available upgrade, CD-ROM, or online technology, or for in-depth technical support, contact ExamWeb Technical Support:

- Phone: 949-566-9375
- E-mail: support@examweb.com

Career Flight Path

Cisco Systems currently has numerous certifications available, and they can get a little confusing. To better understand Cisco certifications, it helps to understand the two divisions that are responsible for them.

Cisco Career Certifications

The Cisco Career Certification program handles most of the certifications that Cisco offers, such as CCNA, CCNP, CCDA, CCDP, and CCIP. All of these programs involve taking written exams that are offered in either VUE or Prometric Testing Centers.

Cisco Career Certifications are broken into four areas:

- **Network Engineering & Design**   These certifications revolve around the basics of Cisco network engineering, not the intricate details of installation and maintenance. These certifications are perfect for sales engineers who will be responsible for explaining the products, but never actually installing them.
- **Network Installation & Support**   These certifications revolve around the basics of Cisco's IOS and the technologies associated with it. These certifications show your ability to install and maintain Cisco equipment.
- **Communications & Services**   C & S currently only has one certification in the Career Certification department, the Cisco Certified Internetworking Professional (CCIP). There is some overlap with the materials found in Engineering & Design and Installation & Support, with added materials in cable, DSL, content networking, and IP telephony.

- **Cisco Qualified Specialists Programs**   The Cisco Qualified Specialists program allows individuals to display competency in a particular technology such as cable, security, Internet solutions, or SNA. These programs typically are used in conjunction with certifications from the other programs.

Cisco Certified Internetworking Expert (CCIE) Program

The CCIE program is completely separate from the certifications we just discussed. It is important to note that none of the certifications found in the Career Certification department is a prerequisite for the CCIE certification. However, without the knowledge required to obtain those certifications, your chances of success in the CCIE program are zero to nil.

The CCIE program has three certifications. Each certification requires a written exam and laboratory exam. Once a candidate has passed both the written exam (which essentially allows them to qualify for the lab exam) and the lab exam, they will have achieved what many believe to be the hardest and most lucrative certification in the industry. Even in today's struggling economy, many CCIEs still maintain a six-figure income.

The three types of CCIE that can be obtained are:

- **Routing & Switching**   This the most popular of the three and also the oldest. A candidate has to demonstrate proficiency in designing and installing some of the most difficult and complex configurations possible.
- **Communications & Services**   The newest of the three certifications, C & S overlaps with R & S, but concentrates in those areas similar to the technologies found in the Career Certification program (cable, DSL, content networking, and IP telephony).
- **Security**   As the name would indicate, the CCIE Security certification indicates an individual's competency with Cisco's security products and technologies, such as the PIX firewall and Cisco's IOS firewall features.

Where Do You Start?

The most basic of all Cisco certifications is the Cisco Certified Network Associate (CCNA). This book prepares you for this certification. All other certifications require either the knowledge contained in the CCNA certification or the certification itself. All Cisco Career Certifications either require the CCNA or highly recommend it. The CCNA is just the beginning. After obtaining the CCNA, a candidate may progress to the CCNP to move forward through the Network &

Installation program, or the CCDA to move forward through the Network Installation & Support program.

Figure B-1 illustrates the path you can take in obtaining the Cisco Career Certification program's certifications and the required exams for each.

There are two approaches to achieving the CCNA certification:

- **Self-study**   Chances are that since you bought this book self-study is the approach you are trying to take. Each section of this book outlines about how much time it should take you to comprehend its contents. With a lot of studying and practice on the sample exams, passing should be a snap!

- **Instructor-led training**   This is a very popular method—as I should know, being an instructor—but it can be quite expensive. At CCPrep.com, for example, a typical CCNA Boot Camp will cost $2,995 plus expenses. However, it is a very effective means of learning new skills.

After CCNA, the choices are numerous, but most of the time the ultimate goal is to achieve CCIE certification. The other certifications are for mere mortals, but to achieve the CCIE will put you in another class. Expect to spend several years in pursuit of this elusive certification, especially if you start out with very little Cisco experience.

For more information on how to obtain your CCIE, please visit CCPrep.com for all the latest details.

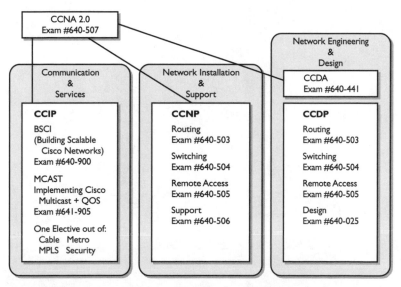

Note: CCNA is highly recommended for CCIP, CCDA, and CCDP but not *required* as it is for CCNP.

FIGURE B.1   Cisco Career Certification paths

Index

INTERNATIONAL CONTACT INFORMATION

AUSTRALIA
McGraw-Hill Book Company Australia Pty. Ltd.
TEL +61-2-9417-9899
FAX +61-2-9417-5687
http://www.mcgraw-hill.com.au
books-it_sydney@mcgraw-hill.com

CANADA
McGraw-Hill Ryerson Ltd.
TEL +905-430-5000
FAX +905-430-5020
http://www.mcgrawhill.ca

**GREECE, MIDDLE EAST,
NORTHERN AFRICA**
McGraw-Hill Hellas
TEL +30-1-656-0990-3-4
FAX +30-1-654-5525

MEXICO (Also serving Latin America)
McGraw-Hill Interamericana Editores S.A. de C.V.
TEL +525-117-1583
FAX +525-117-1589
http://www.mcgraw-hill.com.mx
fernando_castellanos@mcgraw-hill.com

SINGAPORE (Serving Asia)
McGraw-Hill Book Company
TEL +65-863-1580
FAX +65-862-3354
http://www.mcgraw-hill.com.sg
mghasia@mcgraw-hill.com

SOUTH AFRICA
McGraw-Hill South Africa
TEL +27-11-622-7512
FAX +27-11-622-9045
robyn_swanepoel@mcgraw-hill.com

**UNITED KINGDOM & EUROPE
(Excluding Southern Europe)**
McGraw-Hill Education Europe
TEL +44-1-628-502500
FAX +44-1-628-770224
http://www.mcgraw-hill.co.uk
computing_neurope@mcgraw-hill.com

ALL OTHER INQUIRIES Contact:
Osborne/McGraw-Hill
TEL +1-510-549-6600
FAX +1-510-883-7600
http://www.osborne.com
omg_international@mcgraw-hill.com

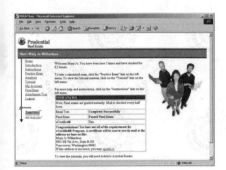